Child Soldiers in Africa

The Ethnography of Political Violence

Cynthia Keppley Mahmood, Series Editor

A complete list of books in the series is available from the publisher.

Child Soldiers in Africa

Alcinda Honwana

PENN

University of Pennsylvania Press

Philadelphia

10 9 8 7 6 5 4 3 2 1

Published by
University of Pennsylvania Press
Philadelphia, Pennsylvania 19104-4112

Library of Congress Cataloging-in-Publication Data

Honwana, Alcinda Manuel.
    Child soldiers in Africa / Alcinda Honwana.
        p. cm. — (The ethnography of political violence)
    Includes bibliographical references and index.
    ISBN-13: 978-0-8122-3911-9
    ISBN-10: 0-8122-3911-3 (cloth : alk. paper)
    1. Child soldiers—Africa.   2. Children and war—Africa.   3. Children and violence—
Africa.   4. Political violence—Africa.   I. Title.   II. Series.

HQ784.W3H66 2005
355'.0083'096—dc22   2005042436

To Nyeleti and Nandhi

Contents

Introduction

The issue of children's participation in armed political conflict has captured the attention of the world during the past ten or fifteen years. Images of boys carrying guns and ammunition flash across television screens and appear on the front pages of newspapers. Less often but equally disturbingly, stories of girls pressed into the service of militias surface in the media. An unprecedented number of children have been drawn into active participation in warfare. Many children are coerced into fighting; others are pushed into it by poverty and crises in their communities; some may be seduced by promises of glory or excitement. Children as young as eight or ten are transformed into merciless killers, committing the most horrendous atrocities with apparent indifference or even pride.

Children's involvement in armed conflict is not a recent phenomenon. In the past, young people have been at the forefront of political conflict in many parts of the world, even when it has turned violent. Today, however, the problem has grown to such magnitude that it has attracted public notice. What is new is not just the visibility of civil wars but also that children are more deeply involved; in some places, they form a substantial proportion of combatants. Analysts of war have pointed out that most contemporary civil wars represent a "total societal crisis." Social order is almost entirely disrupted, and defenseless civilians, especially women, children, and the elderly, are particularly vulnerable.[1]

Reports of children taking human lives are increasingly infiltrating public awareness, not only from conflict zones but also from societies in peacetime. Almost any newspaper or nightly news show in the United States includes a litany of youthful victims and perpetrators of inner-city violence; some cities keep a running tally of the death toll. Isolated cases that occur in white, middle-class settings seem more shocking, such as the Columbine school shootings or the murder of a Dartmouth college couple by two Vermont teenagers. Even younger children can commit murder: for example, three-year-old James Bulger was killed by two ten-year-olds in the United Kingdom. Incidents of children killing children are troubling. The systematic, organized use of children to wage war is even more appalling.

Children get caught up in armed conflict in a whole host of ways. Often, those who manage to avoid becoming soldiers are maimed or killed in attacks on civilian areas. Children are separated from their parents, orphaned, and uprooted from their communities. The displaced may have to seek refuge in other territories. Those children who remain in war zones are subjected to various forms of violence and exploitation. Some are injured by landmines while playing or working. Children are turned into spies or gunrunners, or they work as guards, cooks, cleaners, and servants in military camps. Particularly damaging for future generations is the impact of war on girls. Disadvantaged even in peacetime, girls experience sexual abuse, rape, enslavement, and other tribulations during war. Children witness terrible atrocities and suffer from trauma. Children are deprived of education and basic healthcare. Wars and other forms of armed conflict have profound and lasting effects on young people.

These developments have not gone unnoticed. In recent years, the impact of armed conflict on children has moved to the forefront of political, humanitarian, and academic agendas. The international community has taken several significant steps to address the problem. In 1990, the United Nations established the Convention on the Rights of the Child, which contains important provisions for children affected by armed conflict. In 1994, the UN General Assembly commissioned the Machel study on the impact of armed conflict on children. In 1996, Graça Machel presented a ground-breaking report which made specific recommendations for action. Based on Machel's recommendations, the General Assembly created the Office of the Special Representative of the Secretary General for Children and Armed Conflict in 1997. This office was commissioned to raise awareness and promote the collection of information about the plight of children affected by armed conflict as well as to foster international cooperation to promote respect for children's rights amid such conflicts.

Many humanitarian organizations have launched specific programs to address the issue of children affected by armed conflict and to promote protection and support. The issue became a topic of interest in academic circles as well, producing significant research and publications.[2] The participation of children in war has even become a theme for novels.[3]

The dramatic shift of social roles and responsibilities of children brought about by war is intrinsically linked to the breakdown of societal structures and long-standing moral matrices in contexts of extreme social crisis.[4] Children's involvement in war defies established and generally accepted norms and values with regard to the fundamental categories of childhood and adulthood, as well as the international conventions of modern warfare. In modern societies, childhood is usually associated with innocence, weakness, and dependence upon adult guidance and nurturance. Soldiers, in contrast, are associated with strength, aggression, and the responsible maturity of adulthood. Children should be protected and defended; a soldier's duty is to protect and defend. The paradoxical combination of *child* and *soldier* is unsettling. Children at war find themselves in an unsanctioned position between childhood and adulthood. They are still children, but they are no longer innocent; they perform adult tasks, but they are not yet adults. The possession of guns and a license to kill remove them from childhood. But child soldiers are still physically and psychologically immature; they are not full adults who are responsible for themselves. They live in a twilight zone where the two worlds of childhood and adulthood "rub against each other in . . . uneasy intimacy."[5]

Child soldiers live between a world of make-believe—a child's world of games and fantasy, of playing with guns—and reality—where the playful becomes shockingly lethal and the game turns deadly. Here the ludic is transformed into the grotesque and the macabre.[6] Efforts to theorize the place occupied by child soldiers are not entirely satisfactory, however, for this position is inherently unstable, without sanctioned cultural definition, embodying a societal contradiction, and entirely embedded in conflict. Bhabha suggests that such interstices provide the terrain for the emergence of new strategies of selfhood and identity.[7]

The role-related and ritually defined boundaries between childhood and adulthood that existed in Angola and Mozambique before the onset of civil war were broken down by extreme social crisis. As the social order was disrupted, roles between adults and children were displaced. Children actively create and recreate their roles according to the situations presented to them, and when their communities become engulfed in civil war, they assume roles that under normal circumstances would be filled by adults. In Angola and Mozambique, many children became active soldiers, committing the most horrific atrocities. This dramatic shift is intrinsically linked to the breakdown of society's structures and morality in a crisis such as war.

Outline of Argument

This book focuses on the involvement of children in civil wars in Mozambique and Angola, conveying the experiences of children directly involved in these armed conflicts. It centers primarily on children in military camps: child combatants, sexually abused girls, and other children living within the confines of the military. However, it also discusses children who were victimized by armed conflict in their villages and communities, such as orphans and landmine victims.[8]

Although this study is based on field research from these two countries, its scope extends beyond the borders of Mozambique and Angola. Comparative analyses of various cases highlight their similarities and differences as well as offering broader analytical perspectives on the impact of war on children. In sum, this study situates the phenomenon in Mozambique and Angola within the context of a more far-reaching exploration of these issues.

The book makes four main arguments: (1) the involvement of children in war does not constitute a new phenomenon but has gained new dimensions because of changes in the nature of warfare and current understandings of childhood; (2) children affected by conflict—both girls and boys—do not constitute a homogeneous group of helpless victims but exercise an agency of their own, which is shaped by their particular experiences and circumstances; (3) the healing and reintegration of children affected by armed conflict need to be embedded in local world views and meaning systems in order to be effective and sustainable; and (4) social reintegration of children affected by armed conflict must go hand in hand with larger strategies of social development and the eradication of poverty.

The book outlines the histories of political conflict in Mozambique and Angola and the context in which the involvement of children in the protracted civil wars took place. It also considers issues of research methodologies and the ethical challenges associated with conducting research in conflict and post-conflict situations with vulnerable groups, particularly children.

Chapter 2 discusses the connections between children and war historically and socially, the changes in warfare that have influenced the present situation, and factors such as childhood development and poverty.

Child soldiers find themselves in a position that breaks down dichotomies between civilian and combatant, victim and perpetrator, initiate and initiated, protected and protector. With these multiple, interstitial positions, child soldiers epitomize the condition of simultaneously having multifaceted identities and utterly lacking a permanent, stable, and socially defined place. In this way, they occupy a world of their own. We must go beyond the clear-cut demarcations between child and adult, and between innocence and guilt, to examine the intricate ways in which the condition of the child soldier cuts across established categories.

Warfare is a profoundly gendered phenomenon.[9] It is not just that men become soldiers while women work and wait at home, a popular image based on two relatively well-organized twentieth-century world wars. In European international and civil wars, as well as in African wars, women in the civilian population become targets of recruitment and sexual violence perpetrated by soldiers that is designed to demoralize, humiliate, and immobilize an enemy. Women and girls are raped in front of their male relatives. Sometimes, rape ends in murder. Young women and girls are kidnapped and held in military camps where they are used as laborers, servants, and sexual slaves. In some cases, young women become armed combatants in order to defend themselves or avenge the wrongs done to their kinswomen.[10]

This gendered and sexualized dimension of warfare is seldom understood as a fundamental and pervasive feature of armed conflicts. It comes to public attention primarily in particularly dramatic instances, especially those involving the systematic extermination of combat-aged men as well as the rape of women in the target group.[11] Female survivors of wartime sexual abuse and exploitation seldom speak of their suffering since it is often shameful as well as traumatic.[12] This book examines the situation of girls and young women affected by war.

Boy soldiers and girls forced to serve militias represent anomalies and contradictions. They inhabit an autonomous world with its own rules and relations of power. Yet they come from a civil society ordered by family, kinship, gender, and generation, and, after peace returns, they must reenter a world whose fundamental tenets they were made to violate and whose categories they have defied. How are young women and men who have served and fought with the militia groups to be assimilated back into society? How can they make an orderly transition from child militia member to adult civilian? They have been traumatized by their experiences, by the murders and other acts of violence and violation they have committed, witnessed, and feared or suffered themselves, and by the sudden and total sundering of their previous ties to kin and community.

Civilians lost more than their sons and daughters to the military forces; they lost homes, village, and livelihoods as well. Repeated attacks on civilians in places with no military significance have been a fundamental feature of postcolonial civil wars. In both Mozambique and Angola, substantial numbers of rural residents were displaced, forced to seek sanctuary in more stable regions of their own country or to cross borders to find refuge. Few remained for the duration of the conflict; most returned home as soon as local conditions permitted. The injuries and displacement they suffered were compounded by the devastation they encountered on their return. In Angola, as rural residents tried to resume their lives, rebuilding burned villages, cultivating the fields, and traveling to market, many people—especially children and young people—were injured by the landmines that combatants had left behind. For them, the war continued even in the absence of soldiers.

In Mozambique and Angola, war is generally conceptualized in opposition to society, as a state in which people are rewarded for breaking fundamental norms and social codes. People who have been directly involved in war are not easily accepted back into society, for they are considered to be polluted by the "wrong-doings of the war"; they are regarded as contaminated by the spirits of the dead and carriers of their anger. Those individuals who killed or saw people being killed are potential contaminators of the social body. Danger and pollution are attached to all war-affected persons; being a witness to murder or an unwitting collaborator in atrocities is also dangerous. War pollution is considered a threat to society, so young women and men who served and fought in militias must undergo a process of cleansing as they make the transition from the state of war back into normal society. This reintegration is accomplished with local practices, which differ profoundly from Western psychotherapeutic approaches.

In the context of the civil wars in Mozambique and Angola, reconciliation goes beyond the process of restoring communication and resolving differences among oppositional groups nonviolently; it also encompasses the process of restoring intimate ties that have ruptured, reintegrating war-affected persons into local communities, and resuming normal life. Civil wars have long-lasting effects on whole societies as well as on individuals. The economic underdevelopment that is both cause and consequence of warfare narrows the opportunities available to young people to attain the occupational and family positions that signify full adulthood. The book ends by exploring governmental and non-governmental programs for demobilization, rehabilitation, and social reintegration of war-affected children.

Chapter 1
Civil Wars in Mozambique and Angola

This study draws on ethnographic research undertaken in Angola and Mozambique, two African nations that have experienced prolonged and bloody civil wars. Both countries are former Portuguese colonies that became independent in 1975 after long wars of national liberation. In both countries, the postcolonial government, led by nationalist movements that successfully prosecuted wars of independence, adopted a Marxist orientation and socialist models of development. These policies met with resistance from factions of the former independence movements, which waged war against the incumbent government with material assistance from foreign nations. During these wars, which lasted over fifteen years in Mozambique and for more than twenty years in Angola, thousands of children were drawn into armed conflict. These children of war are the subject of this book.

In Mozambique, the war between the Frente de Libertação de Moçambique (Mozambique Liberation Front), known as FRELIMO, and the Resistência Nacional Moçambicana (Mozambique National Resistance), known as RENAMO, started with the creation of RENAMO in the late 1970s and ended in 1992. After eleven years of armed struggle, Mozambique attained its independence from the Portuguese in 1975. However, it became enmeshed in regional conflicts as Zimbabwean forces fought against British rule in the neighboring colony of Southern Rhodesia. The Rhodesian Central Intelligence Organization in 1977 established RENAMO as a rebel force within Mozambique. Its original assignment was to spy on Zimbabwean guerrillas operating from bases there. Soon its assignment was expanded to include armed opposition to the FRELIMO government in retaliation for its full implementation of UN sanctions against Rhodesia and, more importantly, its support of the armed struggle for independence led by the Zimbabwe National Liberation Front (ZANLA).[1]

The connections between these two territories within the ethnoscape of European colonialism underlaid these developments. Immediately after Mozambique's independence, a number of Portuguese settlers and former members of the colonial army left Mozambique for Rhodesia. The Rhodesian security services recruited the founding members of RENAMO from this group. RENAMO not only assisted Rhodesian forces in their operations against ZANLA inside Mozambique, but it also implemented the agenda of those resentful Portuguese settlers who wanted to unseat the communist government.[2] From 1977 to 1980, RENAMO's role was expanded to include the sabotage of FRELIMO's economic and social policies and the disruption of normal life in rural areas. RENAMO was also deployed against ZANLA infiltration routes into Zimbabwe, although its actions were far less damaging than the direct attacks of the Rhodesian Army and Air Force on economic and military targets in the provinces of Tete, Manica, and Gaza. In response, the Mozambican government forces took the war back to Rhodesia. A well-trained guerrilla force infiltrated the enemy line to operate alongside Zimbabwean nationalists. In addition, Mozambique launched offensive operations against RENAMO bases, which culminated in the capture of the strategically important mountains of Gorongosa in late 1979.

With the independence of Zimbabwe in 1980 following the Lancaster House agreements, which were mediated by the British government, RENAMO lost its Rhodesian support and was taken over by the South African Security Forces. The South African regime had such an interest because the African National Congress (ANC) had a presence in Mozambique and was supported by the Mozambican government in its struggle against apartheid. RENAMO also received support from some groups in Western countries, including the United States.

RENAMO grew rapidly in size and in military effectiveness. By mid-1983, the rebels had regained control over the mountains of Gorongosa in central Mozambique and were operating in eight of the country's eleven provinces. RENAMO's attacks against development and aid projects, roads, bridges and railways, schools, hospitals, farms, and entire villages were characterized by acts of extreme cruelty against civilians. Systematic torture and massacres became tragically frequent, even ordinary events in rural areas, particularly in the southern part of the country. RENAMO's strategy was to disrupt the rural infrastructure, isolate the government in garrison towns, and render the country ungovernable, thereby forcing FRELIMO into compliance with South Africa's security concerns by eliminating the ANC presence in Mozambique. At this stage, RENAMO was primarily the military conduit of the South African regional strategy of destabilization in Mozambique.[3] In spite of its massive cruelty against the civilian population, RENAMO successfully attracted the sympathy of the peasantry, especially in the central and northern regions of the country. Many peasants felt disempowered by the government's antagonism to their rural heritage and traditional authorities and by its policies of forced villagization that coerced peasants into communal settlements with shared farms and social services.[4] Young people, in particular, were attracted to RENAMO because of a crisis in employment. Many youth had migrated from rural to urban areas to find jobs, but in 1984, the FRELIMO government's Operação Produção sent urban dwellers who were considered "unproductive" back to the countryside and closed the doors to "parasites." These returned youth no longer fit into the local social structures, where authority rested with the elders. Furthermore, rural areas lacked food, education, and employment opportunities. RENAMO offered these discontented youth a new purpose in life by putting a gun in their hands.[5]

Warfare in Mozambique peaked in 1987, when RENAMO made significant military gains in the northern and central areas of the country and undertook actions in the southern region. The Homoine massacre in July 1987, in which more than 400 people died, many while they lay in hospital beds, was one of RENAMO's most notorious attacks in the south. During this period, atrocities were committed throughout the country. Most were attributed to RENAMO. However, government soldiers also carried out some abuses.[6] With its economy devastated and development projects paralyzed, the country became increasingly dependent on foreign aid. As a result, the government decided to undertake far reaching economic reforms, abandoning its former Marxist policies in favor of political and economic liberalization. In 1990, a new constitution was adopted, embracing the principles of multiparty democracy.

The FRELIMO government, with its resources dissipated by years of war, was incapable of imposing a military solution to the conflict. RENAMO was also unable to sustain its war effort, because South Africa decreased its support during a process of internal reforms to end apartheid. With this military impasse, a political solution became possible.[7] Following several months of negotiations, the government and RENAMO signed a General Peace Agreement in Rome in October 1992. These negotiations were mediated by the Italian religious community of Santo Egidio and the Catholic Church in Mozambique. The first democratic elections took place in October 1994. FRELIMO won these elections by a wide margin, with strength in the southern and northern regions, and formed a new government. Five years later, in the 1999 elections, FRELIMO maintained its hold on power, though by a narrow margin.[8]

The civil war in Mozambique was one of the bloodiest and most

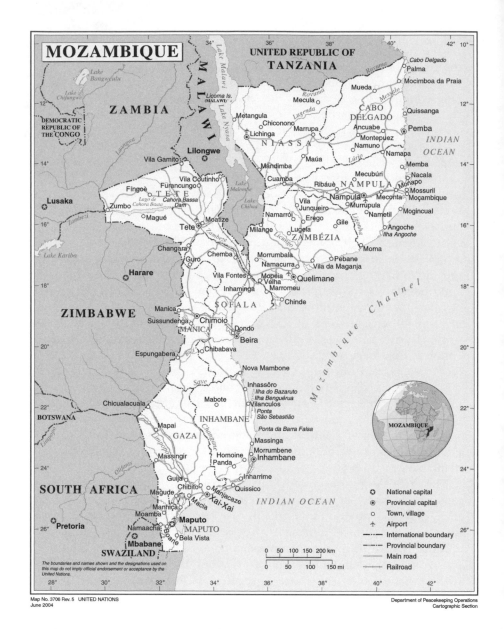

Map 1. Mozambique. Map No. 3706 R.2, United Nations Cartographic Section.
Reprinted by permission of the United Nations.

devastating of its time.[9] The social costs were enormous, and the consequences for the civilian population catastrophic. Hundreds of thousands of Mozambicans died as a result of the war. About five million people were internally displaced by 1989; more than one million became refugees in neighboring countries. Besides the many uncounted children who died as a direct consequence of the war, an estimated 250,000 or more children were either orphaned or separated from their families. School enrollments were reduced by an estimated 500,000, and medical facilities servicing approximately five million people were destroyed.[10] Between 8,000 and 10,000 children in Mozambique participated in the conflicts as soldiers, most fighting with RENAMO.

Since the 1992 agreement, Mozambique has managed to maintain peace. The peaceful democratic transition in South Africa and the continuation of peace in other neighboring nations have facilitated this peaceful atmosphere. Very few incidents of political violence have been reported. In many parts of the country today, especially the rural areas, Mozambicans are still trying to come to terms with the war and reconstitute their lives.

In Angola, civil war lasted even longer than in Mozambique, and peace proved more difficult to establish. Angolans carried on armed struggle against Portuguese colonial rule from the early 1960s until 1974, when the government in Portugal was overthrown. The new government did not pursue colonial wars, and national independence became a real possibility. Three major anti-colonial groups then engaged in a bitter internecine war to gain exclusive access to power and control over the country. These groups were the MPLA, Movimento Popular Nacional de Libertação de Angola (Popular and National Movement for the Liberation of Angola); UNITA, União Nacional para a Independência Total de Angola (National Union for the Total Independence of Angola); and UPA-FNLA, União Popular de Angola–Frente Nacional de Libertação de Angola (Angola Popular Union–National Front for the Liberation of Angola). The MPLA emerged victorious and proclaimed Angola's independence in November 1975. While the UPA-FNLA faded in importance in subsequent years, UNITA reconstituted itself as anti-Marxist and pro-Western to continue its antigovernment insurgency.

UNITA's primary supporters in its war against the MPLA government were the United States and South Africa.[11] South Africa's involvement arose from its interest in maintaining white supremacy and preventing the expansion of Marxism in the region. The United States was interested not only in supporting the apartheid regime in South Africa, a key ally, but also in offsetting any alliances the Soviet Union and Cuba might make on the African continent. At the height of the Cold War, South African troops directly supported UNITA and Cuban troops fought alongside the MPLA. The United States channeled funds and arms to UNITA. Like the civil war in Mozambique, the civil war in Angola was shaped by regional and global forces as well as local and national conditions.

By 1987, there were major battles in the south of the country, culminating in the siege of Cuito Cuanavale (a town in southwestern Angola) by South African and UNITA forces. Although fighting at Cuito Cuanavale ended in a stalemate, the outcome was a psychological defeat for the South African Defence Forces. South Africa had to rethink its military strategy in Angola, given the difficulties it faced in trying to win the conflict militarily.[12] New diplomatic attempts to end the conflict followed Cuito Cuanavale. The next eighteen months were marked simultaneously by the most sustained efforts to achieve a peaceful settlement and some of the fiercest fighting of the entire war.

The first chance for peace came in May 1991, when the government and UNITA signed a ceasefire agreement in Bicesse, Portugal, following mediation by the Portuguese government. The ceasefire held until the elections in September 1992. The first democratic elections in the country's history were deemed free and fair by the international community. The MPLA won a majority of the votes. UNITA refused to accept the election results, claiming electoral fraud. Jonas Savimbi, UNITA's President, ordered his troops to return to war, and full-scale conflict resumed in October 1992.[13]

This brutal war raged on until 1994, taking a heavy toll on the civilian population. In November 1994, a new peace agreement was signed in Lusaka between the government and UNITA. The Lusaka Protocol was aimed at restoring peace in Angola and promoting national reconciliation through a ceasefire followed by complete disarmament and cantonment. In April 1997 a Government of National Reconciliation and Unity, which brought UNITA members as well as representatives of some other political parties into the cabinet, was established. Unfortunattely, this fragile peace did not last long. In October 1998, following disagreements with the government, UNITA went back to war, and the human toll continued to rise. In February 2002, the death of UNITA leader Jonas Savimbi marked a new chapter in Angola's political history, as the People's Movement for the Liberation of Angola (MPLA) and UNITA finally laid down their weapons in pursuit of peace. A peace agreement between the MPLA government and UNITA was signed in April 2003, which ended nearly thirty years of fighting.

The civil war in Angola was devastating to the entire population because it lasted so long, raged across so much of the country, and involved such large-scale atrocities against civilians. Minter estimates that during the 1992–94 phase of the war more than 100,000 people died

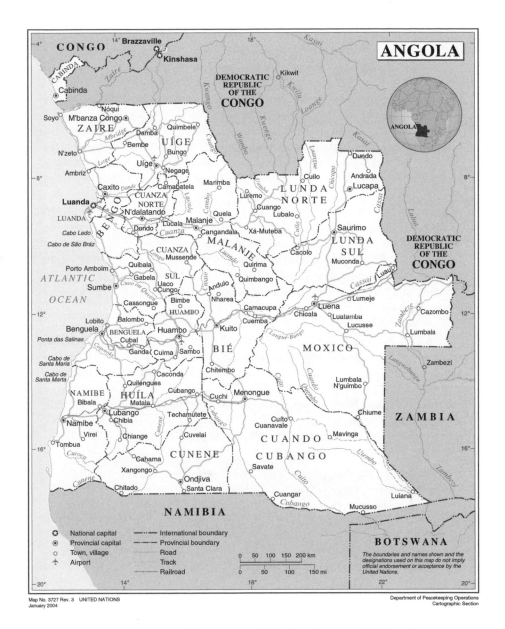

Map No. 3727 Rev. 3   UNITED NATIONS
January 2004

Department of Peacekeeping Operations
Cartographic Section

Map 2. Angola. Map No. 3727 R.2, United Nations Cartographic Section.
Reprinted by permission of the United Nations.

from war-related causes, the number of landmine victims rose to 70,000.[14] According to the 1997 UNDP Human Development Report in Angola, about 280,000 people were living in neighboring countries as refugees, and approximately 1.2 million Angolans were internally displaced, many of them from rural areas to the cities. About half of the displaced population were children under fifteen years of age. As many as one million children were directly exposed to war as civilians and combatants. More than half a million children died, tens of thousands were orphaned or separated from their parents, and many more were kidnapped during military incursions.[15] Even very young children were dragged into armies and militias. UNITA was most active in abducting and recruiting children, but the government forces also used children as soldiers although to a lesser extent. Children carried weapons and other equipment, fought on the front lines, served on reconnaissance missions, laid landmines, and conducted espionage. The 1997 UNDP Report on Human Development in Angola estimated that between 8,500 and 10,000 underage soldiers would be demobilized during the 1996–97 demobilization process.[16]

The war affected many more children indirectly. Malnutrition increased because of a decline in food production and the displacement of farmers. The deterioration of healthcare services during the war resulted in higher infant and child mortality rates. Children were prevented from attending school by displacement and by the destruction of school buildings. In addition to death, physical injury, and trauma, children suffered from the dire poverty, hunger, and social and emotional problems caused by prolonged exposure to political violence.

Challenges of Conducting Research in Post-Conflict Situations

Documenting and analyzing the experiences of children and young people in the context of war and extreme vulnerability poses formidable challenges. This section examines some of the methodological and ethical issues faced by researchers working in contexts of civil war and precarious peace.

Children frequently change their narratives. They may say one thing one day, and the next day they may tell another story entirely, which makes it difficult for the researcher to establish the truth or, more precisely, to decide which version of the narrative to adopt. For this reason researchers must develop skillful ways of cross-referencing children's testimonies. Interviews with witnesses or participants to the same event, as well as with family members, friends, and caregivers such as teachers, trainers, and priests, can be very useful. In addition, the ethnographer may be guided by important social and historical events that help put the child's narrative in context.

The complexities of conducting fieldwork in war settings can, paradoxically, be exacerbated by the presence of humanitarian agencies and NGOs whose raison d'être is the provision of aid and assistance to populations affected by war. The interactions between humanitarian NGOs and the people they support are often based on the unequal relationship between provider and recipient. The agency/client dynamic creates mutual dependency. On the one hand, NGOs need the victims and their stories to fulfill their sense of mission as providers of humanitarian assistance; on the other hand, the victims quickly understand that their status as victims is crucial to obtaining aid. My observations in the field show that populations affected by war are likely to enhance their victim status in the presence of NGOs.

This relationship of mutual dependence is not a problem until the researcher enters the scene. The access of researchers to war zones is often facilitated by NGOs. Humanitarian aid organizations gain early access to conflict and postconflict sites, often by negotiating with the parties in conflict. NGOs are able to develop extensive local networks that allow them to channel support and aid to populations in need. These assets are valuable to researchers who can utilize the contacts of NGOs as a local support bases. Researchers gain access to people, communities, and networks, as well as logistical support—lodging, access to clean water, and sometimes food and transportation to and from the war zone. These resources are invaluable, considering the situation in most war-ravaged regions. In some cases, such as my studies in both Mozambique and Angola, researchers gain access to the field as consultants for humanitarian organizations.

Because of the cooperative relationship between the researcher and the humanitarian organization the researcher is associated with the NGO, even when not employed by the organization. However much researchers attest to their intellectual independence from the organization, the research is perceived as directly related to, or an extension of, the humanitarian work provided by the NGO. Thus, when researchers collect data from local populations they may often be told what victims think NGOs want to hear. Researchers might find themselves collecting recurring, recycled, and sometimes exaggerated narratives of victimization. The relationship between caregiving agencies and researchers especially affects conversations with children, who may believe they must present themselves as helpless and dependent in order to be seen as deserving of assistance. Although this situation is not designed by the humanitarian agencies, it is a consequence of their activities on the ground and poses a challenge to researchers operating in these environments.

While victims are able to exercise their agency in order to maximize their gains, the researcher, too, needs to be aware of the situation and have the ability to filter the information. My experience shows that prolonged or repeated visits to the field, together with cross-referencing to other available sources, help minimize this problem. Although this is a serious issue for researchers, it does not mean that all people touched by war embellish or alter their narratives according to the circumstances.

The influence of humanitarian agencies in conflict and post-conflict settings is so strong that they may be perceived to be replacing or taking up the role of governmental institutions. In these settings, local people commonly say that to resolve a particular problem "an NGO will need to develop a project"; for example, "we are waiting for an NGO to help us deal with sanitation," or "there aren't any recreational facilities for the children . . . we need to discuss this with the NGOs." The NGO-ization of conflict and post-conflict settings might generate a practice or even a philosophy of dependence upon foreign aid, without putting pressure on local institutions to assume their responsibilities and deliver necessary services. Instead of expecting the government to provide for them, citizens turn to NGOs for support. Of course, this is not by chance; the weakening capacity of nation-states to provide for their citizens expands the field of action of humanitarian NGOs that have access to international resources.

This situation has sometimes created clashes between humanitarian agencies and governments with regard to the scope of humanitarian actions and interventions on the ground. I witnessed a typical example of the problem while evaluating the Children and War Project (CWP) sponsored by Save the Children USA in Mozambique in 1995.

This project aimed at documenting, tracing, and reunifying unaccompanied children affected by war with their families. After successfully relocating the children in war-ravaged communities, the CWP faced a problem: in most of these communities, schools had been burned during the war, teachers had been killed or displaced, and education was no longer available. Using some of its resources, the CWP decided to create community schools, holding classes under trees or in buildings made from local materials. Because teachers were not available, the NGO trained some youths who could read and write, all in an effort to keep the children busy. When the reunification project ended in 1995, the NGO asked the Ministry of Education of Mozambique to absorb these community schools into the national educational system. The government refused on the grounds that these schools did not fulfill the minimum standards: most of them operated without proper buildings; the teachers had no formal qualifications and could not be placed and paid within the national qualification and salary scale; and most of the schools taught children of different ages and levels of achievement in the same class. This situation created problems between the NGO and the ministry. An official from the ministry stated that NGOs should recognize the limitations of their humanitarian role and not see themselves as substitutes for the government. He stressed that before NGOs embark on these kinds of initiatives, discussions about follow-up actions should be undertaken with government agencies. This situation is but one example of the clashes that can arise in the course of providing assistance to war-affected children. These problems also affect the work of researchers who need access to both types of institutions. Researchers must be very skillful not to shut down important sources of information and research support.

In Angola, relationships of trust were not easily or quickly established during what turned out to be only an interval of peace in a protracted and bloody civil war. Young demobilized soldiers and their relatives shared personal stories with the CCF teams whom they already knew and trusted. The fact that I was brought in by CCF colleagues facilitated my acceptance. Many of the adults involved with war-affected children took advantage of the opportunity to teach us about local knowledge and practices regarding war trauma, healing, and social reintegration. Openly discussing acts of murder and other atrocities witnessed and committed by former child soldiers, dealing with the guilt that adults felt at their failure to protect their own children and those in their communities, facing the conflicts that still simmered over the injuries suffered and inflicted in the recent past—all required mutual confidence. Indeed, without the field researcher's preexisting relationships with traumatized young people and their caregivers, such project would have been extremely difficult to undertake.

Another question the ethnographer working in war zones faces is, how should these narratives of war and suffering be handled? How do victims of war express their experiences of pain and sexual violence to a stranger doing research? Do people feel compelled to speak, given their vulnerable position? In different circumstances, would they have chosen not to talk? If this is the case, how should the researcher deal with these terrible stories of violence, humiliation, and suffering? I faced these difficulties and dilemmas after gathering children's narratives about their experiences of war, pain, and abuse. How does one translate these gruesome narratives onto paper? What are the boundaries between the need to make these terrible atrocities public and voyeuristic intrusion?

Researchers working on children and war are often faced with the difficult dilemmas inherent in writing about and presenting these horrific stories. Is there a particular language to express a person's pain and suffering without intruding into their private space—the intimacy of the violence, pain, and suffering, as well as the recounting and revisiting of the event that sharing its details with the ethnographer requires? On the other hand, how should the ethnographer handle these narratives without losing the force that such exposures of war atrocities and violence committed against these young women and men bring? Reflecting on these and related questions over the years is part of what kept my field materials in note form for so long.

However, I think that acknowledgement of the informants' agency in the process of telling their war stories is important. Even within the constraints inherent in their situation, they can choose what messages they wish to convey to the world and how they wish to communicate them. They can decide to be silent, to omit certain types of information, and to tailor their narratives. Ethnographers working in these circumstances should be aware of and understand how their positions shape the ways in which the narratives are presented, as well their interpretation and transmission of those narratives to the world. We all—informants and researchers—have agency in these processes.

Research Methodologies

I have been doing research on health, healing, and religion in Africa for the last two decades. Since 1993, my work has focused on the effects of war and on postwar healing of trauma. I have worked intermittently in Mozambique throughout this period and in Angola since 1997. As an anthropologist, I privileged qualitative research methodologies based on in-depth, semistructured interviews with key informants and focus group discussions. I also used participant observation of community events and activities, counseling sessions, and public meetings as a means of acquiring relevant information. I complemented my field research with library and archival research, reviewing published reports and unpublished documents. My interest in the effects of war on children evolved over time as I became involved in various projects about children and armed conflict. Tracing the trajectory of my awareness of and research interest in these issues is important to an understanding of the point of view from which I have written this book.

My first research in Mozambique (1986–87) was a study of traditional religious institutions and their effects on society in three large neighborhoods of Maputo-City: Chamanculo, Xipamanine, and Mafalala. This research focused on indigenous healers and on the Zionist churches that synthesized the Christian message of salvation with indigenous spiritual practices and beliefs focused on healing. I studied these healing rituals as activities carried out within the context of family and community, not as isolated performances or manifestations of a particular belief system. My focus was on culture as dynamic and creative, continuous and shared, and as a fundamental dimension of human societies.

A few years later (1993–94), I continued to develop my research in the same direction, focusing more closely on spirit possession and its relation to the war and wider politics of culture in Mozambique. This fieldwork took place on the periphery of Maputo (in Urban District Number Five, which includes Ndhlavela, Zona Verde, Primeiro de Maio, and Khongoloti) and in two rural districts, Boane and Manhiça, also in the south of Mozambique. Since the civil war had ended in 1992, I was interested in the ways communities negotiated the transition from war to peace by means of spirit possession and belief in the powers of ancestral spirits. Studying the healing strategies adopted by war ravaged people immediately after the ceasefire and then again after the resolution of the civil war was one part of the research I conducted for my dissertation.[17] In the course of this project, I interviewed traditional healers, diviners, and spirit mediums; traditional chiefs appointed by the Portuguese (*régulos*); religious leaders from African Independent Churches and from established religious denominations; war-affected populations, including displaced persons, refugees, children kidnapped and exploited by armed forces, and former soldiers; and as many ordinary civilians.

During this period of research, I became aware of the ways in which the war affected the civilian population as people narrated their wartime experiences, their worries, and their hopes for the future. Among the many problems caused by the war, the situation of children and youth was one of their main concerns. People were worried about the generations of tomorrow and what future would be possible for them after all they had experienced during the civil war. Although the scope of my research then was much broader, I became particularly interested in the effects of war on children. I collected important data and decided to pursue the topic more closely later on.

In 1995, I was invited to conduct an evaluation of the Children and War Project (CWP) in Mozambique, which provided a wonderful opportunity to continue this research. Through this project, I was introduced to a number of children and families who had been affected by the war. I did research in four of the eight provinces in the country where the project operated: Nampula, Sofala, Gaza, and Maputo. CWP undertook the documentation, tracing, and family reunification of unaccompanied children found in military camps at the end of the war. The program focused on children under fifteen, because combatants younger than fifteen, even after fighting in the war for many years, were not formally considered soldiers under international law and, thus, had no access to the official demobilization programs for combatants that were undertaken by the United Nations. Child combatants, like other war-affected children, were taken care of by humanitarian programs provided by non-governmental organizations, such as the International Committee for the Red Cross and the Save the Children Alliance.

The Children and War Project was established in 1988 and carried out in seven of Mozambique's eleven provinces: Cabo Delgado, Nampula, Tete, Sofala, Gaza, Maputo-Province, and Maputo-City. The CWP directly facilitated the reunification of more than 12,000 unaccompanied children with their relatives and helped make family reunification possible for thousands of others between 1988 and 1995. Between 1988 and 1992, most of the reunified children had fled from military camps. Fleeing RENAMO combatants (both children and adults) benefited from an amnesty law passed by the government in 1987. The government established the center of Lhanguene[18] to accommodate the children who took advantage of the amnesty for a preliminary evaluation of their situation and to work out the basic strategies for support and family reunification.

Working on the evaluation of this project helped me to understand better the impact of war on child combatants and the problems involved in their reintegration into society. I read a variety of documents and materials on this issue, and I met with and interviewed a vast network of people involved in this important work, ranging from social services personnel and healing practitioners to war-affected people. My previous research on traditional institutions and the cultural politics involved in the negotiation of transitions from war to peace constituted an excellent background for this research on the social and cultural rehabilitation of children affected by war. Throughout this evaluation, I worked with a psychologist, who focused on the psychological and psychosocial aspects, while as an anthropologist I looked more closely at the social and cultural aspects of these children's rehabilitation and reintegration. During the evaluation of the CWP, we visited some of the provinces where the project operated. We conducted interviews and discussions with the reintegrated children, their families and relatives, and various other members of the community. We also interviewed project staff and government officials, as well as staff from other non-governmental organizations. The review of the project's database and documents was an important aspect of the evaluation. The evaluation team found that, although reunifications were costly because many had to be done by plane or helicopter, the CWP was very successful in reuniting children with their families and reintegrating them into their communities. Central to this project's effectiveness was its choosing of community-level care over institutionalized care for displaced children. The major challenge was providing adequate follow-up support for children in their communities, which were almost always poor and often rural or isolated. This matter is considered in depth in Chapter 6, which examines the future prospects of these children.

Although the evaluation of the CWP reviewed institutional aspects of the project's organization and implementation, my main interest was in the interviews I conducted with young people and their families to gain insight into their lives in the military, their present situations, and their worries and hopes for the future. I had numerous contacts with community leaders, teachers, religious leaders, and other volunteer caregivers associated with the project at the local level. Following the evaluation of the project, I managed to keep in contact with some of these children, conducting further interviews in the southern provinces of Maputo and Gaza.

I returned to fieldwork in Mozambique in 1999 to conduct research on the impact of war on girls and young women, with support from a research grant through the University of Cape Town, where I was a senior lecturer in anthropology. I decided to focus on girls because, as scholars, policymakers, and service providers had begun to realize, a huge silence surrounded the involvement and participation of girls in this and other African civil wars. Access to girls and their stories was extremely difficult, given the taboos associated with rape and the sexual abuse that many of them had to endure. Feelings of shame and guilt and the fear of stigma prevented many young women from telling their stories. I decided to conduct my field research in the province of Maputo, on Josina Machel Island, where I could gain access to the girls through an NGO that was supporting programs for war-affected young women.

During my stay in Josina Machel, I interviewed young women who had lived in military camps during the war. Some had stayed in the camps for six months, while others came home only after the ceasefire agreement in October 1992. All these young women were employed by the national NGO Reconstruindo a Esperança (Rebuilding Hope). This NGO initially dealt with boys, especially former child soldiers, and tried to provide them with work and skills. However, after many young men migrated to the city and to South Africa in the hope of finding work and better living conditions, the organization turned its attention to girls and young women. About ninety war-affected young women, and a few young men, were working with this NGO in 1999. The activities of the young women included agricultural production, dressmaking, and literacy classes. The NGO also provided emotional and psychological support through a group of local elderly women, and two psychologists who visited the island twice a week.

The young women in the program ranged between fifteen and twenty-five years of age. The majority were single, although some had at least one child. I had individual interviews and focus group discussions with some of these young women. Some were not willing to talk about what had happened to them during the war, however. Even in this supportive setting, it was extremely difficult for younger women to talk about the sexual abuse they had suffered and for older women to discuss the girls' experiences. People hardly talk about such taboo subjects within the family, let alone to strangers. I decided to work through this NGO because the program was designed specifically for girls who had lived in military camps and addressed the systematic sexual violence they had endured. Had I attempted to conduct such research elsewhere, it would have been very difficult to find any young women who were willing to admit their involvement in the war and share their stories with me.

Young women on Josina Machel had to tell their stories of living in RENAMO military camps to the NGO personnel in order to be admitted to the program. Possibly, some exaggerated their stories in order to enhance their status as victims. However, considering what is known about the atrocities and abuses committed by RENAMO throughout the country, the narratives told by these young women did not appear unrealistic. During my fieldwork, I also interviewed other women and men in the community: the elderly women who worked for the NGO; some of the mothers of the young women; the religious leader of the local Zionist church; the director of the only primary school in the island; the nurse at the only clinic in the island; and several young men who still worked for the NGO. I also had group discussions with elders. I interviewed the two psychologists and participated in some of their counseling sessions with the girls and young women. I also had a chance to talk to some former child soldiers from the island.

Following my evaluation of the Children and War Project in Mozambique, I was approached by Christian Children's Fund (CCF), another international NGO, to conduct research in Angola on the role of traditional healing practices in the social reintegration of war-affected children. This project researched and documented the concepts, beliefs, and practices related to health, healing, and well-being used by local populations in the aftermath of the war. It focused on practices aimed at the cleansing, healing, and social reintegration of war-affected children. The project was based on the assumption that psychological distress and trauma have a social and cultural dimension. The manner in which people understand and give meaning to their afflictions and problems is generally linked to their culture and worldviews and, therefore, appropriate and effective therapeutic strategies should take these cultural beliefs and worldviews into account.

I worked with CCF national staff and develop a training module ethnographic research that introduced the team to the conceptual and methodological issues of the project. The work in Angola was conducted for nine months in 1997–98, during the peaceful period between the Lusaka Accords of 1994 and the resumption of war in October 1998. Research was carried out in the provinces of Luanda, Moxico, Biè, Huambo, Malange, and Uige. These provinces were fairly representative of the major ethnolinguistic groups in the country, including the Bakongo, Tchokwe, Kimbundu, and Ovimbundu.

During this period, I made two trips to Angola to train members of CCF team and conduct fieldwork in the provinces of Luanda and Biè (July 1997) and Huambo and Malange (February 1998). Members of the CCF team located in the five provinces collected data for the project on a regular basis and followed the situation in the provinces. Data was regularly sent to me for comments and analysis. In addition to correspondence, my visits to Angola allowed for direct discussions and planning subsequent research. This qualitative research project was based on collecting life histories of war-affected children, especially child soldiers, and on gathering data about the social and cultural practices related to the reintegration of children in postwar situations. The life histories were collected through in-depth, open-ended interviews with the children and people close to them, while the ethnographic data was gathered through interviews and group discussions with elders and other community members. From the material gathered both by my direct field research and by the members of the CCF team, I produced a research report for CCF in 1998.[19]

CCF Angola had two main projects going on in the country when we started this research. The first, the Province-Based War Trauma Training project (PBWTT), aimed at facilitating social reintegration of war-affected children into families and communities by training relatives, teachers, adult activists, and caregivers. The training, based on key fundaments of modern psychology, helped caregivers monitor and assist traumatized children. The second program was the Reintegration of Underage Soldiers project (RUS), which focused specifically on the demobilization process and the social reintegration of young combatants. An evaluation in April 1997 showed that these low-cost, community-based interventions conducted by CCF were helping children adjust to life after the war. Through the PBWTT project, adults who worked with war-affected children were given training in child development, the emotional impact of war on children, nonviolent means of conflict resolution, and approaches to healing that emphasize children's emotional expression through dance, drawing, singing, drama, and story-telling. The evaluation concluded that "although there was some training of national staff in Bantu cultural patterns and qualitative research methodology, progress to this date in learning about and documenting traditional healing has been limited" and fell short of what was needed to design culturally appropriate intervention programs.[20] Therefore, CCF decided to enlist outside assistance to undertake ethnographic research on indigenous healing practices as they relate to war-affected children.[21] Knowing of my work on this subject in southern Mozambique, CCF Angola invited me to develop this project. At that time, I was teaching social anthropology at the University of Cape Town in South Africa.

The Impact of Traditional Healing Practices in the Social Reintegration of War-Affected Children project was designed in collaboration with the CCF team in Angola, and was funded by a USAID grant to CCF Angola.[22] The research was carried out in two stages. First, the research teams investigated local cosmological beliefs and practices regarding health, healing, and the wellbeing of individuals and groups. The teams gathered valuable information from interviews and discussions with elders, traditional authorities, religious leaders, and local government officials about notions of childhood, transitions to adulthood, the connections between children and warfare, the role of the spirits of the dead in the lives of their kin and other living people, and the relationships between the mundane and the transcendent, between human beings and the environment, and among human beings in society. We focused on people's perceptions and understandings of the war and the instrumental use of children in the conflict, as well as their points of view regarding mechanisms for the reconstitution of the social fabric in peacetime. The second stage focused on case studies of children directly affected by war, recording their life histories and examining the different therapeutic strategies that were employed to resolve their afflictions. Life histories were recorded from interviews with children and their relatives, teachers, friends, and neighbors. Although the plan was to follow up selected cases to evaluate the effectiveness of different therapeutic approaches based on the particular conditions of each child, that goal proved difficult to accomplish in a formal way. Partly because the first stage of work took more time than expected, CCF staff relied on their long-established contacts with war-affected children to compile retrospective accounts rather than collecting longitudinal data.

The project met with a favorable response. People appreciated our effort to investigate local beliefs and practices and to learn from elders, chiefs, and traditional healers. Teams carried out the research in the centers and communities where CCF staff was already working. For example, at the Transit Center, created by the International Organization for Migration (IOM) in Viana, we were able establish contact with officials working with former child soldiers and conduct interviews with young, recently demobilized soldiers waiting to be reunified with their relatives. I also conducted training workshops in Kuito, in the province of Biè, for members of the CCF provincial team and undertook field-work by interviewing traditional healers, war-affected children, and their relatives. Research in each province was supervised by a member of the central CCF team and carried out by CCF field staff trained for this purpose. CCF teams, with at least two persons per province, worked from August 1997 through April 1998, with a mid-term evaluation and analysis under my supervision in February 1998. The research was carried out in Portuguese and in local languages. CCF team members were fluent in the languages of the areas in which they operated. While all members of the CCF teams contributed enormously to the project, I am especially indebted to Carlinda Monteiro, who played a critical role in the development of the project; she accompanied me on all my field trips, helped to interpret the information gathered, and provided very useful insights.

Unfortunately, in part because of its concentration on demobilized soldiers, this research project did not manage to record as many voices of girls and young women as planned. People would not talk about the situation of girls as easily as they did about boys. Also, while boys were available to talk, girls were usually busy with household chores or the care of younger siblings. I realized that a fuller, more gender-balanced picture was vital to complement the studies of former boy soldiers and provide a more complete account of the consequences of war for young people. This desire to complete the knowledge about how girls are affected by war led me to conduct in-depth research with girls and young women on Josina Machel Island in Mozambique, which I have described above.

Working in two countries in conflict and postconflict situations over a period of more than a dozen years enabled me to gather comprehensive information and analyze underlying patterns in the experiences of war-affected young persons and their communities.

Chapter 2
Historical and Social Contexts

In recent decades, children and youth have featured centrally as both the targets and the perpetrators of violence. In nearly every war and civil conflict, children are among the principal victims. The situation has worsened in recent years because civil wars and conflicts without clearly defined state actors have grown more prominent, and children suffer more in these irregular conflicts. Not only are they injured by bombs and other instruments of violence used against civilians, but all too often they are drawn into direct participation in armed combat. Children fight as soldiers and are abducted into servitude and for sexual exploitation. Young people suffer from the spread of AIDS and other diseases exacerbated by combat. They are among the most bereft of victims when conflict ends, in need of rehabilitation and assistance to continue lives that have been so profoundly interrupted.

In order to analyze the causes of this problem, we must place contemporary developments in historical perspective. The involvement of young people in warfare is not a recent phenomenon; it is deeply rooted in the history of all civilizations. In Europe during the Middle Ages, upper-class boys who hoped to become knights served as squires. Around the age of thirteen, the boy was apprenticed to a knight. He was taught skills with the sword, lance, and shield and learned the duties and responsibilities of knighthood. Squires engaged in mock battles against each other and against dummies. A squire also served his mentor. He looked after his master's horses, polished his weapons and armor, and served him at meals. As a squire grew older, he was expected to follow his master into battle and protect him if the knight fell in combat. Some squires were rewarded with knighthood for performing an outstanding deed on the battlefield.[1] Italians called the young soldiers who followed knights into battle on foot *infante*, which literally means "child," and collectively these children made up the *infanteria*, or infantry.

Across Europe, most of the children who were mobilized into armies served in groups under a few adult commanders, rather than each one serving at the side of a knight or expert soldier. The Children's Crusades of 1212 included thousands of boys and girls between the ages of ten and eighteen who joined together believing that God would deliver Jerusalem into their hands. Most died on their long march because of the harsh conditions. Those who did return came home in shame.[2] Children and youth swelled the ranks of Napoleon's army, which was one the first military forces to recruit massive numbers of soldiers from the common classes; boys as young as twelve took active roles as soldiers. The British navy under Nelson included many naval cadets and midshipmen of fifteen, as well as younger cabin boys and "powder monkeys."

Young people have been at the forefront of warfare and political conflict in many parts of the world. Children and youth have often fought in revolutions with strong ideological motivations. Stories of wars of national independence often feature the heroic deeds of children of both sexes who were too young to join the armed forces or even the guerrillas. Sometimes such actions are attributed to youthful idealism. During the Chinese Cultural Revolution, Red Guards between the ages of eight and fifteen carried out some of the more violent acts.[3] Today, children participate as combatants in conflict zones around the globe, in places as diverse as Afghanistan, the Balkan region, Cambodia, Colombia, Northern Ireland, Palestine, and Sri Lanka. The scale of the contemporary problem is unprecedented, both in the numbers of young people involved and in the degree of their participation. Indeed, the magnitude of children's involvement in war is such that the international community has begun to take actions to address the problem.

The nature of warfare and political violence has changed over the past several decades. We have witnessed a shift from conventional warfare between states, in which soldiers fight soldiers, to civil wars within states. Civil wars are fought mainly by proxy, use guerrilla and other irregular fighters, and target defenseless civilians. Young civilians are frequently abducted and forced to join the military. In many conflict zones in Africa, Asia, Europe, and Latin America, young soldiers constitute a significant proportion of the armed groups and become instrumental in committing the most horrendous atrocities. The participation of children and youth in armed conflicts is a defining feature of our times.

Why are young people increasingly being used in armed conflict and political violence? What factors contribute to their involvement in wars? What makes them so vulnerable to being recruited, or even volunteering to take part in these activities? There are many questions, but so far very few answers.

Children and youth are in a process of formation and development, and, thus, vulnerable and in need of guidance and nurturance from society. Militias turn the mutability of youth to their own purposes, developing them into soldiers instead of facilitating their transition to adulthood. Young people's vulnerability to recruitment into armed groups in wars and other violent political conflict is exacerbated by a number of social, economic, and political conditions. In many countries, extreme poverty and the breakdown of societal structures and services have a tremendous impact on the ways young people adjust to problems in their lives. As conflict, migration, and poverty cause families to dissolve and communities to disintegrate, the young are forced to improvise their own survival strategies, becoming street children in cities or joining gangs, armed groups, and the military. In many social contexts, deficient or nonexistent educational and vocational training facilities, the lack of healthcare and sanitation, and the absence of employment opportunities contribute to making membership in armed groups attractive to young people. Political and religious ideologies can also play a part in their decision to participate in such conflicts.

Clearly, mobilizing children in combat or visiting violence, illness, and exploitation upon them holds terrible consequences for their development and for the peace and stability of generations to come. While the recruitment of children and youth into armed conflict arises from social crisis, its consequences entail even more profound social and cultural dislocation.

This chapter analyzes the connections between children and war historically and socially. It examines the involvement of children in military activity and recent changes in warfare that have magnified the extent and intensity of the child soldier's participation in combat. It also poses questions about the evolution of the concept of childhood, asking whether the dominant contemporary conception, which is based on European history and social institutions, has much relevance in non-Western societies' view of children's participation in war. No single and universal concept of what it means to be a child exists. This study emphasizes the diverse ways in which the concept of childhood is socially and culturally constructed in specific contexts. How effective are the existing and proposed provisions of international humanitarian law in protecting children from war and armed conflict? Most were designed for traditional warfare, not for modern wars in Africa and other postcolonial settings. Finally, the massive use of children in armed conflicts after the Cold War is considered, highlighting some of the factors that drive children into war and that make armed groups abduct children to fight and serve. The analysis of the phenomenon of the child soldier is located within the context of the social, economic, and political breakdown of the postcolonial state in Africa.

Comparative Perspectives on Children's Participation in Warfare

In Mozambique and Angola, large numbers of children were used as soldiers by rebels and government forces. RENAMO exploited at least 10,000 child soldiers, some as young as six years old. In Angola, a 1995 survey found that 36 percent of children had accompanied or supported soldiers, and 7 percent of Angolan children had fired at somebody.[4] But the conditions of these civil wars, while extreme, were more visible than they were unusual. The instrumentalization of children as soldiers extends far beyond Mozambique and Angola. Many other recent and current conflicts in Africa take advantage of young combatants; Algeria, Congo, Liberia, Rwanda, Sierra Leone, and Uganda are just a few.

The Lord's Resistance Army (LRA), a rebel movement fighting against the government of Uganda, has become notorious locally and internationally for its use of child soldiers. Children as young as eight are kidnapped, abused to the point of submission, and turned into merciless killers. In the LRA base camps, gruesome initiations take place in which new recruits are forced to kill another child—often a sister or brother—or be killed themselves. Girls become "wives" of soldiers; younger children run errands and carry loot.[5] The whole Great Lakes region of Africa has been immersed in conflict for decades, and children have become active participants in and victims of violence in Rwanda, Burundi, and the Republic of Congo. In the Democratic Republic of Congo (DRC), where all parties to the armed conflict use children, some as young as seven, the forced recruitment of children increased so dramatically in late 2002 and early 2003 that observers described the fighting forces as "armies of children." In the neighboring Horn of Africa, conflicts in Ethiopia, Eritrea, and the Sudan brought many young combatants to the front lines.[6] In West Africa, the civil wars in Sierra Leone and Liberia that began in 1991 were fought by thousands of child soldiers. In Liberia, both the United Liberian Movement for Democracy (ULMD), led by Roosevelt Johnson, and the National Patriotic Front of Liberia (NPFL), led by Charles Taylor, relied heavily on child soldiers. According to the 1994 Human Rights Watch report "Easy Prey: Child Soldiers in Liberia," many children approached the warring factions seeking food and protection; some wanted to revenge the killing of their families by the opposition.[7] The warring parties did not turn these children away but used them in the most brutal possible way. Child soldiers were actively recruited or abducted to serve as the chief cadre of the Revolutionary United Front (RUF) of Sierra Leone.[8]

The massive instrumentalization of children in combat exists outside postcolonial Africa, in other regions of the world marked by violent political conflict. In Latin America, children have been directly involved in civil wars since the 1980s. In Peru, children and youth fought in the Shining Path rebellion.[9] In civil wars in Guatemala, El Salvador, Nicaragua, and more recently Colombia, armed groups and paramilitaries—including irregular forces that support existing governments and those that oppose them—continue to recruit and use children under the age of fifteen. The problem is particularly severe in Colombia, in such regions as Alto Naya and Tierradentro. According to a 2003 report by Human Rights Watch, more than 11,000 children were fighting in irregular armies, including paramilitaries and urban militias. Children interviewed by Human Rights Watch said they joined when they were fourteen or younger. Both girls and boys said they received military training at around age thirteen and that participation in combat came soon afterwards.[10]

In Asia, the Khmer Rouge of Cambodia was notorious for its use of young soldiers. A Sri Lankan rebel group, the Liberation Tigers of Tamil Eelam (LTTE), makes extensive use of children in its war against the Sinhalese government. During 2003 alone, the LTTE recruited more than seven hundred children to add their ranks as soldiers.[11] Children play active roles in armed conflicts in Kashmir, the Philippines, and Burma (Myanmar). In Afghanistan, child fighters have been involved in the successive insurgencies against the Soviets, the Taliban, and the American and European Coalition forces. Muzamil Jaleel, a Kashmir academic commenting on the impact of armed conflict on children, said that for many children in Kashmir, "A" means army; "B," bullet; and "C," curfew.[12]

In the Middle East, the conflict between Palestinians and the State of Israel has been profoundly marked by young people taking their destiny in their own hands. Here, as in many national liberation movements, youth have played key roles on the ground and redefined the conflict through their actions. Palestinian youth sparked confrontations with Israeli troops in the West Bank and Gaza. The *intifada* in the Israeli Occupied Territories featured young people as the primary catalysts of strife. Their motivation to participate in the conflict comes from the geopolitical, social, and economic issues that define their lives.[13] The so-called suicide bombers are only the most shocking example of the turn toward violence by young people in the face of despair.

Europe is not exempt from involving children in armed conflict, just as not all civil wars occur in postcolonial contexts. In Central Europe, the conflict in the Balkans exposed many young people to violence and war. In the fighting in Bosnia, Herzegovina, and Croatia, a deliberate policy was to rape teenage girls and force them to bear the enemy's child. A European Community fact-finding team estimated that more than 20,000 Muslim women in Bosnia had been raped since fighting broke out in April 1992.[14] As Gilboa pointed out, in Bosnia "humanity turned beastly. There were no rules, boundaries, or fear of reprisals. Women were the perfect target: subjugated, accessible, and relatively defenseless. Sexuality became a means to control. In this war, the animal act of rape became part of the strategic plan."[15]

The widening scale and deepening intensity of the participation of children and youth in armed conflict makes the problem qualitatively different from the past. Profound changes in the nature of warfare have contributed to the increasing involvement of children in war. These changes arise not only from the way wars are fought but also from new military technologies. In the past, for example, heavy and unwieldy weapons limited the usefulness of children on the front lines, but today's arms technology has developed in such a way that small boys and girls can handle weapons like M16 and AK-47 assault rifles.[16] They are light and very simple to use and can easily be stripped and reassembled. Hand grenades, landmines, and other forms of explosives, while dangerous to handle, are easily carried and thrown or planted by children. These and other deadly weapons have become cheap and widely available.

At the same time, contemporary views and understandings of childhood and child protection have developed in the opposite direction, toward a definition of children as dependent and vulnerable human beings who are entitled to life, sustenance, health, and well-being. Families, communities, nation-states, and international bodies are held responsible for creating conditions that facilitate their growth both directly and indirectly. The development of a global social consciousness supporting the protection of human rights has profoundly affected the way children's participation in wars is perceived today. International legal frameworks for child protection have developed significantly in recent decades.

The new civil wars in which young people are active participants do not resemble the old wars that shaped the Geneva Conventions. These international rules of warfare, initially agreed by European states in 1949, seek to mitigate the excesses of war and guarantee the humane treatment of civilians and of captured and wounded belligerents. The First Convention applies to wounded and sick members of the armed forces in the field; the Second Convention concerns wounded, sick, and shipwrecked members of the armed forces at sea; and the Third Convention focuses on prisoners of war. The Fourth Convention deals with civilians in times of war. The principles of the Geneva Conventions were based on respect for the life and dignity of human beings. All civilians are entitled to respect and protection from the military operations of the conflicting sides without any invidious distinctions, whether allied with friend or foe, at home or in contested and occupied territories.[17] The conventions presume that wars are fought between nation-states by regular armies under government control, and establish a very clear distinction between civilians and belligerents. The Geneva Conventions reflect the realities and concerns of wars in Europe, particularly the Second World War. These rules do not apply neatly to postcolonial wars in Africa or to wars in Latin America, Central Europe, the Middle East, and Asia. The Geneva Conventions have been found inadequate to protect the victims of modern military conflicts.[18]

In order to take recent changes in warfare into account, the Geneva Conventions were revised in 1977 with two Additional Protocols. The Additional Protocols extended the scope of the conventions, limiting the use of violence and protecting civilian populations by strengthening the rules governing the conduct of hostilities. The First Protocol Additional to the Geneva Conventions (Additional Protocol I) concerns international military conflicts; the (Additional Protocol II) focuses on local conflicts such as civil wars. These protocols oblige warring sides and combatants not to attack civilians and civil structures such as schools and hospitals, and they attempt to force military operations to comply with humanitarian law.

Academics have debated the extent to which the new wars that emerged in the post-Cold War era are fundamentally different from the old wars between states, which were fought by armed forces for state interests—the type of war theorized by Clausewitz.[19] Some authors consider new wars basically different from their predecessors; they characteristically are violent and criminal, predatory, and moved by private economic interests.[20] As Kaldor put it, "New wars, which take place in the Balkans, Africa, Central Asia and other places, could also be described as organised crime (illegal or private violence) or as massive violations of human rights (violence against civilians)."[21] She enumerates their characteristic features: they "use techniques of terror, ethnic cleansing or genocide as deliberate war strategies. In the new wars, battles are rare and violence is directed against civilians. Violations of humanitarian and human rights law are not a side effect of war but the central methodology of new wars. Over 90% of the casualties in the new wars are civilian and the number of refugees and displaced persons per conflict has risen steadily."[22]

Other analysts believe that such a distinction cannot be so neatly demarcated, because the available information about recent and ongoing wars is incomplete and often biased, and the historical research on traditional wars tends to be disregarded. The differences between them might be less pronounced than usually argued.[23] For example, as Benhabib points out, the dividing line between civilian and military targets had already been erased during the aerial bombings of World War II. She says that "it was the democracies of the world . . . that first crossed that line and initiated total war. . . . The civilian population at large became hostage of the enemy during the bombing of London by the Nazis and then of Dresden, Hiroshima and Nagasaki by the Allies."[24] While scholars disagree about the degree of such differences,[25] they generally accept the idea that modern civil wars present particular characteristics, or have developed features of traditional wars to an extreme rarely seen in the past. Moreover, in recent decades, the development of a global social consciousness of human rights and the sanctity of human life, particularly in the more affluent societies, has affected the way academics, policymakers, and societies in general perceive and understand violence, warfare, and civilian protection. This shift explains the recent revision and strengthening of international humanitarian law, as well as the frequency of "humanitarian interventions" in recent years.

Recent civil wars tend to obliterate distinctions between civilians and belligerents in ways rarely witnessed before.[26] As Cock pointed out, in these kinds of civil wars the separation between the battlefield and the home front becomes blurred. The traditional idea that war compels men to go into battle in order to protect the women, the children, and the elderly who remain safe and secure at home no longer holds.[27] Civilians—and especially children—have increasingly been incorporated into military activities in ways that defy established conventions about civilian protection in times of war. Civilians are forced to perform military tasks.[28] People who belong to no political faction—especially children—are abducted, given weapons, and sent into combat without proper military training or equipment. In different phases of the war, civilians find themselves being used by one side or the other, as military control of their village or town shifts back and forth from one faction to another.

Modern wars are mostly internal rather than between states, although they involve a number of transnational actors. They also involve multiple political and military actors from paramilitary groups organized around a charismatic leader, warlords who control particular areas, organized criminal groups, units of regular forces or other security services, and mercenaries and private military companies.[29] These wars mobilize military forces that have less formal and institutionalized training than conventional combatants.[30] As Ignatieff points out, "[W]ar used to be fought by soldiers; it is now fought by irregulars. This may be one reason why postmodern war is so savage, why war crimes and atrocities are now integral to the very prosecution of war."[31] Soldiers cutting off women's breasts and men's genitals, chopping off arms, legs, hands, feet, ears, and noses—all these atrocities that defy human imagination— have become common features in contemporary wars.[32] Children are easy prey and particularly vulnerable to military recruitment in these conflicts.[33] Many children are given arms and forced to fight without proper training and preparation for such tasks. Boys are trained to kill on command. Two young men describe how they were inducted as boys:

From Mozambique:

After four months of training they put me to a test. They put a person before me and ordered me to shoot him. I shot him. After the test they considered me good and they gave me a gun[34]

From Angola:

I was trained for three days on how to march and run. Then they gave me my weapon and I got used to fighting. The orders were to kill anyone we caught and to bring back anything they had on them.[35]

The uncontrolled proliferation of small arms and light weapons,[36] the indiscriminate use of land mines,[37] the illegal trade in minerals by armed groups that target civilians,[38] the systematic use of extreme cruelty and sexual violence as weapons of war, and the phenomenon of "warlords" (local strongmen who mobilize armed forces on the basis of personal loyalty and terror) have all become defining features of these new wars.[39] These wars are ultimately, and often immediately, moved by the economic interests of political factions and military commanders. Some analysts argue that they represent a form of "privatisation of violence."[40]

These developments in the methods of warfare must also be understood within the context of more global trends and interactions. One of the typical features of the new wars is the key role played by diasporic groups and a vast array of global actors: foreign mercenaries, strategists, volunteers, corporate business interests, diaspora supporters, neighboring states, the media, and the like. As these many groups interact and local and transnational concerns are enmeshed, ideas and values about what constitutes acceptable warfare practices are constructed and reshaped.

Contemporary civil wars are protracted, lasting years if not decades, and they render defenseless civilians—particularly children and women— especially vulnerable. "Children, women, the elderly, granary stores, crops, live-stock—all have become fair game in the single–minded strug-gle for power, in an attempt not just to prevail but to humiliate, not simply to subdue but to annihilate the 'enemy community' altogether. This is the phenomenon of 'total war.'"[41] Indeed, these wars constitute a total crisis in people's lives because they destroy not only material pos-sessions but also the moral fiber and sense of dignity of a people. No wonder, then, that some parents found themselves compelled to give their own children to the military, and honorable leaders and teachers became involved in the recruitment of children into the military. The tales of war of Mozambican and Angolan children are not very different from the experiences recounted by children in many conflict zones around the world. From Croatia to Afghanistan, from Sierra Leone to Cambodia, from Nicaragua to Palestine, and from Sri Lanka to the Democratic Republic of Congo, the similarities in recruitment strategies are striking.[42] The use of children as fighters in these wars clearly violates international laws. Despite international treaties intended to ensure so-called just war and respect for human rights, "dirty war tactics—those that use terror against both civilian and military populations to try to control political acquiescence through fear—are a major form of war-fare today."[43]

International Humanitarian Law and the Protection of Children

Several international agreements have been put in place to protect the rights of children and prevent their participation in armed conflicts. The First Protocol Additional to the Geneva Conventions provides that involved parties shall take "all feasible measures in order that children who have not attained the age of fifteen years do not take a direct part in hostilities and, in particular, they shall refrain from recruiting them into their armed forces."[44] In 1979, the International Year of the Child, nations began discussing a comprehensive document defining chil-dren's rights. After ten years of negotiations, the United Nations adopted the landmark Convention on the Rights of the Child in 1989. The con-vention's fifty-four articles reaffirm the fundamental place of the family in society and set global precepts for a child's inherent right to life, sur-vival, development, and freedom of thought, regardless of race, reli-gion, or gender. The document asserts that the best interests of children must become a high priority for governing and legislative bodies. To date, 191 of the 193 countries in the world have ratified the treaty; the United States and Somalia are the two holdouts. The Convention on the Rights of the Child defines a child as a person below the age of eighteen, unless the law applicable to the child provides otherwise.[45] However,

Article 38(2) of the Convention provides that involved parties shall take "all feasible measures to ensure that persons who have attained the age of fifteen years do not take a direct part in hostilities."[46] This language is somewhat stronger than the First Additional Protocol, emphasizing that states are to take measures not simply in order that children not be drawn into armed conflict but to "ensure" that this does not occur. The adoption of the age of fifteen conforms to the provisions of the First Additional Protocol.

The African Charter on the Rights and Welfare of the Child, promulgated in 1990 by the Organization of African Unity, defines a child simply as a person younger than eighteen years of age.[47] Article 22(2) of the African Charter does not stipulate a different age for nonparticipation in armed conflict, merely stating that involved parties shall take "*all necessary measures* to ensure that no child shall take a direct part in hostilities and refrain in particular from recruiting any child."[48] Here the language is even stronger than in the 1989 UN Convention, which required states to take "all necessary measures" rather than just "feasible" ones.

The decision to make fifteen the minimum age for recruitment and participation in hostilities was controversial and subject to intense debate. Many humanitarian organizations and pressure groups considered fifteen years of age too young for military enrollment. In 1994, the UN constituted a working group to examine the issue, and debates on the need to increase the minimum age to eighteen lasted for more than six years. The Optional Protocol to the Convention on the Rights of the Child on the Involvement of Children in Armed Conflicts,[49] making eighteen the minimum age for military recruitment, was proposed at the sixth session of the working group in January 2000 and adopted by the UN General Assembly in May 2000. The protocol applies to both national armed forces and non-state armed groups and would require nations to rehabilitate former child soldiers. However, while compulsory recruitment below the age of eighteen is prohibited, voluntary recruitment at sixteen years of age is permitted. The United States, the United Kingdom, and Australia were responsible for weakening the protocol by insisting that the panel agree to a minimum age of sixteen for voluntary, noncombatant recruits.[50] These countries insisted on a lower age for voluntary enlistment in order to allow for the enrollment of sixteen-year-olds into educational institutions operated by the military.[51] Although these nations may ensure that sixteen-year-olds enrolled in military training programs will not serve in combat positions before they turn eighteen, this exception opens the door for pretexted voluntary recruitment into military positions that may well draw sixteen- and seventeen-year-old boys into armed conflict.

Some humanitarian organizations expressed disappointment with the failure of the international community to reach a straight-eighteen position. They believe that by failing to raise the age of voluntary recruitment of children to eighteen, governments continue to base their positions primarily on narrow military interests rather than on the best interests of children. The new protocol also creates a double standard by prohibiting all recruitment of children under eighteen, but allowing the recruitment of volunteers under eighteen. This exception raises an important issue with respect to the connection between voluntary and forced recruitment. In practice, the distinction between voluntary and forced recruitment is blurred; in some circumstances, it is entirely absent. Governments and armed groups can find space for underage recruitment by considering and labeling it "voluntary." Although in some cases, young people do volunteer to join military institutions, not all alleged volunteers make truly voluntary choices. Indirect and coercive mechanisms can be used to persuade young people to join the military. Intimidation, social pressure, physical protection, the opportunity for revenge, access to food and shelter, security, and adventure are some of the inducements.

In Mozambique and Angola, boys were encouraged by intimidation and social pressure to join the armed forces. They did so in search of physical protection, access to food and shelter, and the possibility of taking revenge against those who had killed their relatives and destroyed their communities. The dividing line between voluntary and forced recruitment can be very imprecise and ambiguous. The distinction between conscription for service in combat and recruitment for noncombatant roles can also be blurred. The formal distinction can be used as an expedient to justify the presence of children in military bases and camps where, although they are ostensibly noncombatants, they are trained to carry arms, are left to defend the camp against attack and to guard captives, are sent on looting missions, and participate in raids on civilian areas. Children in the military, especially in irregular armies, are easily drawn into combat.

Raising the minimum age for military involvement and clarifying the ambiguities inherent in the distinctions between voluntary and forced recruitment and between combat and noncombatant roles will certainly strengthen international laws protecting children from armed conflict, but alone they have little practical significance to the myriads of children in many areas of the globe where these laws are not understood or recognized. These changes have had little impact on the situation of children aged six, seven, ten, and twelve who were and still are being recruited to be soldiers in many conflict zones. The problem of children's recruitment for participation in war was never specific to the age bracket between fifteen and eighteen, but involved many children under fifteen. So, why focus so much energy and years of debate on that particular age group? The point of contention was the fact that the USA, the UK, and Australia were interested in maintaining the age limit of fifteen for enrollment into military schools, an issue well removed from the pressing need to protect children abducted in war zones. Most of the people I spoke with in the field were not aware of these debates, and when I mentioned them people would say that they would rather have the international community focus on ways to stop the recruitment of younger children under the age of fifteen rather than start by raising the existing minimum age, which was not observed anyway.

The central problems regarding international humanitarian law concerning the involvement of children in armed conflict are not matters of definition but of public acceptance and effective enforcement. International conventions and protocols are based on the voluntary agreement of nation-states and work effectively when countries and their people make compliance a political priority. Agreements regarding children are peculiarly subject to popular consent, for parents, adults in civil and military institutions, and young people themselves must cooperate to ensure their implementation. The question is how to establish better connections between developments at the international level and needs at the local level. Many children well under fifteen years of age were being systematically recruited and coerced into military activities during the six years that marked the debates over age limits for the Optional Protocol, and they continue to be recruited. This testimony comes from Burma (Myanmar) in 2003:

Fourteen-year-old Kyow Zeya should have spent the last three years at school. Instead, he was forced to become a child soldier in the Burma Army. Grabbed by Burmese soldiers at a bus stop near the capital, Rangoon, on his way to visit his aunt at the age of 11, he was told if he did not join the army, he would be imprisoned. "I had no choice," he said.[52]

The success of the Optional Protocol so far has meant very little to the thousands of younger children who are abducted to take part in warfare.

Other significant international instruments for the protection of children include the Rome Statute of the International Criminal Court, adopted in 1998, and the International Labor Organization (ILO) Convention on the Worst Forms of Child Labor, adopted in 1999. The Rome Statute makes it a clear crime to recruit—conscript or enlist—children under fifteen years of age, or to use them in hostilities in both international and intrastate armed conflicts, whether on behalf of a government or any non-state armed group.[53] The ILO convention lists "forced or compulsory recruitment of children for use in armed conflict"[54] among the worst forms of child labor. These treaties were rapidly ratified by the international community. The Worst Forms of Child Labor Convention was the most rapidly endorsed labor convention in history, with 147 states ratifying by November 2003. In April 2002, the Rome Statute reached the necessary sixty ratifications needed to bring it into force.

The UN Security Council has passed a number of resolutions aimed at protecting children from armed conflicts. Security Council Resolution 1261 of 1999 stressed the responsibility of all states to bring an end to impunity and their obligation to prosecute those responsible for grave breaches of the Geneva Conventions. In its Resolution 1379 of 2001, the Security Council urged member states "to prosecute those responsible for . . . egregious crimes perpetrated against children." In 2003, Security Council Resolution 1460 endorsed the UN Era of Application Campaign, led by the office of the Special Representative of the Secretary-General for Children and Armed Conflict. Involving various UN agencies, it ensures more systematic monitoring and reporting on the recruitment and use of children in armed conflict and other types of abuses and violations committed against children in situations of war. While many agencies, organizations, and activist groups have, over the years, been able to gather information about the situation of children in the areas where they operate, so far these efforts have not been effective in enforcing international laws and ensuring that violators cannot act with impunity.

International humanitarian law has been unable to secure the protection of human rights in times of war. The central challenge is how to make international humanitarian law understood, recognized, and enforced in places where children are recruited into armed conflicts on a daily basis. Even the current international laws and agreements requiring nation-states to prevent children under eighteen from military involvement are not widely known or observed. Beyond strengthening international laws, it is vital to reinforce local understandings and norms about notions of childhood and child protection from war, as well to consider the intersections between international and local understandings. Local communities and civil groups must become actively involved in monitoring conflict situations and making efforts to stop the abuse of the rights of children. Effective protection from direct involvement in armed conflict requires the harmonization of local and global understandings of these rights. Effectively translating these rights into local worldviews and meaning systems and making them recognizable and locally sanctioned are vitally necessary steps. A marriage between international law and these more localized norms of child rights and protection is critical. Only a coordinated approach involving both global and local strategies can create an environment conducive to the effective protection of children against armed conflict in places where such protection is most needed. I believe that all societies, under ideal circumstances, strive to protect their children. The biological bond between parent and child is strong and guarantees the survival and continuity of the society. Societies have elaborate mechanisms for childrearing and for structuring the transition from childhood into adulthood. Children are the generation of tomorrow—the new leaders, parents, teachers, and productive workers—and must be properly prepared to run society. In different societies, these values, norms, and practices take different forms that reflect to particular social, economic, and cultural contexts, but they are all aimed at the same goal. What happens when a society's values and norms are turned upside down and young people are abused and turned into criminals and merciless killers? What kinds of political, social, and economic disruptions make that inversion possible?

The involvement of children in war arouses strong emotions. The outrage that some foreign observers express may be based on a false universalization of the position of children and youth in their own societies: contained within primary and secondary educational institutions, preparing for adult occupations, and largely excluded from the freedoms and necessities of economic independence. In societies like Mozambique and Angola, the boundaries between adulthood and childhood have traditionally been more fluid than in European societies. Of necessity, children are actively involved in economic activities; the transition to adulthood is gradual, variable, and responsive to the particular situations of young people, their families, and communities. Universalizing definitions of childhood are often not applicable in many African conditions.

Childhood as Social and Cultural Construction

Contemporary studies of childhood are increasingly committed to the idea that childhood constitutes a social artifact rather than a natural biological state. Childhood as a social category constitutes a relatively recent concept. Philippe Aries locates the genesis of the modern conception of childhood in the eighteenth century, together with bourgeois notions of family, home, privacy, and individuality.[55] As childhood and adulthood became increasingly differentiated, each elaborated its own symbolic world. In modern Western societies, the major tenet of contemporary understandings of childhood is the assumption that children evolve through established phases of development and that childhood stands in opposition to adulthood.[56] By this conception, child development is generally taken to be a natural and universal phase of human existence, one shaped more by biological and psychological considerations than by social factors.[57]

In international humanitarian law, children often appear as pre-social beings and passive recipients of experience who need to be segregated from the harsh realities of the adult world and protected from social danger until they reach the age of eighteen.[58] Thus, childhood appears as a transitional stage, and its temporal dimension is robbed of immediate status as children are seen as something in the "process of becoming rather than being."[59] Children are perceived as knowing less than adults, rather than knowing something else that is specific to their particular situation and surroundings.[60] Therefore, children need to be nurtured and enlightened; they are immature and incapable of assuming responsibilities. In this sense, childhood should constitute a carefree, secure, and happy phase of human existence.[61] Although this notion of childhood is often generalized and even universalized, it derives from a Western and middle-class view of childhood that is not categorically shared around the globe.

Numerous authors have demonstrated the importance of understanding childhood as a social construction. As James and Prout pointed out, "the institution of childhood provides an interpretative frame for understanding the early years of human life. In these terms it is biological immaturity rather than childhood which is a universal and natural feature of human groups."[62] However, notions of childhood cannot be understood in universal terms. They vary across societies, as they are attached to culture, class, gender, and other types of social relations. Notions of childhood also change over time. Hendrick refers to the shifting notions of childhood in nineteenth-and twentieth-century Britain, from an idea of childhood fragmented by urban/rural location and class to one that was much more uniform and coherent.[63]

In many social contexts, the notion of childhood diverges dramatically from this view. Unlike middle-class children whose parents and families are in a position to support them until they are able to sustain themselves (in many cases well over the age of eighteen), many children around the world assume work and social responsibilities at an early age. They participate actively in economic productivity, in household chores, and in the care of younger children. In Angola and Mozambique, as in many other contexts, children are often portrayed as strong and resilient, as survivors who grow in difficult conditions.[64] Being a child in this particular setting may have little to do with age (although people sometimes refer to age limits) and is centrally linked to social roles, expectations, and responsibilities.

In Angola, among the Tchokwè, children are identified through the roles they assume; they are even named according to their occupation

and roles. For example, *tchitutas* are girls and boys around the age of five to seven, whose role is to fetch water and tobacco for the elders and take messages to neighbors. *Kambumbu* are children (especially girls), seven to thirteen years of age, who participate actively in household chores and help parents in the field or with fishing and hunting. *Mukwenge wa lunga* (boys) and the *mwana pwo* (girls), around the age of thirteen, have to pass the rites of initiation. In Mozambique, young girls become wives as early as thirteen or fourteen years of age and become mothers soon after; they are introduced to the roles and responsibilities of married life and motherhood. In such a societal context, emphasis is placed on roles rather than on age. As seventy-five-year-old Sonama, an elderly Angolan, pointed out:

In the past there wasn't this thing of saying that this person is eighteen years of age or ten years of age and, therefore, must do this and that. The elders in the family identified the passing of time through the seasons: the time to plant the maize; the time of the harvest, etc. And in this way children just grew freely, and parents would know what tasks to assign to them depending on the way they were growing. Some children grow faster than others, both mentally and physically.[65]

These examples show the different ways in which childhood can be understood and constructed socially and culturally.

Societies define childhood as dissimilar from adulthood and devise processes to articulate this transition, which takes place in different ways and at different stages in diverse cultural settings. The transition is often seen as a process rather than a single event. It is often composed of a series of gradual transformations, or initiations. The initiatory dimensions do not necessarily take place at the same time. For example, in describing the rites of passage from childhood into adulthood, Grimes identifies several ritualized moments: the *rites of childhood,* which follow birth and precede entry into adolescence; the *adolescent initiations,* which articulate the transition from childhood into adolescence; and the *adult initiations,* which negotiate an exit from adolescence and entry into adulthood.[66] However, these divisions are not rigid; they vary cross-culturally and over time. Like childhood, notions of youth and adolescence are social constructs. What defines youth? Is it age, biology, social roles, social expectations and responsibilities? Or is it a combination of all or some of these factors? For example, in some social settings, an unmarried forty-five-year-old who doesn't have a job and lives in his parents' home might be considered to be in a state of prolonged youth because he does not assume the roles and responsibilities associated with adulthood. On the other hand, a person can reach manhood or womanhood without necessarily becoming an adult. Such a notion of adulthood is primarily understood in terms of social roles and responsibilities.

Among the Tchokwè, initiation processes involve both a physical and a social dimension. The former focuses on adult masculinity and femininity at an immediately physical level through biological changes in the body, and the latter effects an induction into the roles and responsibilities of social adult personhood. The *mukaand* circumcision rituals transform boys into men by defining adolescent masculinity in terms of hunting capacities and sexual prowess. However, the assumption of the roles and responsibilities of manhood is articulated through the *mwiingoony* ritual complex, which takes place after circumcision.[67] For the transition to be properly established, society has to prepare young people to assume these new roles. The ritualized moments of the initiation constitute symbolic enactments of the transition. The initiation is gradual and progressive; it starts at home at an early age and continues well beyond the ritual performance. Multistage, multidimensional, and prolonged initiation processes also occur in Mozambique and in many other contexts in which societies mediate the transition from childhood into adulthood.

The majority of children who participated in the wars in Mozambique and Angola were forcibly recruited, many at a very young age, before making the normative transition from childhood into adulthood. They had no opportunity to prepare socially for adult roles. The rituals of initiation, which symbolically establish this transition, encompass both the physical and the social aspects of a child's development. Becoming an adult is understood to mean more than a certain physical strength and to include a sense of responsibility, of right and wrong, of good and bad, which is acquired through social preparation that is supposed to start at home and continue throughout the initiation process.

Many adults in Mozambique and Angola mentioned that communities in the aftermath of war are still dealing with the serious disruptions the wars caused in the life course of young people. Beyond the massive killings and material destruction, beyond even the transformation of particular children into merciless killers, the wars left a deep moral crisis. Because children were abducted from their homes and schools to fight, the initiation rituals and systematic preparation of young people to become responsible adults ceased. A whole generation was seriously affected. Youth were not only denied their childhoods but also the possibility of becoming responsible and morally grounded citizens. Frequently, adults say that young people no longer have respect for social values and norms: "Children these days do not listen to the elders";[68] "there is no notion of good and bad among young people;"[69] "with the war, initiation ceased to be performed and this is what we see."[70] The absence of initiation practices created a lapse in the process of maturing into an adult person. In addition to the family and community initiation rites, institutions such as the school, the church, and associations for children and youth play a role in the initiation of children into adult roles. But these institutions were also seriously disrupted by war. Young people have to make sense of their world and make their own transition into adulthood within an environment of societal chaos. In this process, many youngsters construct their own imaginary spaces and symbolic worlds with the means available to them. War and political violence are some of those means.

Why Are Children Used in Wars as Soldiers?

The shortcomings of international humanitarian law and the breakdown of local normative and value systems in times of war are not enough to explain why children were and continue to be involved as soldiers in armed conflicts. Several social scientists have recently examined this question. Some consider the phenomenon of child soldering a response to the shortage of manpower as the adult reserve is exhausted by war, poverty, and disease.[71] Others have attempted to explain the occurrence of child soldiers as an expression of cultural propensities and environmental breakdown.[72] Patrimonial politics and traditional cultural forms of initiation and rites of passage to adulthood have also been used to explain the phenomenon.[73]

Other analysts think that the systematic preference for children as soldiers is based on the assumption that children make good soldiers because they are especially susceptible to ideological conditioning; they are easier to manipulate and control; they are readily programmed to feel little fear in combat or revulsion at atrocious acts; and they can simply be made to think of war and only war. Their abductors and commanders believe that children possess excessive energy so that, once trained, they carry out brutal attacks with greater enthusiasm than adults.[74]

I believe that armies of children were created neither by chance, nor from a merely shortage of manpower, not because of the ease of indoctrination. In Mozambique and Angola, there seems to have been a concerted and well-thought-out strategy to use and manipulate children into warfare. In my view, the creation of child soldiers does not constitute an isolated, random incident. Child soldering is part of a warfare strategy that is shared across lines of combat and war zones around the globe. The similarities between what happened to children during the wars in Cambodia, Uganda, and Sierra Leone and what happened in Mozambique and Angola are very striking.

In recent years, anthropologists have pointed out that locality is produced by a combination of internal and external forces and developments.[75] Appadurai's notion of *ethnoscape* is especially helpful. Appadurai uses the term *ethnoscape* to capture the idea of a transnational *ethno,* or group identity, which is constructed as people migrate, interact, and reconfigure their own histories and collective selfhood. Thus the *ethno* assumes a "slippery, non-localized quality."[76] Nordstrom draws on this notion to develop the idea of "war-scapes" to describe the interconnections between local and global networks in war situations. The notion of "war-scapes" permits us to go beyond the individual expression of war in a specific context to understand a global culture of war. As many groups interact, local and transnational concerns are enmeshed in the political and social construction of conflict that is continually reconfigured across time and space."[77] This process of interaction occurred in Mozambique and Angola, where intricate networks of local and global interests played key roles in the conflict. Information about tactics and technologies is transmitted from one war to another through soldiers, military advisers, and mercenaries. Media reports and popular war films also spread this type of information.[78] South African military and several other global players were instrumental in supporting RENAMO and UNITA during the war. In this transnational process, ideas and values about acceptable war practices are established. It is precisely in this context that I consider the spread of the child soldering phenomenon.

Furthermore, I contend that the issue of child soldiers cannot be explained in terms of Africa's precolonial history or cultural traditions. Scholars who have examined the involvement of children in African civil wars as a cultural phenomenon have sometimes confused the extreme actions people take during wartime with a stable, unchanging cultural tradition. People attempt to cope with the disruptions of war by drawing upon their entire cultural repertoire, including spiritual rituals of initiation and healing; insurgent groups deliberately appeal to and employ cultural elements that they proclaim as traditional in order to mobilize popular support and establish their legitimacy; and civil wars often reveal the fault lines within social structures and exacerbate preexisting tensions between groups. However, that does not make wars and the atrocities they involve traditional *em* religiously, ethnically, or culturally based *em* or expressions of deep-seated social conflicts. Rather, the recruitment of children into the military in war represents a real rupture of historical continuity, a profound disruption of social order, and a violation of moral norms.[79]

All societies aim to protect children from war and danger, not only because parents instinctively protect their offspring but also because generational succession guarantees the continuity of society. For example, in southern Africa during the precolonial period, the Zulu, a social group renowned for its military might, did not allow children who had not yet been initiated to become warriors. They were not eligible for *ukubuthwa*—drafting into Zulu military regiments—before the age of eighteen or twenty.[80] In West Africa in the Kano region, only married men were enlisted into the army. In *Children of War*, Singer also refers to an example from northern Uganda, in East Africa. He quotes Olara Otunnu's explanation of the notion of *lapir*, which "denotes cleanliness . . . and attracts the blessings of the ancestors."[81]

Before declaring war the elders would carefully consider their *lapir*—to be sure that their community had a deep and well founded grievance against the other side. If this was established to be the case, war might be declared, but never lightly. And in order to preserve one's *lapir*, strict injunctions would be issued to regulate the actual conduct of war. You did not attack children, women or the elderly; you did not destroy crops, granary stores or livestock. For to commit such taboos would be to soil your *lapir* with the consequence that you would forfeit the blessing of the ancestors, and thereby risk losing the war itself. . . . [82]

Beliefs about purity reinforced norms against endangering civilians, including children.

In my view, the phenomenon of the child soldier can best be understood as rooted in the crisis of the postcolonial state in Africa. Processes of globalization and economic restructuring of the world economy have permeated African communities.[83] Constrained by debt and structural adjustment programs, African economies, like those of most developing countries, have been restructured and undergone serious cuts in basic services reducing the size of the public sector. Inequalities have widened and livelihoods have become more insecure, straining and weakening the social fabric. Household and community capacities to nurture and protect the young have declined, and social norms and value systems to protect children have weakened. This trend has resulted in the commodification of children and a revaluation that has induced an increase in child labor, including child soldiering.

Many children and youth in Africa find it difficult to pursue livelihoods that would enable them to become economically independent and, thus, make an orderly transition from childhood into adulthood. At the same time, their labor is becoming increasingly important to family livelihood strategies. Armed conflict and HIV/AIDS are precipitating a crisis in the family, an institution that has been the cornerstone of African societies but whose capacity for adaptive change to create meaningful, sustainable, and coherent patterns of everyday life is now being seriously threatened.

This crisis in the African postcolonial state creates the basic conditions in which phenomena such as child soldiering flourish. The crisis is also coupled with ethnic tensions over power sharing, identity, and access to resources. The incapacity of the state to respond to the situation and to provide for and protect its citizens is apparent. The collapse of social and economic structures in rural areas and the massive migration of young people to towns in search of employment and livelihoods, often without success, contributes to driving them into soldiering. Thus, the increasing development of armed conflicts into which youth and children are drawn is a direct symptom of such a crisis. In Mozambique and Angola, the crisis was exacerbated by external pressures, especially the South African apartheid regime's destabilization efforts through its direct support of rebel movements. During these wars, children and youth became vulnerable to recruitment because of the lack of opportunities in the countryside. Ethnic alliances and a general disenchantment with the state for its rejection of traditional authorities and cultural values prompted some village chiefs to help recruit young men to join the rebel forces. Boys and young men also volunteered to serve the government. For many, the possession of a weapon was often their only means of access to food and a sense of power.

Conclusion

Children's participation in war is not a phenomenon specific to our times; children have been involved in war since the Middle Ages. Yet the problem has gained new proportions today. The differences between old and new wars highlight but do not fully explain this change. While the extent and degree of the differences between past and present international and civil wars is debatable, it is clear that contemporary warfare presents new features and develops old features to an extent rarely seen before.

International humanitarian law and local notions of childhood determine the way we understand these phenomena today. The recognition that international humanitarian law is unable to protect children from war and prevent their recruitment into armed forces calls for a reexamination of the notions of childhood behind such agreements and the real capacity to enforce them, given the different socioeconomic and cultural contexts in which laws are drawn up and conflict takes place. The way forward lies in reinforcing norms and value systems for child protection based on indigenous local worldviews and meaning systems.

Finally, I contend that the participation of children in war is not based on African precolonial history and culture and does not result from shortages in manpower. Rather, the phenomenon is deeply rooted in the social and economic crisis that the continent faces, which results to a significant degree from pressures associated with globalization. These pressures attenuate the community's capacity to nurture and protect children, and they increase the vulnerability of children to involvement in armed conflict.

Chapter 3
Recruitment and Initiation

At the age of ten, Marula[1] was kidnapped by RENAMO insurgents during a rebel attack on his village in Gaza province, southern Mozambique. His father and his younger sister also were kidnapped along with other villagers. They walked for three days, carrying military equipment and items looted from the village, before reaching the RENAMO camp. There the family was separated. While his father was sent to the men's ward and his sister to the women's sector, Marula was ordered to join a group of young boys. A few weeks later, Marula started military training. He was not allowed to see his father and sister, but they managed to arrange secret meetings on a few occasions. During one of these meetings, they agreed to run away together. But they were caught attempting to escape. Marula was ordered to kill his own father, and so he did. Following this first killing, Marula grew into a fierce RENAMO combatant and was active for more than seven years. He does not even remember how many people he tortured, how many he killed, how many villages he burned, and how many food convoys and shops he looted. After the war, he returned to his village, but his paternal uncle, the only close relative who survived the war, refused to welcome him home. The uncle, whose brother Marula had killed, could not forgive his nephew. Eventually, through the skilful intervention of his uncle's wife, Marula came to stay in the house despite his uncle's disapproval.[2]

What are we to make of Marula and his disturbing story?

It is difficult to regard Marula as simply a victim who was compelled to kill and, therefore, bears no responsibility for his act of parricide. Yet Marula's responsibility is not the same as that of a boy who kills his father for some imagined benefit. Civil war and social peace create quite distinct moral conditions. The very ground upon which action is conducted differs in the two situations, even though they represent two states of a single, albeit deeply divided society. How can we understand moral responsibility in the disruptive and distorted conditions of civil war? Rather than conducting a philosophical inquiry into the degrees of guilt that can be attributed to children who are coerced into active participation in civil wars, this study examines the actual conditions under which child soldiers lived. What can we learn from their own accounts and from others about the new identities they developed in these interstitial positions and the type of agency they were able to exercise? We should remember that only the survivors can tell their stories.

It is clear from former child soldiers' accounts of their recruitment into militias that coercion predominated. Many boys like Marula were kidnapped or forced into military camps. The context of civil war made detachment from armed conflict impossible, even if enlistment was ostensibly voluntary. Once in the militia, boys were initiated into violence through a deliberate process of terror. Terrified themselves, they were prepared to inflict terror on others. As Marula's account shows, these were not two separate phases in which boys were first brutalized by soldiers and then forced to brutalize civilians. Rather, the infliction of suffering on others was part of their own initiation into violence. Marula's act of murder irrevocably severed him from his immediate family; he violated fundamental kinship ties with his own hand. Thereafter, his action was both sign and cause of his commitment to the militia. In such situations, the roles of victim and perpetrator become confused. This confusion occurs not only in the relations between armed combatants and civilians in civil wars but also as a contradiction within the position occupied by child soldiers in militias.

Many former soldiers saw these circumstances as excusing them from responsibility for their actions. Fernando, who was only nine at the time he entered the military, explained: "My first military assignment was to attack a village and steal cattle . . . we burnt down that village . . . With my gun I killed the ammunition chief. . . . I am very sad about my story; but I had no choice."[3] His argument is echoed by many other demobilized youth. Sadness about a past that could not have been changed is an important theme in their recollections. Although the moral responsibility of individual soldiers may be severely limited by the constraints under which they fought, it is not entirely absent. The consequences of such acts cannot be evaded. In both practical and spiritual terms, child soldiers are marked by their participation in violence and death.

Programs promoting the demobilization of soldiers and their reintegration into civil society recognize that boys who grew up in the militias face special problems. They have been socialized into violence rather than into the identities developed through work and family in peaceable times. Their relatives and covillagers recognize that young men who have been changed into instruments of death must be transformed in order to return to family and community life. Otherwise, they face risks and pose dangers to themselves and others.

Careful analysis of the stories that young men tell about their lives confirms these viewpoints. Within the militias, child soldiers were not devoid of agency; these boys were agents in their own right. They adapted to the conditions into which they had been forced and attempted to survive and even succeed. Their agency however, is of a specific type. Drawing on De Certeau's distinction between strategies and tactics, I argue that child soldiers display "tactical agency" devised to cope with and maximize the concrete, immediate circumstances of the military environment in which they have to operate. They are not in a position of power; they may not be fully conscious of the ultimate goals of their actions; and they may not anticipate any long-term gains or benefits. All three characteristics that would, in De Certeau's terms, make their actions strategic are absent.[4] Nonetheless, they are fully conscious of the immediate returns and they act, within certain constraints, to seize opportunities that are available to them. These actions are likely to have both beneficial and deleterious long-term consequences.

This chapter examines how boys were recruited by warring militias and initiated into violence. It analyzes their lives within the confines of their military activity, their fears, sorrows, pains, and joys. It ends by considering the interstitial subject position and tactical agency of these young combatants in the context of political violence. First, though, we consider the problematic conjunction of child and soldier in the specific cultural contexts of Mozambique and Angola.

Child/Soldier: A Graphic Representation

The term *child soldier* is an oxymoron that signifies the violence that this position does to established social categories. Here a clarification of the specific meaning of the term *soldier* in these civil wars, especially when preceded by the term *child*, is necessary. The soldier in these contexts was often not a regular soldier of the sort who serves in state-sponsored, centrally controlled, and well-disciplined armed forces. Rather, the term refers to the type of fighter who often fills the ranks of guerrilla and rebel groups, inadequately trained and outfitted, often operating under the influence of drugs. Such soldiers harass, loot, and kill defenseless civilians indiscriminately. Not only do they show their victims no mercy, they may even fail to distinguish between friends and foes, kin and non-kin. In southern Mozambique, these soldiers were known as *matsanga*. This term signified the military forces commanded by Andrè Matsangaíssa, RENAMO's first president and military leader.[5] RENAMO militiamen were associated with violence, terror, and indiscriminate killings. Although government soldiers were reported to behave in a similar fashion, in the southern region this was considered to be more of an exception than the rule. Many reports attest that RENAMO used terror as a matter of policy and strategy.[6] In Angola, similarly, the insurgent group UNITA was reported to have been more active in abducting children and using boys as soldiers than was the government, although the MPLA forces are also reported to have recruited children. Most child soldiers are transformed into this type of irregular combatant.

We also need to clarify the meaning of the term *child*. As discussed in the previous chapter, in Mozambique and Angola, as in many other societies within and beyond Africa, children are portrayed as strong, resilient, and active persons who grow even under difficult conditions.[7] Children are synonymous with wealth because of the contribution they make to the productive work of the family and as a source of security for the future. Thus, children are social actors with an active presence of their own.[8]

The definition of childhood in these African cultures has little to do with age, although people sometimes refer to age limits. Rather, the positions of children are defined through social roles, expectations, and responsibilities. Among the Tchokwè ethnolinguistic group in Moxico province in Angola, children are identified with what they do or are supposed to do, and each position carries a distinct name. In Mozambique, girls as young as thirteen or fourteen years of age become wives and become mothers soon after. Marriage and motherhood introduce them to the roles and responsibilities of adult womanhood. In such a societal context, emphasis is placed on roles rather than on age. As children mature, adults tailor their expectations to each child's particular pattern of growth.

Initiation rituals guiding young men and women through the transition to adulthood reflect this variability and unevenness. Among the Tchokwè, initiation processes have distinct physical and social dimensions. One focuses on the attainment of adult masculinity and femininity through biological changes in the body-self, and the other effects an induction into the roles and responsibilities of social adult personhood. The ritualized moments of the initiation constitute symbolic enactments of the transition to adulthood. However, initiation is a gradual process; it starts at home at an early age and continues well beyond the performance of rituals.

Warfare and soldiering are generally perceived as activities for the initiated. Indeed, the transition to adult manhood is often marked or brought about by military service. The age of conscription in many countries is eighteen, and international law specifies that youths under the age of fifteen should not be recruited or drafted into armies. In

Western societies that lack rituals marking early adolescence, military service often functions as an initiation ritual for young men. The transition from civilian into soldier constitutes a carefully designed process of reconfiguring identities.[9] This passage is especially dramatic in situations of armed combat, when boys move from being protected to risking their own lives to protect others. Military conscripts submit to a training regimen that encourages and rewards competitiveness, insensitivity, and aggression. Dominance is encouraged, but only over the enemy; obedience to superiors is inculcated. The physical condition of soldiers is enhanced to suggest power and strength. Soldiers are taught to manipulate arms, to prepare for combat, and to kill.

The military institution is a locus for the creation of a specific form of masculinity. Cock posits a direct connection between masculinity and militarism: "[T]he army is an institutional sphere for the cultivation of masculinity; war provides the social space for its validation."[10] Prevailing notions of masculinity provide powerful tools for changing boys into soldiers. Women generally occupy marginal positions because military discourse and ideology are heavily drawn from gender definitions that cast women as weak, prohibited from aggressive behavior, and subordinated to men. Although in Angola and Mozambique girls were also abducted to participate in civil war, only boys were subjected to military training and authorized to kill.

While the conditions under which the taking of human life is considered acceptable vary from culture to culture, killing is generally seen as an extreme measure reserved for highly circumscribed circumstances. When licensed by the state, the responsibility for killing lies with initiated men whose military training prepares them not only to commit such acts on command but also to cope emotionally with the consequences of their actions. In the civil wars in Mozambique and Angola, young men were initiated into violence through military training, but the discipline of a regular army was absent. The use of lethal force was not clearly directed and controlled, and soldiers were not emotionally prepared for violence except by experiencing violence themselves. The conditions of civil war generated a distorted, destructive, and problematic form of masculinity that was not aligned with civil society in peacetime.

In Angola and Mozambique, from where the majority of the children who participated in these wars were abducted, many at a very early age, they were not socially prepared to assume the role of soldier. Many older people recognized that, beyond the massive death toll and material destruction, the war created a crisis in moral values. Respect for rules and norms, for adults and the elderly, and for the orderly process of maturation had been eroded. According to an Angolan *kimbanda* (healer), "[W]ith the war, initiation rituals for the young ceased to be performed."[11] War is viewed as a very serious affair, so soldiers need to be well trained for such a tremendous task. Being prepared to fight a war is understood to go beyond physical strength and mastery of weapons to include a sense of responsibility, of right and wrong, and of good and bad war practices. Angolans and Mozambicans believe that a set of war ethics should be acquired through initiation that takes place outside the context of combat. Some Mozambicans and Angolans have stated that moral as well as martial knowledge was provided by older to younger men growing up in peacetime. This initiation enabled them to become valuable members of society. "But today things are upside down, nothing works normally anymore, it is complete chaos."[12] Some elderly people in Mozambique and Angola asserted that the absence of these initiation rituals creates a serious lapse in the process of maturing into an adult person. The other institutions that guided boys and girls into adult roles were also seriously disrupted by war. Young men and women have to make sense of their world and navigate their own transition to adulthood within an environment of societal chaos. In this process, many youths construct their own imaginary spaces and symbolic worlds with whatever means are available to them. Civil war and political violence have become centrally important and yet socially isolated arenas for young men's self-definition.

The Recruitment of Children into the Military

How did children become involved in these armed conflicts? What immediate circumstances effected their recruitment into militias, and how were they socialized into the role of soldier? The nightmare condition of the child soldier required breaking down the socially established barriers between childhood and soldiering. The interstitial position of the child soldier is achieved through a careful process of initiation into a new culture of terror and violence that starts with their forcible recruitment.

Many of the children—boys and girls—who participated in the wars in Mozambique and Angola were brutally abducted from their families and forced to follow the soldiers into the military camps. Some were captured by rebels during raids on villages. Fernando is a fourteen-year-old from the district of Chokwè, Gaza province, in Mozambique.

I was kidnapped at my house by armed bandits (RENAMO soldiers) in the night, while sleeping together with my two brothers. . . . They tied me up and took me away together with my two brothers. . . . While doing this some [soldiers] were burning down the village and after that they took us all to a base [military camp] . . . we walked to the base . . . some time later I was sent for [military] training. . . .[13]

One former young soldier recalls that he was abducted from his home by a group of UNITA soldiers on a beautiful moonlight evening. His family was sitting outside in the courtyard when "Suddenly we heard gun shots and we all ran to hide inside the house. The soldiers came into the house and asked everybody to line up outside. Then they told me to go with them. I was taken to a military base and shown how to operate with guns."[14] He was eleven years old.

Zita, from the district of Macia, Gaza province in Mozambique, shared his recruitment story with me. He was abducted by RENAMO soldiers in his village, Chilengue (near the Bilene beach), and taken to the Kalanga area. He was twelve years old when he started his military training at the RENAMO camp of Ngugwè. After the training, Zita participated in various military incursions. He couldn't remember how many. But he remembers taking part in the notorious attack on Taninga on 3 February 1987, in which dozens of civilians were killed.[15]

Girls were also abducted and taken into military camps. Although in Angola and Mozambique very few girls were sent to the front lines as soldiers, many of them were kidnapped and kept in the military camps. Here is the testimony of Maria, a girl from Josina Machel Island in Mozambique:

I was kidnapped with three friends of mine when we were in the bush looking for firewood. A group of RENAMO soldiers stopped us, and forced us to go with them to the military base. We had to carry the products they had looted . . . we walked for three days until we reached the base. I lived in the base for three years. During the day we had to cook, clean the base and look for firewood and water. During the night soldiers came to take us to sleep with them . . . a soldier per night . . . The lucky ones were those who were chosen by an "officer" who had a hut for them to live in, and who protected them as his wives.[16]

Astro was twelve years old when he started his military training with UNITA in Karilonge, Huambo province. He was picked up on the street.

I was walking. . . . When I was near the railway line, UNITA soldiers came and said, "Hey boy, come with us, we want you to do some work for us." It was a lie. They took me to N'gove . . . and there I did my military training, which lasted only five months due to an attack we suffered from the government troops. . . . My training should have lasted eight months.[17]

Ernesto was even younger when his village was occupied and he was taken as a soldier.

I am 10 years old, and I am from Chibuto, Gaza Province [in Mozambique] . . . the bandits [RENAMO] occupied our village. They had a base there. We lived with the bandits until one day FRELIMO [government] soldiers attacked the

[RENAMO] base. We had to run to the bush with the bandits . . . to Inhambane province. When we arrived there I was trained as a soldier.[18]

Balto, a young man from Huambo who served in the government army, told me that government soldiers took him from his uncle's home. There were five soldiers who ordered him to go with them. The soldiers had already abducted three other boys. Balto says he was inside the house and there was no way he could have escaped.[19]

Traditional leaders were reported to have been involved in the recruitment of child soldiers, particularly in the Angolan provinces of Biè, Huambo, and Malange. In colonial times, *sobas* (chiefs) had to collect taxes from the population. Now they were expected to furnish young recruits to UNITA and in some cases, especially in Biè, to the government army as well.[20] There are several accounts of *sobas'* participation in recruitment. Lopes was twelve years old in 1993, when he was selected at school to be sent to the UNITA forces.

Sobas had to provide UNITA with soldiers from their *sobados* [areas of jurisdiction of the *sobas*], so they would ask the teachers to give them children. I was taken from school straight to the UNITA base [military camp] where I had military training for three months before starting to go on missions.[21]

Domingo from Malange in Angola was taken into UNITA's army from school. The UNITA soldiers who attacked the school that day took him and four other boys from his class. The soldiers killed his teacher on the spot because he was wearing a MPLA tee shirt. Domingo and his three classmates were made to march a long distance until their reached the military camp; two of them died during the long journey.[22] Dunga was captured by UNITA soldiers when he was on his way to visit his brother-in-law. "They told me to go with them. . . . Later I managed to escape and returned home. But the UNITA soldiers asked the *soba* to show them my house and, in the evening, they came and took me for the second time."[23]

Other, less powerful, members of local communities participated in recruitment. In some cases, teachers and parents had to give their pupils, sons, and daughters to the *soba*, who then sent them the militia. Ben remarked: "UNITA asked the *sobas* to give a certain number of boys (periodically). Parents were responsible for encouraging the boys to stay with UNITA, and to return them if they escaped. If the boys escaped and were not returned to the *soba*, the families would suffer."[24]

Parents were also directly coerced to send their sons into the militia. The mother of a child soldier explained that her son was kidnapped and then sent back by a commander because he was ill. When the UNITA troops who had abducted him found out that he was back home, they blamed it on her and her husband. "They said that I prevented him from joining the military. . . . I said no, the boy was very ill. My husband is a *catequista* [religious leader] . . . and the UNITA soldiers harassed him, and he had to let them take our son."[25] In these circumstances, parents were unable to protect their own offspring. Children's confidence in the ability of their parents to protect them quickly faded. As sixteen-year-old Nelson said: "[A]t night I would dream that my father would come to rescue me,"[26] but unfortunately that never happened.

In a striking reversal of normal generational relationships, adults sometimes surrendered to the power of guns wielded by very young soldiers. Children had to become killers or be killed. In the context of such profound social crisis, parents might view their children joining the armed forces—government or rebel—as a way of protecting both their children and themselves. Guns gave these children the ability to defend themselves and their relatives, as well as access to whatever food, clothing, and shelter the armed forces provided.[27]

In southern Mozambique, village chiefs do not seem to have been involved in the forced recruitment of boy soldiers as frequently as they were in some provinces of Angola. There are accounts of local chiefs who supported the rebels or the government, but the extent to which they had a direct hand in recruiting young combatants is not clear. In other areas of the country, especially in the central and northern regions, a stronger link between traditional authorities and the rebels was reported.[28] The difference seems to depend mostly on whether the area was controlled by one force or another or changed hands frequently, and not from any fundamental differences in social structure. The area of southern Mozambique on which my research focused was generally under government control. Villages more hotly contested or under firmer rebel control were also those areas in which chiefs might have played a significant role in the recruitment of boy soldiers. Traditional authorities were called upon to serve the rebels or the government by furnishing boys to the military forces in both Mozambique and Angola.

Not all child soldiers were forcibly recruited; some boys volunteered to join the military. Pitango was fifteen years old when he joined the government forces in the province of Biè, Angola.

I started military service in 1994. I volunteered to join the government army because we were suffering a lot in my village. . . . I wanted to defend my province and help my family with the products that I could get from the military ambushes. When you have a gun you can defend yourself.[29]

Fonseca was thirteen years old when he joined the government army.

I got into the FAA [government army] in July 1994. I volunteered; no one
forced me to join. The *soba* only said that he had been instructed by the government to encourage all young people to join the army and fight for their country.
I volunteered to avoid being *rusgado* [picked up in the street] because they
could be nasty to you.[30]

In his village, young men were pressured to "volunteer."

Both accounts point to intricate connections between voluntary and
forced recruitment. Although some young people volunteered for ideological reasons and were aware of the strategic objectives of the war they
were waging, many were responding to the more immediate conditions
that civil war had created in their communities. Former boy soldiers
listed insecurity, vulnerability, and lack of food among the reasons that
led them to volunteer. Indirect yet coercive mechanisms were used to
persuade young people to join the military. Intimidation and social
pressure pushed some boys; others were drawn in by the potential to secure physical protection, opportunities to take revenge for the killing of
relatives, access to food and shelter, and sheer adventure.[31] Particularly
important in the context of civil war is the sense of security and power
that the possession of a gun provided. As one young man pointed out,
"[N]o one messes with you when you have a gun."[32] In some cases, the
main attraction of the militia seemed to be wearing military gear and
carrying an AK-47.

There seems to be communal complicity in the recruitment of child
soldiers, if only that parents, teachers, and chiefs were, or felt themselves to be, impotent and incapable of doing anything to prevent these
young children from being forced to participate in war. Having a child
join the military was a strategy for protection of the child, the family,
and the community.[33]

Initiation into Violence

Military training of new recruits is designed to break down the boy soldier's ties to other people and create a new, warlike persona. As Roberts
aptly stated: "A soldier must learn to dehumanise other people and
make them into targets, and to cut himself off from his own feelings of
caring and connectedness to the community. His survival and compe-
tence as a soldier depend on this process."[34] The heavy physical exercise
of military training pushes children to high levels of physical exhaustion
in order to create mental states conducive to ideological indoctrination.[35]
Many young former soldiers in Angola mentioned the Jura (a form of ritual celebration adopted by UNITA) during which young soldiers were
forced to sing and dance non-stop the whole night through. The practice

was aimed at making them forget about home and about their parents, brothers, sisters, and friends. Induced forgetting, along with the isolation of the camps, constitute a strategy to disconnect recruits from their past and cut their ties with society—family, friends, and community alike.[36] In both Mozambican and Angolan military camps, marijuana and bullet-powder were reported to be widely used to induce forgetting or insensibility, to enhance morale, and to make soldiers fearless when performing horrible deeds.[37] Young boys who had been forcibly inducted often had to endure long periods of darkness, severe beatings, and deliberately instilled terror to impress on them that there was no going back. Intense psychological pressure was placed on recruits to remold their identities.[38]

Terror and fear, evoked by horrific acts of violence during military training, were centrally important instruments in the dehumanization process. Often new recruits were both agents and victims of such violence simultaneously. Boys in training received their weapons, not when they had learned simply how to use them, but when they demonstrated their willingness to kill. Fernando, a former child soldier from Mozambique who fought alongside RENAMO, recounted his story:

I've run, I've turned somersaults and climbed trees. Then they taught me to dismount and mount guns. After four months of training, they put me to a test. They put a person before me and ordered me to shoot him. I shot him. After the test they considered me good and they gave me a weapon and a gun. And they told me that from that time on I was chief of a group of other children. . . . My first task was to attack a village and steal cattle for the base. We burnt down the village. We killed cattle. We returned to the base. Some weeks after that, they ordered us to ambush a convoy which was passing by Maluana.[39]

Young Fernando demonstrated his transformation into boy soldier by killing a person "put before him" whom he was ordered to shoot; he was rewarded by being named chief of a gang of boy soldiers who attacked villages and convoys, killing other persons whose presence he does not even acknowledge.

Boys were initiated into violence by committing such acts. Young recruits lived under constant fear of being accused of wrongdoing, of treason, or of attempted escape. Repeated and merciless killing was the only way to avert the possibility of dying.

A significant number of new recruits tried to flee from the camps, but only a very few succeeded. The father of a boy who was abducted described his son's history:

When RENAMO soldiers attacked our neighborhood (First of May), in Maputo's Urban District No. 5, they kidnapped a number of youngsters, amongst them was my son Paulo. He was only nine years old. He was taken to Chinhang-wanine military camp, where he was forced to drink water from a skull after days of walking. Paulo managed to escape after nine months of captivity.[40]

Paulo's father does not know exactly how his son managed to escape from the RENAMO camp. Successful escapes were rare, and the penalty for failed escape attempts was execution. Almost all the young men I met who had fought with UNITA and RENAMO mentioned being forced to watch the execution of those who had been caught attempting to escape.

Whoever did not want to fight was killed. . . . They would slice the throat of those who did not want to fight. . . . I was trained for three days on how to march and run. Then they gave me my weapon and I got used to fighting. The orders were to kill anyone we caught and to bring back anything they had on them.[41]

Significantly, this account conflates the execution of recruits who attempted to escape and the acts of murder that those who remained were compelled to perform. Some recruits witnessed the execution of boys to whom they had the closest of ties.

My brother and I were together in the same camp. My brother was caught while trying to escape and was tied to a tree and killed. I was watching, but I had to keep myself from crying because if they had discovered that we were related I could have been killed too.[42]

In this instance, the boy soldier hid his grief and his kinship with the victim in order to escape the same fate. Witnessing executions was not regarded as a sufficient deterrent to escape, however. Some new recruits were ordered to kill others who had fled but were recaptured. Former child soldiers who recounted their participation in such executions, even as witnesses, eloquently described their meaning:

I saw someone being killed (in the parade). He was my friend and was also a soldier, and one day while he was trying to flee someone denounced him and he was caught. He was imprisoned for a few days. . . . One day they brought him to the parade; they tied his arms and legs against a post, then blindfolded him and then shot him. The executioner then sucked his blood. I felt very sad; it was terrible to witness all that.[43]

Recruits who witnessed such executions realized that the same fate could befall them. Equally important, their identities and their ties to fellow soldiers were narrowed from personal friendship to terms defined entirely and exclusively by the militia. "It was terrible to witness all that." In such ritualized acts of murder, boy soldiers were unable to act humanely, and they vividly experienced their own powerlessness—except as killers.

Marula's experience of being ordered to execute his father after a failed escape attempt was not unique. The murder of close relatives was a method used by the militias of both Mozambique and Angola to turn boys into soldiers. Relatives of a kidnapped child in the camp were killed in the child's presence, precisely to cut the child's kinship ties, eliminate the child's desire to escape and rejoin the family, and demonstrate the unlimited power of the commanders. Several cases of children who were forced to murder their relatives are in the testimonies from Angola.

A young soldier in Huambo mentioned that during the long walk to the base, the mother of one of his friends was unable to keep up with the march, as they had been walking for four days and she was carrying a heavy load. The commander took his gun, gave it to the boy, and ordered him to kill his mother.[44] In other instances, RENAMO soldiers would go out and look for the relatives of children they had abducted and kill them in their villages.

Noel, a twelve-year-old boy from Nhamatanda, Mozambique, recounted that he was forcibly recruited to join RENAMO when he was only seven. During training, he mentioned to his fellows that his father was a captain in the government army and would come and rescue him. When this information reached the RENAMO commanders, they sent soldiers back to Noel's village to kill his father. His father was away from home, so they killed Noel's grandfather. They made sure that Noel got the news and threatened to find and kill his father as well.[45]

Recruits were forced to attack and loot their own towns and villages precisely to impress on them the impossibility of going back. More symbolic means of transforming the identity of the boy soldier were also deployed. Children were sometimes given new names and forbidden to use their birth names, traditional names, or nicknames that related to their past experiences at home with family, relatives, and friends. Some new names signified the aggression boy were to display in combat: "the strong," "Rambo," "the invincible," "Russian," and "the powerful." Others were ordinary names, but were different from boys' birth names in order to mark their new identities.[46]

This initiation into violence was a ritualized process that often drew upon spiritual practices conducted in peacetime and turned them to warlike, even fatal purposes. For example, in the camps young recruits were made to suck or drink the blood of the people they or others had killed, which was believed to make them fearless and immune to remorse. Blood sucking was a common theme voiced by former boy soldiers. Many of them mentioned this practice without being asked about it. "I saw many people being killed, many dead bodies. . . . My friend who tried to escape was killed in front of me. They drank his blood . . . I saw it. They do it in front of everybody to discourage those who want to flee."[47] Domingo, a former soldier from Malange, engaged in a dialogue with me:

Domingo: "Escapees who were found were generally killed. They were tied to a post and all the troops would be called to watch. They were killed, and the killer had sometimes to drink the victim's blood. The blood was said to be good for the person not to feel remorse."

Honwana: "Do you think it [drinking the blood] works?"

Domingo: "Yes, it works."[48]

Another former soldier mentioned that the ritual drinking of blood still affected him. "I used to drink the blood of the people I killed. . . . Today I cannot look at red wine because I feel like killing and sucking blood again."[49] The drinking of blood apparently functioned as an initiation rite. Eduardo, a seventeen-year-old from Kuito, recalled: "I drank blood on the day I finished my military training, in the swearing-in ceremony. We all had to drink two spoons of blood each. They told us that this was important to prevent us from being haunted by the spirits of the people we might kill."[50]

Echoes of traditional religious beliefs and practices are audible in these testimonies. Militia commanders deliberately used features of local peacetime initiation rituals in the initiation of recruits into violence in order to make boy soldiers fearless and to mystify the taking of life. Herbal medicines were sometimes given to recruits in order to enable them to fight courageously and protect them from death during combat. Local healers, called *kimbandas*, treated soldiers in the Angolan camps. Commanders often sought the aid of healers to win battles and shield them from injury. Antonio Sula from Cangumbe said that they used *mufuca* (a tail of an animal prepared with remedies), which they would shake to protect them in situations of danger, However, not all commanders and soldiers had access to these special treatments. Eduardo remarked: "I don't think all commanders were protected by the kimbanda. . . . I saw many commanders die in combat." Recruits were also treated by healers, especially if they were upset by ritualized killings during training. Sam, a young former solider, recounted: "In order not to be afraid of fighting the war we had to kill a person at the parade. . . . Those who cried in the evening [after having killed] were treated by the *kimbanda*s."[51]

Blood sucking and *kimbanda* treatments are clearly linked to local ritual forms and healing practices. The sucking of human and animal
blood is, in many societies, an integral part of the initiation of healers,
diviners, chiefs, and other individuals who are called to perform functions that situate them above ordinary mortals.[52] Because UNITA saw itself as a political movement attached to the masses, it appropriated and
manipulated a language and set of symbols that resonate deeply with
local systems of meaning in order to achieve its own objectives.[53]

Together with strenuous physical exercise, manipulation of weapons,
and the imposition of strict discipline, these practices represent a powerful ritualized initiation into a culture of violence and terror. However,
while initiation may have transformed some boys into strong and fierce
combatants, it did not facilitate their social transition into responsible
adulthood, at least not in terms of locally accepted standards. Elderly
Angolans and Mozambicans saw the violent and terrorizing acts of many
child soldiers as falling well outside what they considered acceptable
and responsible adult behavior, even in times of war.

In his analysis of the civil war in Mozambique, Alex Vines reported
that

young RENAMO soldiers as little as 10 [years of age] seem to have been put
through psychological trauma and deprivation, such as being hung upside down
from trees until their individualism is broken, and encouraged and rewarded
for killing. Some commentators believe that massacres in southern Mozambique
are committed by these child combatants, who have been programmed to feel
little fear or revulsion for such actions, and thereby carry out these attacks with
greater enthusiasm and brutality than adults would.[54]

To former boy soldiers, their commanders, and contemporary commentators, the extremes of violence to which boy soldiers were subjected and the atrocities they committed against others seem closely
related.

Spaces for Maneuver within the Terrain of Warfare

Child soldiers assumed new identities in the militia camps and through
their participation in civil war. If these identities did not fulfil the norms
of fully responsible adult manhood, then what sort of identities were
they? What kinds of actions were condoned for boy soldiers? How did
they create and sustain viable identities amid their horrific experiences
of warfare?

Bhabha's mapping of the interstitial spaces that such persons occupy
offers a useful conceptual approach to these questions. As he put it,

"These 'in between' spaces provide the terrain for elaborating strategies of selfhood—singular and communal—that initiate new signs of identity, and innovative sites of collaboration, and contestation. . . ."[55] The category of child soldier is located in the unstable position between childhood and adulthood. Their intermediary position is visible in their accounts of daily military life. Despite the indoctrination and dehumanization they experience during the initiation process, these young men manage to develop a world of their own, situated within this ambiguous state of being simultaneously children and soldiers. In the previous section, I brought their vulnerability to the fore, showing how they are manipulated into becoming fierce combatants and merciless killers. This section conveys the ways in which these children create imaginary spaces for themselves within a context of violence and terror. How do they find space and time to play children's games, miss their relatives, and cry over their pains and sorrows? How is this twilight position enacted out their daily life?

Narratives of former boy soldiers are suffused with expressions of their feelings: their fears, sorrows, sadness, loss, pain, expectations, and hopes. Fear was the most pervasive of these feelings. Child soldiers expressed fear of being taken to the battlefield to fight, fear of being killed, and fear of their commanders. The relationship between boy soldiers and older commanders was founded in terror. Any wrong move, however slight, could result in death, possible not only in combat but also in the camps where soldiers were kept under constant surveillance. These forms of death were confirmed in the narratives of former soldiers. The fear they felt was in contrast to the sense of security they had previously enjoyed at home.

During the war I was very scared of going into combat. I thought I was going to die. Before going on missions, I always thought of my parents and asked in silence for them to pray for me. . . . In my quiet time I would always be longing to be home with my father and my mother. I often remembered the things we did together as a family.[56]

Some of the narratives report cruel commanders who ordered soldiers to risk their lives while they themselves were ritually protected. This situation represents a potentially fatal inversion of ordinary relations between the generations.

The war is not good. I will not recommend it to my future child. In the war you have no say. You are always under the orders of the commanders, and they can make you do just anything. I was very frightened when I took part in a twenty-four-hour combat to recapture Mbanza-Congo from the government forces. We were under intense fire for twenty-four hours. In the end we had to withdraw because our ammunition was gone. That day I thought I was going to die because I was not protected by the kimbanda. All the chiefs were well protected. I saw them being treated by the kimbanda.[57]

Commanders also punished new recruits who were not training for battle, for acting like ordinary boys.

Our commanders were really mean and nasty. We were very scared of them. One day, while we were still doing our military training, we got permission to go bathe in the river, but we stayed there for quite a while because we started playing, swimming and enjoying ourselves. Time just flew. Our instructor came to look for us. He was so furious that he shot my friend, who died on the spot. I feel so sad when I remember all these things.[58]

In the military camps, the most innocent of pastimes became the occasion for the most brutal of murders.

These accounts of fear are suffused with pain: not just physical pain, which no doubt was common in the camps and in battle, but also emotional and psychological pain.

One day during a combat, my friend was shot and died next to me. I managed to take him to the margin of the nearby river. Together with other friends, we buried him. He was my best friend . . . In the war nobody could cry; if the commanders saw you crying they would take measures.[59]

Responding emotionally to the death in battle could provoke execution in the camps. Former soldiers frequently spoke of the pain they felt at the death and devastation their own militia inflicted. These feelings were most acute when the victims were known and intimately connected to them.

I felt very, very sad when I found out that most of my relatives were killed in an attack to my village, carried out by one of our groups. Those who didn't die disappeared. I didn't feel like fighting with them anymore because UNITA killed my own family . . . I was living with this big pain inside my heart, but I couldn't say anything. I just did what I did, because I was forced to do it. I didn't fight because I wanted to.[60]

Many of these young men had problems living with this pain, as well as with their awareness of the pain they had inflicted on others. A few boys claimed that, when their commanders were absent, they had acted humanely. However, this claim was made in the context of asserting their helplessness at other times:

If the commander told me to go for a mission and kill everyone, sometimes I felt compassion for the people and, if the commander was not there, I would let them run home instead of killing them. It was very hard to kill, and then look at all the dead bodies.[61]

Looking at dead bodies seems to be described here as a form of cruelty inflicted on boy soldiers by commanders.

Former child soldiers commonly expressed remorse for the atrocities they and their militia had committed, but insisted that they were unable to act differently, given the circumstances.

When we were on our reconnaissance missions, we often killed the people who came across our path. Many of them didn't do us any harm. I didn't like that, I was very sad to witness and be part of that, but I couldn't say anything because many of my colleagues had smoked *liamba* [marijuana].[62]

Being aware of the randomness of the violent acts they committed seemed to reinforce boy solders' sense of helplessness, as if the senselessness of the war reinforced their own impotence. Some attributed their irresponsibility to their drug-induced state, as well as their immaturity.

Most of us [those who carried out these attacks] were children. The boys had guns and they smoked marijuana mixed with bullet powder. That is why they were able to be so ruthless and kill so many people. When I think of that I become very depressed.[63]

This former soldier uses the third person to refer directly to perpetrators, but in the more general statements he includes himself among them.

How did boy soldiers cope with the feelings of remorse and horror that they could not fully exclude from their consciousness? How did they cope with their separation from family and friends and their isolation in the camps? Some former soldiers mentioned that, in their spare time, they would sit down and talk with their friends about things far removed from the environment of warfare.

During the war we had some days of rest, one or two days a week in which we would stay in the camp. We couldn't go far because to go out one had to request a *guia de dispensa* [authorization] and that was not easy to get. But during that time we tried to meet with our friends and the people from our village or nearby villages who lived in the camp.[64]

Recalling the experiences they had shared before the war made fellow soldiers from the same home village similar to kin. Often, too, friends could talk about their relatives and assuage their longing.

In the military camps, in our free time, especially at night before going to sleep, we would sit down and chat with our friends. Our conversations were about our relatives, and our friends who stayed at home. I often felt *saudade* [missing or longing] for my family, my mom and my dad, my brothers and sisters.[65]

Such conversations had to be carried on secretly because the military commanders did not want boy soldiers talking about their homes and families. Longing for home, commanders rightly understood, might lead to escape attempts.

We couldn't talk about our homes and our relatives; if they heard us talking about that they immediately thought that we were planning to escape and would punish us. We used to talk in secret, when it was safe to do so. . . . I once managed to escape together with my friend, but because we didn't know the area very well we ended up in another UNITA camp. We were both severely beaten by the soldiers.[66]

Conversations about home were dangerous as well as consoling.

Such accounts juxtapose the pervasive fear and longing with the occasional diversions the child soldiers enjoyed in camp.

In the war I had my friends Luis, Dino, Nelo, Marino, and Nando. When we managed to get time together, we played our games like *pessonha* and soccer. We also talked about our families and our villages. We wondered whether our parents were alive or dead . . . I was often ill there. I had headaches and diarrhea. When I was frightened by something my heart would beat very, very fast.[67]

When we had a chance, we would play music—somebody had a radio—and dance in our barracks. We couldn't play it too loud, though. The chief of our group was not so bad; sometimes he allowed us to have a bit of fun. Sometimes we would also play soccer, but not so often. Life there was not a happy life.[68]

In both these accounts, misery frames the occasional attempt to assuage it.

Abducted child combatants found ways of protecting themselves and coping with the hardships of wartime. They often deceived their commanders by telling outright lies, playing tricks, or obscuring the truth. Some adopted such stratagems immediately.

When I was kidnapped, I gave the soldiers a false name, not my real one. I didn't want them to know my family and make my parents suffer.[69]

Many sought simply to avoid the risk of death in combat:

When I was afraid of going to fight I would pretend to be ill . . . but sometimes it didn't work. They would insist that you go even if you were really ill. My friend once escaped death. He was ill and the commander let him stay in the camp. The other three who went on the mission died. He escaped because he stayed in the camp. It was his lucky day.[70]

Neither feigning illness nor really being ill guaranteed a young soldier's exemption from combat, however; this soldier attributes his sick friend's survival to luck.

Recruits found more ways to beat the system as they grew to know it better. "During the war, one had to pretend to be stupid to be left alone.

Those who were smart and spunky were always controlled by the chiefs and given heavy and hard tasks."[71] Feigning weakness and stupidity was a way of evading onerous duties. Boy soldiers used such stratagems not only to evade onerous tasks but also to avoid objectionable acts—implicitly, in this account, acts of violence that they would regret.

When they asked you to do something really bad and you didn't want to do it, you had to pretend that you didn't understand very well what they wanted, or you had to do it the wrong way, so that they would ask someone else to do it. But, that was very risky because if the chief was vicious you could be severely punished for it. It was a gamble.[72]

In contrast, some soldiers acted secretly to employ the militia's tactics for their own benefit—or, at least, reported that others did so.

I knew of a group of boys who found a way of fleeing from the camp late at night. They would go out and loot goods for themselves, and sleep with girls in the nearby villages. They would hide their looted things in the bush. The commanders didn't know they were doing that. If caught, they could be imprisoned or even killed.[73]

Some young men expressed pride in taking risks to claim moments and relationships for themselves.

I was working as the security of a commander. I had to carry his bags and guard his house. When the commander was drunk and asleep, I would leave him and run to see my friends, and a girl I met there. We liked each other a lot. We had to keep our relationship secret because the big soldiers could take her from me, if they found out that I was seeing her.[74]

Victims or Perpetrators?

Questions of responsibility pervade these narratives. Consider seventeen-year-old Ben's account of his situation and feelings, which uses both individual and collective terms for perpetrators.

During the war I was very sad because of all the violence and killings we had to do. Now I continue to be sad because some people here in the village say that I was responsible for the people killed in the war because I belonged to UNITA. They despise me. I am afraid of them.[75]

Soldiers who had returned home were aware that others held them responsible, directly or indirectly, for the suffering that civil war inflicted. This young ex-soldier seems to feel powerless both to have avoided committing atrocities and to avoid being punished for them afterwards. Other soldiers are haunted by remorse, which they associate with the unquiet spirits of those they killed. Nineteen-year-old Nelito lamented:

"I didn't want to fight; they forced me to fight and kill people . . . Now I am not well; I act like a crazy person. . . . The spirits of those I killed in the war are haunting me and making me ill."[76] Former soldiers who share such a belief system cannot escape the consequences of their actions, even if they claim they were unwilling killers and had no other choice under the circumstances.

Accounts given by demobilized boy soldiers are filled with descriptions of actions they took in order to avoid causing suffering to themselves and others. Boy soldiers expressed pride in creating their own space for maneuver, even as they proclaimed their helplessness. Indeed, their identification with their victims underlines, rather than excuses, their moral responsibility.

Conventional Western philosophical and legal formulations of these questions can be applied to child soldiers in civil wars only with grave difficulty. We begin by asking, should we consider these child combatants victims, helpless boys who were coerced into violent actions? Or should we consider them perpetrators, fully culpable and accountable for their actions? The extenuating circumstances and internal emotional states of children vary from case to case. Here, we are not concerned with a war crimes tribunal or a trial for crimes against humanity, and so such matters need not be adjudicated in individual cases. Nor are we engaging in a merely philosophical exercise. We are called, instead, to account for civil wars that enlist children in horrific violence and distort both their development and that of their societies. From this perspective, boy soldiers are both victims and perpetrators. The processes in which they become involved transform them from children into something else—not quite soldiers, but rather child soldiers, an oxymoron that generates an ambiguous association of innocence and guilt. Although these boy soldiers cannot be considered fully responsible for their actions, they cannot be seen as entirely deprived of agency either.

Social theorists agree that agency involves the exercise of power. What sorts of power could and did these boy soldiers exercise in an environment of civil war? How can we distinguish between the things they could and could not control, the actions they could choose to commit or avoid committing? Giddens's reformulation of the concept of human agency in his theory of structuration is helpful here.[77] He considers agency to be the capability of doing something, rather than simply the intention of doing something. "Agency concerns events of which an individual is the perpetrator, in the sense that the individual could, at any phase in a given sequence of conduct, have acted differently. Whatever happened would not have happened if that individual had not intervened."[78] For Giddens, the agent is a person with transformative capacity, the power to intervene or to refrain from intervention in ways that matter. Agency is intrinsically connected to power; to be able to act otherwise, the individual must be able to exercise some sort of consequential control over himself and others. But that power can be constrained by a range of circumstances. Indeed, choice is always exercised within a specific situation defined by given constraints. Giddens's theory starts from the assumption that all human action is framed by social structures that shape relations of power. Many former soldiers claim that they "had no choice." Yet recognition of the constraints under which they acted need not mean, in Giddens's terms, the dissolution of agency as such. Giddens conceives power as presuming regularized relations of both autonomy and dependence between actors in contexts of social interaction. All forms of dependence offer some resources whereby those who are subordinated can influence the actions of their superiors. This view of agency and power makes these young combatants agents in their own right because they can, at certain moments, mobilize resources to alter the activities of others and, thereby, of themselves. They can pretend to be ill to avoid certain tasks; they can plan to escape; they can deliberately fail to perform their duties properly. This interplay constitutes what Giddens calls the "dialectic of control."[79]

In order to make sense of the agency of these young soldiers within this dialectic of control, I also draw on De Certeau's analysis of trajectories, strategies, and tactics. In *The Practice of Everyday Life*, De Certeau tries to describe the complex modes of action of "consumers," a euphemistic term that he uses to identify the dominated, the subalterns.[80] He sees the actions of consumers as intricate trajectories that are indirect and errant, that obey only their own logic. However, he realizes that to represent these actions as trajectories fails to do justice to them, because although this term suggests movement, it also involves a "plane projection, a flattening out" which fails to capture the three-dimensional bricolage and the intricate meanderings of these actions. In order to avoid this reduction, he suggests a distinction between strategies and tactics. De Certeau defines strategy as the calculation or manipulation of force-relationships that becomes possible as soon as a subject of will and power, such as an army, can be isolated from its environment. A strategy "assumes a place that can be circumscribed as 'proper' (*propre*) and thus serve as the basis for generating relations with an exterior distinct from it (competitors, adversaries)."[81] A tactic, on the other hand, is a calculated action that is determined by the absence of the proper (a spatial or institutional locus under the subject's control) and takes place on a territory that is not autonomous. "The place of a tactic is the space of the other . . . it must play on and with a terrain imposed on it . . . it is a manoeuvre within the enemy's field of vision . . . it operates in isolated actions, blow by blow. It takes advantage of 'opportunities' and depends on them . . . this gives a tactic more mobility, to be sure, but a mobility that must accept the chance offerings of the moment, and seize on the wing the possibilities that offer themselves at any given moment."[82] As De Certeau recognizes, tactics are the "art of the weak."[83] Subordinated subjects must constantly manipulate events in order to turn them into opportunities. Drawing on Clausewitz's discussion of deception, De Certeau states that "power is bound by its visibility," while trickery and deception are only possible for the weak. Therefore, while strategies come from a locus of power, tactics arise from the absence of a locus of power.

These young combatants exercised tactical agency to cope with the concrete, immediate conditions of their lives in order to maximize the circumstances created by their violent military environment. They acted from a position of weakness. They had no power base, no locus (*propre*) from which to act within the confines of this militarized territory. As De Certeau suggests, their tactical actions arose "blow by blow," seizing the openings any given moment offered. Their testimony demonstrates that this is precisely how their actions unfolded. Child soldiers managed to create a little world of their own within the political violence and terror in which they had to operate. They seized spaces for secret conversations about home and their loved ones. They found time for play, music, and laughter. Equally important, they managed to modify the military actions in which they were expected to engage. They deceived their superiors with false identities, escape plans, and feigned illness. They pretended to be stupid in order to avoid being deployed on dangerous missions. These actions were almost always indirect, taken behind commanders' backs; direct refusals to kill were, they knew, potentially fatal. Boy soldiers could not act for themselves but only through the dialectic of power in their relationships with their superiors. No wonder, then, that former boy soldiers spoke as though whether they lived or died, killed or were killed, was determined by random factors they could neither predict nor control. They acted in the moment, without a strategic logic that would make sense of their wandering trajectories. They might kill on one occasion and show mercy on another.

A substantial proportion of former boy soldiers were fully aware of the atrocities they had committed. A few even exceeded the demands of their military assignments. Some acted out of vengeance, greed, immaturity, impulsiveness, or jealousy, while others did so with the expectation of being rewarded by their commanders. Aggressive acts against the enemy could be recompensed with the friendship and protection of commanders. Although few would admit to it, some soldiers undoubtedly found a thrill in killing, in wielding weapons and exercising life-and-death power over others more powerless than themselves. The story of Timangane illustrates this fact. Timangane was initially forced to kill and quickly became a ruthless killer, not sparing anyone who crossed his path. As Boia Júnior who interviewed him pointed out, Timangane was so efficient as a killer that

after a while the commander of the base no longer bothered to check whether his order would be carried out because he knew it would be. Timangane had lost count of how many people he had killed. He would dehumanise his victims [and in the process] dehumanise himself. Timangane identified with his commander. In his dreams . . . he saw himself in the skin of his commander, and . . . had the power to decide about life and death.[84]

Many of these young soldiers had no prospects of returning home after raiding and burning villages, killing defenseless civilians, and looting food convoys. They felt that they were constrained to live as militia members forever. Their own actions, no matter how coerced, had irrevocably sundered them from previous kinship and village ties. Those soldiers who were abducted at a young age—some as young as five or six—never had the chance to develop any idea of life outside the context of war; they were too young when they were taken by militia, and the civil war went on too long. Premature recruitment forced them to grow up within a culture of terror and violence. The military and the war became all they knew of life, and they tried to make the best of it. These child soldiers were conscious tactical agents who responded to the demands and pressures of their military existence.

By contrast, the exercise of strategic agency requires a basis of power. It also requires mastery of the larger picture, some comprehension—however inaccurate—of the long-term consequences of actions in the form of political gain, benefits, or profits. The majority of child soldiers seem to have entirely lacked such a perspective. Many demobilized soldiers regarded their service in the militia as a waste of time. Those who had worked hard in hopes of reward were disappointed. "We suffered a lot. The things that they promised to us we never saw. No, we don't want to return to war. That is why we were so happy when we were called for demobilisation."[85] Others were even more demoralized, feeling they had lost years of their lives for nothing.

If I could I would have told those who gave orders to start the war to talk amongst themselves and stop the war. Because of the war, I cannot be a truck driver. I needed to have studied, but I lost my time in the war. When I came back, I learned that my father died. Now I cannot study. I have to work to help my mother and my younger siblings.[86]

I wasted my time in the military and now I can't manage to study to learn a profession. . . . When I think of all this, my heart beats and becomes very sore and I am unable to sleep at night.[87]

After years of fighting and enduring adverse conditions, they have nothing: no jobs, no skills, no education, no homes, no parents, no food and shelter—not even a gun that would make looting possible. They have become completely dispossessed, completely powerless.

Conclusion

This chapter has explored boy soldiers' daily experiences of war and political violence. These tales of terror, violence, and survival constitute shared experiences that link young men who fought on opposite sides of civil wars that extended beyond their local and regional communities.[88] I have argued that armies of child soldiers exist not simply because of a shortage of manpower but through the concerted actions of local leaders responding to global forces. The initiation of young men into violence is a carefully orchestrated process of identity reconfiguration aimed at cutting links with society and transforming boys into merciless killers. Despite the fact that the majority of these boys had been forced to enter the military, they were not empty vessels into whom violence was poured or from whom violent behaviour was coerced.

We might say that, having started out as victims, many of them were converted into perpetrators of the most violent and atrocious deeds. Yet such a linear progress does not fully represent the complex, intertwined, and mutually reinforcing acts of violence of which they were both victims and perpetrators. Some boy soldiers were most victimized in the very act of murdering others; the more closely connected they were with their victims, the more intense and complete was their own victimization. But their identification with those whom they mercilessly killed was not redemptive; rather, it wed them more irrevocably to the identity of soldier.

As boys are transformed into child soldiers, they exercise agency of their own, a tactical agency or an agency of the weak, which is sporadic and mobile and seizes opportunities that allow them to cope with the constraints imposed upon them. Tactics are complex actions that involve calculation of advantage but arise from vulnerability. Tactical agency is often all that is possible for persons who occupy interstitial positions. They operate with a myriad of signifying practices, similar to "wandering lines,"[89] which only make sense within their own logic, the logic of the "in between." They take a series of actions, each seemingly disconnected from the other, that makes no sense except in relation to their own unstable location on the terrain of power. By virtue of this contradictory condition, they are able to maneuver on the field of battle and seize opportunities at the moments they arise. Despite being deprived of a locus of power, they navigate within a multiplicity of simultaneous spaces and states of being: children and adults, victims and perpetrators, civilians and soldiers.

This view of the position and tactical agency of child soldier resembles Mbembe's analysis of the ways in which postcolonial subjects assemble and make use of multiple, fluid identities, which need to be "constantly revised in order to achieve maximum instrumentality and efficacy as and when required."[90] Multiple identities allow boy soldiers to manipulate their situation and deploy deception and trickery in order to achieve small and temporary gains. The social logic and process of initiation that defines child soldiers also opens to them a limited field for the exercise of tactical agency within the totality of war.

In Ahmadou Kourouma's 2002 novel, *Allah n'est pas obligé*, which is set in West Africa, the main character says, "M'appelle Birahima. J'aurais pu etre un gosse comme les autres. . . . un sale gosse ni meilleur ni pire que tout les sales gosses du monde . . . j'ai tue pas mal des gens avec mon kalachnikov. C'est facile. On appuie et ça fait *tralala.* Je ne sais pas si je me suis amusé. Je sais que j'ai eu beaucoup de mal parce que beaucoup de mes copains enfant-soldats sont morts." This is translated into English as "My name is Birahima. I could have been a boy like any other. . . . A dirty boy, neither better nor worse than all the other dirty boys of the world. . . . With my Kalashnikov (machine gun), I killed lots of people. It is easy. You press and it goes tra-la-la. I am not sure that I enjoyed it. I know that I suffered a lot because many of my fellow child soldiers have died."[91]

Chapter 4
Young Women

Anita, a twenty-three-year-old woman in Josina Machel Island in southern Mozambique, told me her war story, which began when she was fourteen:

We were all asleep when they came to our house. This was 1991? I can't remember exactly . . . maybe 1990 . . . I am not sure. They forced the door open and started to beat all of us. There was my father, my two younger brothers, and I. Other members of our family were [away]. The soldiers tied my father inside the house. The commander of the group raped me. They took everything they wanted from the house and then burnt it, killing my father. My brothers and I were forced to go with them. We walked to the main road where the shops are and joined others who were emptying the shops. We walked for days to get to the base . . . The soldier who raped me at home said that I was his wife, and so he kept sleeping with me throughout our journey to the base. Once there, he took me to his quarters. I then realized that I was his fifth wife.[1]

This chapter explores the experiences of girls, like Anita, who were abducted and held captive by militias.

Public awareness of the impact of armed conflict on children focuses almost entirely on boys and young men, as do governmental, nongovernmental, and international programs to demobilize and reintegrate former combatants into society. Girls and young women usually become visible in news stories about civil wars as civilians who are victimized by irregular soldiers. Otherwise, girls are subsumed within the civilian populations who are displaced from their homes or injured by landmines. They are lumped into aggregate categories and included in statistical reports along with adults of both sexes. But the experiences of girls and young women like Anita whose families are torn apart, whose means of education and livelihood are destroyed, and whose home places are riddled with landmines, have some distinctive characteristics related to both their youth and their gender. The voices of these young women deserve to be heard. Even less publicized outside of these conflict zones is the more direct involvement of girls and young women with the military forces. Although sexual assaults by soldiers on village women during raids were not absent from the civil wars in Angola and Mozambique, they were not the whole story of girls' suffering at the hands of the military. These wars were distinguished by the blurring of the line between civilians and combatants and by the use of terrifying violence within militias as well as in their conflicts with opponents and civilians. So, too, were the kidnapping, captivity, and sexual exploitation of girls and young women pervasive features of these postcolonial civil wars.

This chapter examines young women's experiences of war. It focuses on the impact of political violence on girls and young women, many of whom were forced to become involved well before the age of eighteen. The chapter conveys some of their untold war stories: stories of killings, kidnappings, beatings, exploitation, and of rape and other forms of sexual violence, as well as stories of fighting, looting, and serving the military. In addition to discussing the rape and sexual abuse that girls and young women suffered during war, the chapter examines other aspects of their involvement as fighters, domestic laborers, looters, victims of landmines and displacement, and witnesses of violence and terror. While sexual violence is an important feature of their experiences of war—and this intimate violation of their dignity and sense of self often initiated them into other forms of violence—exclusive focus on the sexual dimension of violence has often obscured the complexity of their roles and experiences in armed conflicts. The chapter further discusses the processes through which these young women try to reconstitute themselves and their lives in the aftermath of war. While the ethnographic material presented in this chapter is drawn mainly from research carried out in southern Mozambique, it also brings in case material from Angola, especially on landmine victims and displaced women and girls. The chapter examines the Mozambican and Angolan cases against the backdrop of the experiences of many other girls and young women in the context of other wars around the globe.

Studies focused on women and war are vitally important, because war is a field normally conceptualized in terms of male discourse and characteristics. Men are seen as the principal protagonists. Women are usually featured as victims or as loyal supporters who keep the home fires burning and nurse the wounded. Yet, women's roles in war, as numerous studies have demonstrated, go far beyond these. They are complex and contradictory, and require careful analysis. We must break the silence about women in this context and reinterpret war in the light of women's involvement.

By focusing mainly on the experiences of girls and young women who lived in the confines of the military in southern Mozambique, the chapter goes beyond approaches that focus only on women in uniform, formally attached to military institutions, or on civilian women outside these institutions. It analyzes the impact of war on young women forcibly recruited from their homes to live in military camps. While they may have been subjected to military training, few of them were fully used as soldiers in the frontlines. At the same time, their civilian status changed, as they learned to live as soldiers, and their daily life became conditioned by war. Like the boy soldiers discussed in the previous chapter, girls abducted into militias are also placed in a twilight position between civilian and military life. The chapter explores their lives in captivity and what is currently known about the experiences of girls and young women in contemporary civil wars.

Women, Gender, and War

Gender relations, identities, and roles are fundamental to the ways in which women experience war. The concept of gender, defined as a social construct of what it means to be male or female, implies that, while the biological attributes of sex are universal, the way in which biological differences are interpreted and understood is a social phenomenon. Anthropological and sociological studies show that gender is not uniform across and within societies.[2] Gender constructs are historically and culturally specific. Masculinity and femininity are neither the only nor necessarily the primary ways in which people are defined. These terms are not even mutually exclusive, although they are constituted in relation to one another. Furthermore, masculinity and femininity are not singular or stable in cultural discourses and social practices. As Moore notes, cultures exhibit a multiplicity of gender discourses that vary contextually.[3]

Gender relations occupy a central place in discourses of war. Men are generally associated with conflict, while women are associated with peace. The prototypes are the man who leaves home to fight as an avatar of a nation's sanctioned violence and the woman who stays home, works, cares for the children, and weeps for the dead. Elshtain examined the myths of men as "just warriors" and woman as "beautiful souls" and showed how these stereotypes have served to establish and perpetuate woman's social position as noncombatant and man's identity as warrior. However, women are not invisible actors in war situations; they "have structured conflicts and collaborations, have crystallized and imploded what successive epochs imagine when the subject at hand is collective violence."[4] Turshen maintains that the invisibility of women's participation in warfare can no longer be sustained. Beyond their unacknowledged, behind-the-scenes contributions to the prosecution of war, women take sides, resist, fight back, and become active soldiers. As Turshen puts it, "even when they don't see active service, they often support war efforts in multiple ways, willingly or unwillingly."[5]

According to Cock, the debate about the role of women in war has been dominated by two competing perspectives, the sexist and the feminist views. Sexism postulates that women are excluded from war because of their physical inferiority and unsuitability for fighting; they are better off being defended and protected by men. One variant of the feminist approach also excludes women, but on the grounds that women possess innate nurturing qualities; they are creative, sensitive, caring, and more inclined to justice, pacifism, and equality. The other variant of feminism sees the exclusion of women from war as a result of men's monopoly on power. All these perspectives, as Cock clearly states, concur that war is understood as the domain of men and the military is conceived as a "patriarchal institution from which women are excluded and by whom women are often victimized."[6]

Cock points out that war is not the exclusive domain of men. The reality is that women have increasingly been involved in war and incorporated into armed forces worldwide. This trend is related both to changes in the technology of warfare and to changing attitudes about gender roles. However, the way men and women live and experience war is strongly affected by definitions of masculinity and femininity that continue to dominate military discourses.[7] The role that women play in wartime and within military organizations is often shaped by an ideology that still casts women as weak and places them in traditional feminine roles as wives, mothers, and nurses who are responsible for domestic chores. Even when women participate directly in the conflict as combatants, female soldiers are often faced with additional stresses; they must struggle to assert themselves in the organization, and they are subjected to sexual violence, harassment, and abuse.[8]

The issue of women and war is usually considered in terms of female soldiers, or women in uniform. Little attention has been paid to the more general relationship between women and armed conflict. This chapter looks at women who do not wear military gear and are formally not part of the military institution, but who participate directly and actively in war.

Survivors of Captivity in Military Camps

In Mozambique, girls and young women played a variety of roles in warfare. They served as guards, carriers of ammunition and supplies, messengers, spies, "wives" and sexual partners, and sometimes as fighters on the front lines. They were used as domestic labor and performed tasks such as carrying water, searching for firewood, cooking, cleaning, and other daily chores. Sexual violence and abuse was a fundamental feature of their experience of captivity. Unlike the cases of Sierra Leone and Liberia, where girls served as combatants, in Mozambique few were active in combat. Many undertook military training, but served essentially as guards in the camps and took part in reconnaissance and looting missions. Although the young women I interviewed were abducted by RENAMO and forced to live in RENAMO's camps, girls under seventeen years of age also served in the government army.[9] Some girls and young women also joined the military simply in order to survive.

In Angola, interviewing girls and young women about their participation in war was not easy. Unfortunately, the research undertaken with the Christian Children's Fund in 1997–98 did not record many girls' voices. Studies of the impact of armed conflict on children in Angola point out that girls and young women were directly involved in the war. They cleaned the camps, washed clothes, prepared food, entertained the troops, and responded to the soldiers' sexual demands.[10] There have been reports that women and girls were forced into sexual relations and marriages with UNITA commanders and combatants. Refusals were met with punishment, and attempts to escape often meant death. Human Rights Watch (HRW) contends that girls were often victims of sexual abuse by government soldiers in the field, and occasionally were obliged to provide services. However, HRW was unable to document the use of girls as soldiers by government forces.[11] A report by the Institute for Security Studies (ISS) also noted that girls as young as thirteen became porters, camp followers, and sexual servants for UNITA. "Indeed, girls were often required to render sexual services and the majority was abducted for the primary purpose of serving as 'wives' to the male soldiers."[12]

The participation of girls in war, their exploitation, and their sexual victimization are still surrounded by silence and secrecy, not just in Mozambique and Angola but also in many conflict and post-conflict situations throughout the world. We know very little about their roles and experiences in war and about the physical and emotional consequences of their involvement. Very few young women were comfortable talking about what happened to them during war times. Stavrou acknowledges that this silence makes it difficult to determine the impact of armed conflict on girls in Angola. "Often young women are afraid to reveal their involvement in the war, for fear that they will be discriminated against by community members. . . . [Data] is gathered from word of mouth, and when these former girl soldiers are approached they shy away from questions which probe their past lives. It would seem they would rather let it go."[13]

Families are equally cautious about disclosing information concerning the participation of girls and young women in the war. The sexual abuse that women suffer is a taboo subject in these communities, even for mature women, because of the social implications that such situations can have for a young woman's future and the family's honor. Because of their intimate and private nature, sexual matters are generally surrounded with silence even under ordinary circumstances. People hardly talk about these issues within the family, let alone to strangers. Extreme situations, such as rape and sexual slavery, are even more difficult to discuss. Honor and shame matter in these communities. Dishonor does not depend entirely upon whether a young woman consented to or resisted unsanctioned sexual relations, and it involves not only her but her whole family as well.

Silence in these circumstances can be seen as a powerful language, a language impregnated with meaning. As Das points out, silence is an act of conscious agency. By examining women's experiences of violation during the Indian Partition, Das asserts that agency has nothing to do with the linguistic competency of the women to express themselves. On the contrary, their agency lies in their refusal to put words to the experience, in the ability to hold it inside and be silent about it. Das reminds us that in reading history, it is important to appreciate silences, to delve into the cadences and rhythms of silence, because historical accounts very rarely record and consider the victim's point of view.[14] When histories are written and when glorious battles are made into legends, the stories of victims, such as the accounts of these girls, are glossed over and discounted as exaggerations.[15]

During my research in Mozambique, I was able to speak with young women through my involvement with a national non-governmental organization supporting girls who had been affected by the civil war.[16] The distinctive characteristics of Josina Machel Island, where I conducted this research, shaped the experiences analyzed in this chapter. We cannot readily generalize from these findings to all young women captured by militias in Mozambique, much less in Angola. But the specific conditions that prevailed on the island made the research possible, in part through a local organization that established a unique program to aid young women after the armed insurgency ended.

In colonial times, Josina Machel was called "Mariana Island." This small island, located in the district of Manhiça about 100 kilometers north of Maputo, has a land area of 196 square kilometers and about 10,000 inhabitants. Unfortunately, its poor infrastructure and relative isolation did not protect it during the civil war. Fertile soil, abundant crops, and flourishing cattle breeding made the island a prime site of contention between the government and rebel forces. Military incursions into the island started in 1985–86, but the most difficult years of war were 1989 through 1992. RENAMO troops raided the island frequently, taking both food and captives. Islanders responded by creating a local militia to defend themselves, incorporating all men between the ages of eighteen and forty-five. But the resistance did not enable them to escape mass killings, labor exploitation, and sexual abuse. Many women, including young girls, were taken from their homes to military bases where they were held captive, some for months and many even for years. As the situation worsened, a government battalion was stationed on the island to protect the population.

Josina Machel Island is now mainly a community of women. The female population significantly exceeds the male, and many households are headed by women. This situation is not entirely new, although it was seriously exacerbated by the civil war. Male labor migration to the diamond and gold mines of Witwatersrand and Kimberley in South Africa began in the mid-nineteenth century. For generation after generation, young men left home to find work and earn money to marry. According to local tradition, "You become a man after having been in South Africa." Men remained away from home for long periods, generally for eighteen months at a time. Some migrants eventually returned permanently. Others created second families in South Africa while sending remittances home. Still others settled permanently in South Africa, especially during the long Mozambican civil war.

The massive wartime killings of adult men tipped the gender balance in the island even further. The migration of young men to South Africa in search of employment continues in the postwar period, even though it is illegal. Men also move to urban centers, finding employment in Maputo, the capital, or small towns in the region. Women now constitute a majority on the island. They manage the day-to-day affairs of their families and the community. Therefore, it is not surprising that they have established a program to assist young women who were kidnapped and held captive in military camps during the war.

Reconstruindo a Esperança (Rebuilding Hope) began, like many postwar non-governmental programs, by assisting former soldiers, especially boys, to learn skills and find jobs. It shifted its focus to young women who had been affected by the war because so few young men remained on Josina Machel Island. When I conducted this research in 1999, about ninety young women were employed by the organization and engaged in such activities as agricultural production, dressmaking, and literacy classes. Reconstruindo a Esperança provides emotional and psychological support through a group of local elderly women, and two psychologists visit the island twice a week. The young women in this program have become accustomed to sharing their experiences with each other and with the women who work for the organization, so they were more comfortable speaking to me than most young war-affected women would have been.

The young women I interviewed range in age from sixteen to twenty-five. Most are single, although some have at least one child. I also spoke with other people in the community: the elderly women who work for the NGO; some of the young women's mothers; the religious leader of the local Zionist church;[17] the director of the only primary school on the island; the nurse at the only clinic; and a few young men, former soldiers, who still work for the NGO. I did individual interviews and held focus group discussions with some of the girls. I also had group discussions with the elders, both male and female. I interviewed the two psychologists and participated in some of their counseling sessions.

What were the common themes in the experiences of these girls? How were they abducted, and how did their sexual violation by soldiers signify their captivity and subordination? What work did they do while they were held in the camps? What was their experience of captivity? How did these girls manage to cope and survive? Were they just victims, or did they, like boy soldiers, exercise tactical agency?

Sexual Enslavement by the Militia

In southern Mozambique, the majority of the military camps in which abducted children—both boys and girls—were held had a particular spatial configuration. They were divided into two sectors: the military sector, where soldiers lived and were trained and other military activities occurred; and the civilian sector, generally located around the military area and divided in different sections called *muti*.[18] Civilians were placed into the different *mimuti* ("mi" is a plural prefix). In some camps they had tents; in others they had to sleep outside, or build their own huts. The huts were structurally precarious, given the temporary nature of the camps; they had to be dismantled quickly and moved to another location if enemy forces appeared nearby. Civilians were carefully distributed among the different sections so that families and people from the same villages were separated. This strategy aimed at deterring contacts and group escapes from the camp. The civilian sections of the camp performed various tasks, from looking for water, firewood, and foodstuffs to the cleaning of the whole camp, including the military sector. While civilians were confined to their sections, soldiers moved freely between the different *mimuti*.[19] In the civilian sector, soldiers could get food, water, girls for sexual satisfaction, and eventually wives. In reality, in these camps, kidnapped civilians were enslaved to the militia.

Although girls were abducted and taken to military camps in much the same ways boys were, their experiences in the military were marked by one profound difference: they were raped and held as sexual slaves. This fact was so commonly understood that many young women took their listeners' knowledge for granted and avoided mentioning the specifics in their retrospective accounts. As one seventeen-year-old put it:

I was taken with my parents from our home in this island in 1989 . . . RENAMO soldiers kidnapped us, and took all our cattle. We were taken to the military camp. My father, my mother, and I were separated. I suffered a lot while I was there. I am not going to tell you everything that happened to me in the military camp because it was very ugly.[20]

What this ugliness and suffering signified was left unsaid. An eighteen-year-old Mozambican woman speaks of sexual assault indirectly, recounting the suffering that her militia inflicted on villagers, first by taking food and then by raping village girls.

There was a lot of famine in the war. Sometimes, we didn't have any food to eat, and we had to loot the villages. We would get there and attack the village, and grab all the goats, chicken, cassava and millet we could find. The villagers couldn't say or do anything. Those who tried to resist were beaten or even shot. Sometimes, we would tell them to cook a meal for us. The soldiers would sleep with the girls. Many girls cried and shouted, but nobody could do anything to prevent it.[21]

Her account slips from the hunger she experienced in the camps to the looting of villages; famine seems to victimize militia girls and villagers alike, even as she recounts her participation in the raid. Significantly, she speaks of the rape of village girls in the context of their resistance to these assaults. So, too, had girls like her suffered sexual assault at the hands of the commanders, but she does not say so explicitly. Civilians whose villages were invaded and those who were kidnapped by militias occupied similar positions: even if girls "cried and shouted," "nobody could do anything to prevent it." Captive girls could not save themselves or other girls—whether in villages or in the camps—from sexual violation.

A nineteen-year-old was more forthright about her own experience, perhaps because she had a child.

I was taken by force by *matsanga* (RENAMO soldiers) in 1991 during one of their attacks on the island. Our first assignment was to loot the shops. They burnt all the shops after we emptied them. Then they forced us to go with them and carry the loot to the military base. We walked for three days. . . . On our journey to the base the soldiers killed many people, those who got tired of walking and carrying heavy loads, the elderly. . . . When we got to the base I was chosen by one of the commanders to be his wife. . . . In 1992, when I was twelve years old, I gave birth to a baby girl.[22]

Female captives were immediately forced into service. Their obedience to orders and their physical capacities were tested, and any sign of defiance or weakness was met with summary execution. Participation in and subjection to violent acts were closely allied. The dominance of soldiers over captive girls was established and demonstrated right from the start.

Ntombi, who was eighteen years old when I interviewed her, was kidnapped in 1991 when she was only ten. She and the others who were kidnapped on the same occasion walked for about five days carrying heavy loads. In the military camp, Ntombi and many young girls lived in a tent with three older women. She remained at the base for about six months before managing to escape. During the day, the girls had many tasks to do. At night the soldiers came to the tent and picked whomever they wished. On her second night at the base, Ntombi was taken by a soldier. "He was a big man, and it was very painful," she said. The rape was her first sexual experience. The next night, another soldier picked her to abuse. She still remembers the night in which two men raped her.[23]

Maria, a seventeen-year-old whose kidnapping story was discussed in Chapter 3, also spoke of sexual abuse as it affected the girls as a group. Maria was abducted with three of her friends while looking for firewood in the bush near her village.

The nights were dreadful because we were there to be used by the soldiers. A soldier per night. . . . the lucky ones were those who were chosen by an officer who had a hut for them to live in and who protected them as his wives.[24]

This account of kidnapping and coercion foregrounds the "dreadful" sexual exploitation the girls endured. Having forced sexual relations with a different soldier every night was the fate of most, while a "privileged" few became the sexual slaves and property of commanders. There was a sexualized hierarchy in the camps; ordinary soldiers usually had to share girls, but officers had exclusive access to multiple concubines (wives). The protection they offered these young women—from other soldiers, as well as from the enemy—was, perhaps, the reason why these women were referred to as "wives."

The story of Anita that opens this chapter shows how she became the so-called wife of a RENAMO commander. Her ordeal began with her rape in the presence of male relatives and continued for over a year. She became the commander's fifth wife and gave birth to his baby while in captivity.

We [the wives] lived together in a hut he made recruits build for us. He could do that because he was a commander. I got pregnant and gave birth to a baby girl. I was helped by the other women. . . . after me he had two more wives, two girls younger than me. Only one of us didn't have children from him.[25]

Giving birth in captivity was a grueling experience for women. "I thank God for not getting pregnant while I was there," said Dinha.[26] Conditions in the military camps were so harsh, with insufficient shelter, shortages of food and water, and a lack of basic hygienic conditions, that it was inhumane to raise children in those circumstances. Dinha recalls that the women and children often had to run from the camps to escape the attacks of the government forces. Babies and toddlers were dragged around, crying and screaming. Since noisy children might reveal the group's position to the enemy, unscrupulous soldiers would simply shoot them.

Another important aspect of Anita's account is the mutual support among captive girls who lived together as sexual chattel of the same officer or commander. While this kind of camaraderie was Anita's experience, rivalries between women for alliances with powerful men in the camps have also been reported. It was important to be placed under the wing of an important officer or commander for protection and for access to the spoils of looting. Older woman mentioned that in the RENAMO military camps some girls died as a result of disputes between soldiers over who would possess them. Soldiers quarreled when they both wanted the same girl. Those quarrels could end in the death of one of the soldiers, but sometimes the girl was killed so that neither soldier could have her. Conflicts also arose when soldiers who took captive girls as wives found out that the women had sex with other soldiers while the "husbands" were away in combat. Disregarding the forced nature of these sexual encounters, the men would beat the women and sometimes take their lives.

Utas discusses the protection soldiers offered to women with whom they had sexual relations in his study of young women the Liberian war. As he points out, "whatever 'choiceless decisions' introduced these young girls into the war system . . . they soon got used to the system, and thus created different ways to cope with it. . . . The struggles among young women were often over access to important fighters, mastering one's 'mates,' and the search for protection. . . ."[27] A Colombian woman quoted by Human Rights Watch makes the same point. Although girls might not be openly forced into these relationships, in such contexts their choices are heavily restricted, as powerful soldiers have "life-or-death" authority over them.

When girls join the FARC, the commanders choose among them. There's pressure. The women have the final say, but they want to be with a commander to be protected. The commanders buy them. They give a girl money and presents.

When you're with a commander, you don't have to do the hard work. So most of the prettiest girls are with the commanders.[28]

In Angola, there were reports of girls being forced to have sexual relations with soldiers. "If you do not accept, they will take you to a place, and then kill you. Even if you don't want to, you are forced to."[29] The most powerful soldiers who wanted to have sex with the girls would send foot soldiers to fetch a girl.

In Mozambique, some residents of Josina Machel Island referred to sexual abuse of women in the island by the government military brigade stationed there during the hard years of the war. According to an elderly woman from the island:

Even our soldiers [the government army] who came here to defend us, they abused women too. Young women were forced to sleep with them; they threatened them with their guns. . . . some even abused married women. There were also relationships that developed between some women and the soldiers. Some marriages were destroyed because of that.[30]

This account shows that rape was an atrocity perpetrated by both sides. Adulterous relationships also developed between some women and government soldiers stationed on the island.

This phenomenon raises the issue of the more complex and subtle relationships that might have developed between women and the military during wartime. Some abducted women lived in the RENAMO camps for more than five years. After several years in captivity, some girls established relationships with soldiers and ended up settling with a partner, as newly abducted girls became the rape victims. Some young women gave birth to more than one child by the same soldier, and these families grew in the military camps in an environment of war.

The stories of Felista and Judite exemplify this pattern. Felista was about sixteen years old when she was kidnapped from the island by RENAMO troops in the late 1980s and taken to a military camp. She had to endure rape and was later chosen by one of the commanders to be his wife. Felista lived with this commander, and they had three children in the camp before the war ended war in 1992. Then Felista returned to the island with her commander. She asked her family and community to forgive her husband for the atrocities committed during the war and to accept him as one of them. As she explained to me during our conversation, "[T]his was the man who took care of me during the war . . . the father of my children."[31] What made this case difficult was that Felista's husband had commanded several incursions into the island. Nevertheless, Felista's family and people on the island forgave him, and he established himself with his family.

Judite was abducted when she was very young and lived in the camp for about six years. During this period, Judite established a relationship with a RENAMO soldier whom she describes as her husband. When the war was over, Judite returned home and informed her family that her husband from the camp intended to come and ask for her hand in marriage. He wanted to marry properly, with the blessing of her family.[32]

Other women learned over time to ameliorate their situation by pairing up with powerful soldiers on an occasional or regular basis, even though they did not settle into permanent relationships. In the camps, women found ways to adjust to their new lives, some more successfully than others. Muianga points out that well-fed and well-dressed women were those "adopted" by or "married" to powerful soldiers, who benefited from the spoils that were looted from towns, villages, and factories.[33] These women themselves became powerful and subjugated other women in the camps. They required services from them, such as cleaning; searching for water, firewood, and food; cooking; and childcare. The wives of powerful commanders held special positions in the camps as leaders of women's affairs, nurses, counselors, teachers, and political advisors.[34] In the midst of the war, despite the turmoil and transience, the military camps had rigid hierarchies and internal organization. Women played a variety of roles and invented institutions to mirror normal life.

Sexual Violence as a Tactic of War

Is rape a new feature of civil wars? How widespread and systematic was sexual violence during the war in Mozambique? Are these accounts incidental episodes, or are they part of a more complex war strategy? The issue of sexual violence against women in general and in times of war in particular has been the subject of many studies. Although there might be variations in scale, apparently rape and sexual abuse are not exclusive to "new" civil wars. Susan Brownmiller's book *Against Our Will* shows how women have been direct targets of rape in wars throughout history.[35] During World War I, acts of rape reportedly committed by German soldiers as they marched through Belgium were the subject of intense Allied concern. The German film *Befreier und Befreite* (*Liberators Take Liberties*), produced by Sander and Johr, exposes the mass rapes that occurred in the vicinity of Berlin in 1945 at the end of World War II.[36] Cautious estimates indicate that 110,000 women in the area were raped; less conservative estimates suggest that as many as 900,000 women were raped and abused.[37] We now know that Allied as well as Japanese forces engaged in forced prostitution during World War II. The testimonies of Korean "comfort women" in the mid-1990s drew attention to the role of women as sexual conscripts, who were subjected to rape by as many as ten soldiers.[38] In the early 1970s, newly independent Bangladesh was the stage of mass rapes of Bangladeshi women by Pakistani soldiers.[39]

Seifert characterizes the two prevailing popular explanations for this phenomenon as the "sexual urge" argument and the argument that brutality against civilians and sexual violence against women are "regrettable side effects" of war and not part of an overall military strategy. With regard to the first argument, clearly, rape and sexual violence, especially in the context of war, are not sexual but aggressive acts. The humiliation, abasement, and domination of the victim and her group provide satisfaction to the perpetrator. Rape is an act of aggression and violence through sexual means, rather than "an aggressive manifestation of sexuality."[40] In the same vein, Brownmiller asserts that rape constitutes a conscious process of intimidation by which men keep women in a state of fear.[41] The idea that rape results from a loss of masculine sexual self-control is untenable. Rape has nothing to do with natural sexual impulses. Rape represents a violent aggression that attacks the "intimate self and dignity of a human being."[42]

The second explanation, which regards rape as a regrettable side effect of war, is often put forward by the military establishment, but it is also questionable. In the context of civil wars such as the one in Mozambique, the distinctions between civilians and belligerents and between the battlefield and the home front were systematically blurred, as civilians became primary targets of violence and were often forced into performing military tasks. Coerced and abducted civilians became directly involved in military activities and lived within the confines of military life. This situation affected not only the girls from Josina Machel Island, but also female victims of rape in Bosnia-Herzegovina and many other civilians around the world. Girls and young women were and still are made to fight as soldiers on the front lines; to serve as messengers and spies; to carry ammunition; to participate in reconnaissance missions; and to perform a myriad of domestic roles. The aggressions and violations perpetrated against these groups cannot be considered the mere side effects of war. They are very much part of war itself.

Sexual violence is, without doubt, one of the most frequent human rights abuses committed during wars. It constitutes an important weapon, which is generally regarded as inevitable in warfare. Sexual violence cannot be seen solely as an assault on the body. Feminist scholars have long espoused the view that rape and sexual violence, wherever they occur, constitute major political acts.[43] They are an attack on the "body politic," aimed at controlling an entire sociopolitical process by crippling the enemy group.[44]

Advocates of human rights and women's rights have documented sexual violence against women during the war in Mozambique.[45] As McKay and Mazurana assert, both sides raped and sexually abused girls and young women. Such tactics were adopted early in RENAMO's history. The Gorongosa documents captured in 1981 contain minutes of discussions between RENAMO and South African officers suggesting that detachments of women be placed in RENAMO camps to "entertain" soldiers.[46] The accounts I heard demonstrate that sexual assaults against women went well beyond what might be described as forced prostitution or a response to the "need" of men to satisfy their sexual desires. Kidnapping and rape were used as instruments of subordination against masses of civilians, subjecting women and whole families to captivity and terror. Many rapes were carried out in front of the families of the victims. Relatives were often forced to watch soldiers rape their wives, mothers, sisters, and daughters. In my conversation with Inocêncio Diniz, director of Josina Machel Island's primary school (the only school in the entire island), he referred to cases in which husbands were forced to lie on the floor and soldiers raped their wives on top of them, using them as mattresses.[47]

Sexual assaults were not confined to mature women; very young girls were kidnapped, held captive, and repeatedly raped in the camps. This practice seems to have been deliberate; soldiers preferred younger girls, whom they referred to as "tender meat." This moving account by a sixteen-year-old says it all:

The day of my arrival in the military camp, exhausted as I was, a soldier came for me. . . . I was only eight and I was a virgin, but he didn't pity me. . . . I don't believe he had any pleasure raping me because I was like a dead body; the only difference was that I was crying and screaming . . . I still don't know where I got the energy to cry.[48]

Rape was a violent instrument of subordination. Magaia's book on peasant tales of war in Mozambique illustrates this premeditated use of violence and terror. The book begins with this story:

To demonstrate the fate of the girls to those who were going back [to the camp], the bandit chief of the group picked out one, the small girl who was less than eight. In front of everyone, he tried to rape her. The child's vagina was small and he could not penetrate. On a whim, he took a whetted pocketknife and opened her with a violent stroke. He took her in blood. The child died.[49]

Such stories circulated among war-affected people in the region, instilling the terror that such public acts of sexualized violence no doubt were intended to do.

What prompted such extreme sexual abuse of children? In the

Mozambican civil war, dirty tactics were a main form of warfare used by the RENAMO rebels. Reportedly, government forces also committed atrocities, but most were perpetrated by individual soldiers or small groups of soldiers, not as a matter of deliberate strategy. Unfortunately, that pattern is more often the exception than the rule. Most acts of sexual violence committed against these young women do not constitute isolated incidents of assault perpetrated here and there by individual soldiers seeking sexual gratification.[50] They were part of a carefully designed strategy aimed at terrorizing the civilian population.

The experiences of Mozambican women are shared by many other women, young and old, in conflict zones around the globe. Evidence of sexual assault on women in the context of modern warfare is rapidly accumulating in studies of women and war. This tactic has been employed in many conflicts in Central Europe, Asia, and Latin America, as well as Africa. Rape and other forms of sexual violence were deployed in the former Yugoslavia as a weapon of ethnic cleansing, designed to humiliate women and emasculate men. Repeated rape intended to result in pregnancy was used to fragment family and community by destabilizing a group's sense of ethnic integrity.[51] "One Croatian woman described being tortured by electric shocks and gang-raped in a camp by Serbian men . . . who filmed the rapes and forced her to 'confess' on film that Croatians had raped her."[52] MacKinnon refers to reports in Zagreb that accused UN troops of forcing refugee women to provide sexual services in exchange for aid.[53]

Rape has become an instrument of warfare in many areas beyond Central Europe. In Peru, female activists are commonly raped during interrogation and security sweeps through emergency zones.[54] In Burma, women have been abducted and subjected to sexual violence.[55] During the 1994 genocide in Rwanda, more than 5,000 women, many of whom were adolescent girls, were impregnated through rape. The Lord's Resistance Army in Uganda is known to abduct girls and force them to provide sexual services; some girls are married off to rebel leaders. The widespread use of sexual violence and abuse of girls in Northern Uganda and in Sierra Leone have been more recently documented in reports by Human Rights Watch.[56]

There is no doubt that rape constitutes a direct attack on a woman's physical integrity and personal identity. In Nordstrom's words, rape touches "the core constructions of identity and ontological security in its most personal and profound sense."[57] The act of rape takes away the victim's control of her own body. It makes victims feel unworthy and inferior.[58] It destroys fundamental assumptions about the safety of the world, the positive value of the self, and the meaningful order of creation.[59]

The rape and sexual violence that marked these women's war experiences destroyed their sense of self-worth. However, in prolonged captivity, some women managed to develop complex and intimate relationships—not necessarily based in systematic violence and abuse—with soldiers and fellow captives. These relationships helped them find ways of surviving within the hostile environment of war. There are real differences between the sexual violations that occur when soldiers pass by, attack, and rape women in their villages and the systematic violations that take place in the context of military camps where victims and perpetrators cohabitate and interact at many levels on a daily basis. As time goes by, abuse can be transformed into a complex relationship in which the victim accepts the logic of the abuser or the abuser's group and eventually conforms to it, sometimes to the point of becoming fond of the abuser or one of his colleagues. Some women who lived in these camps for several years became emotionally involved with their abductors (even their rapists), as shown by Judite and Felista's stories.

How does the sexual violation that these women suffered differ from those who were raped and left in the villages? How do these women feel about it? In the end, what experiences weigh most in their assessments of the life in the camp: the abuses and violations, or the steady relationships they eventually managed to foster during captivity? What are the distinctions, if any, between a single act of rape and the relationships of dependency between victims and perpetrators that are developed in military camps? These questions need further investigation in order to explain the situation of women living in military camps during these wars. Because of the long stay of many women in the camps, their regular interaction with the military, and of the dynamics of warfare in these locales, experiences of sexual violence and exploitation merit special consideration.

The sexual violation of young women has devastating effects. The experience of captivity and sexual slavery destroys a girl's sense of home and security, of self-worth and power, of the possibility of safe interpersonal relationships—indeed, of any future at all. People in the island say that the war left profound marks on young people, particularly on their sexual behavior.

Many elders complain about sexual promiscuity among youth. There were also more general complaints about young people's lack of respect for the elderly and for traditional cultural values. According to David Ntimane, bishop of one of the local Zionist congregations, "Boys learned to abuse girls during the war; there is no respect. Girls got used to sleeping with many men during the war. Virginity? We can no longer speak about virginity here. There is no courtship; they just want to sleep together straight away."[60] The mother of a young woman who was kidnapped and raped by RENAMO soldiers commented: "Because there aren't many men in the island girls give themselves to men very easily. Most of these men do not have serious intentions. They just want to sleep with them, but do not want to marry them. They say they are 'second hand' because they were RENAMO soldiers' 'wives.' They just use and abuse them."[61] A twenty-year-old woman whom I interviewed concluded, "Men only want to take advantage of girls like me, who were forced to be 'wives' of soldiers during the war. Therefore, for us it is very difficult to marry. . . . My childhood was destroyed by the war, and now my adult life is suffering the consequences of the war."[62] Young men and women who were not directly involved in the military as combatants and captives have also been affected by the changes in the terms of intimate relationships that were a consequence of warfare.

Military Activities and Militarization of Girls

The militarization of girls and young women is an important feature of contemporary armed conflicts. Various studies of the role of young women in fighting forces have revealed their increasing involvement in direct combat on the front lines.[63] In the Mozambican armed struggle for independence during the 1960s, women constituted the Destacamento Femenino (women's military wing, commonly known as "DF") and were trained to handle weapons and to take part in military operations. Some were deployed in combat; others served as military instructors, as spies or intelligence officers, and in other support positions. However, the number of women directly involved in combat was still very small. In the context of the revolutionary struggle for liberation against colonialism, the active participation of women in the movement and in the guerrilla war enabled them to develop a new identity that challenged existing gender relations and promoted their emancipation and more gender egalitarian relations. Women saw themselves participating equally with men in the struggle to end colonial rule.[64]

During the recent civil war between the government and RENAMO, many girls and young women were forcibly abducted to take part in warfare. Many sources clearly show that RENAMO made greater use of children as combatants than government forces did.[65] Conscription laws in Mozambique did not establish any distinction between male and female recruits and, since independence, young women have been conscripted into the DF, the women's department of the army.[66] The Moamba garrison in southern Mozambique was one of the training centers for female recruits. They performed a variety of roles in army offices as administrative staff; they were also nurses, instructors, and spies. The evidence does not show that they played a role in active combat.

Some young women in RENAMO camps were given military training and learned how to handle weapons. However, there are few reports of their direct involvement in combat. Those women who were given guns guarded the camps, accompanied civilians on transfers of military supplies, and prevented captives from escaping during expeditions to find water and food. RENAMO also had its Destacamento Femenino, comprising dynamic young women who went through military training. According to Muianga, the wives of powerful commanders were also members of the military wing. While girls and young women were engaged in warfare in Mozambique, direct combat was not a major feature of their activities. Human Rights Watch also reported finding no evidence of the extensive use of girls and young women in combat in Angola.

In other contexts, girls and young women were and are directly engaged in military combat. In Colombia, for example, irregular paramilitary groups systematically recruit girls and young women to serve as fighters. Girls are not spared the hardships of military life and perform the same roles as boys. They undergo military training, learn how to fight and kill, and take part in combat. According to Human Rights Watch, many girls in Colombian paramilitary groups emphasized the egalitarian character of guerrilla life when compared to their position in civilian life.[67] Young women from Sri Lanka were also active in combat. After formal training, girls were not immediately given real weapons; they started with a piece of wood that functioned as a dummy gun. Only after they were judged to be comfortable carrying it at all times were they issued rifles.[68] Participants testified to the extent of their involvement in combat in Sri Lanka.

The day I was given the cyanide [capsule] I was very happy because no one would catch me alive—abuse or harass me. This was for my safety. I felt good to carry this around my neck. One day another leader didn't have her capsule. I don't know what happened; she didn't explain. She said that she wanted to use mine. That day, I never ever thought I would be caught, so I gave mine to her. I was fighting in a war. Four soldiers captured me. They surrounded me and I gave up. I had no cyanide so it was easy to surrender.[69]

In Sierra Leone, reported by, young girls went through training and took part in combat.[70]

Compared to the number of men directly involved in hostilities, many fewer women fight actively on the front lines. Yet, military discourse and practice is still very male. Military training is a process of "socialization into masculinity carried to extremes,"[71] and combat constitutes the core of that socialization. Combat epitomizes the "masculinity/militarism nexus"[72] and constitutes a fundamental dimension of the development of manhood and male superiority. Combat is "the ultimate test of a man's masculinity."[73] The notion of combat in modern warfare is highly ambiguous, however. According to Cock, the ambiguity arises because combat exclusion laws, such as those in the U.S., fail to take into account the blurred distinctions between combatant and noncombatant roles, as well as the less precise demarcations between "front" and "rear."[74] However, as Enloe points out, the myth of combat dies hard.[75] Therefore, it is not surprising that, despite the increasing involvement of women in warfare and military activities, their participation in combat is still limited because the military institution protects its core values. As Elshtain asserts, among women, direct combatants are the ferocious few and the noncombatants are the many.

In Mozambique, RENAMO did not spare unarmed girls from participating in military incursions. These young women frequently went on missions with armed men. They were most often deployed on excursions aimed at pillaging and looting villages. Soldiers also ambushed and raided private cars on the highway and convoys of trucks carrying goods to and from Maputo, the capital, and the rest of the country. Young women carried military equipment on the way to these raids and toted the booty back to the base.

One young woman recounted how, after successfully ambushing a convoy of trucks, her militia unit kidnapped civilians specifically to transport the loot.

I participated in an assault in the national highway number one in which we ambushed a convoy of several trucks full of goods. We got several new motorbikes, bicycles, bags of maize meal, rice, dried beans and sugar, oil and soap. There were lots of goods; we were all very happy. The operation was a great success. But we couldn't carry all those goods; there were lots. So the soldiers went and attacked a nearby village and abducted people to carry the goods to the base.[76]

She includes herself in the "we" who conducted the ambush and felt "very happy" about the bounty they had seized. But she says that "the soldiers" kidnapped civilians—many of whom were probably young women like her—to carry the loot home. Her language suggests that, by the time she participated in this mission, she might have identified with the militia rather than with these new captives.

Another young woman also spoke in the first person about her role in such raids. "I took part in various attacks. Our role was to wait until the soldiers finished the ambush and gave us green light to start taking the goods. Sometimes, we walked for days before we got to villages and roads to launch our assaults."[77] This story makes a distinction between the young women's work in looting and transporting goods and the more aggressive role of the soldiers in these attacks, but it refers to these attacks as "our assaults."

Some young women described unsuccessful ambushes in which they took part.

In my first assault we attacked three cars on the national highway number one. The soldiers killed everybody, but we only managed to get some food, nothing else. In the second attack we assaulted a passenger bus. They burnt the bus with the people inside. Again we didn't manage to get anything, because all the goods were burnt together with the people and the bus.[78]

Her diction suggests disapproval of the soldiers' precipitous and destructive acts, but more out of disappointment at not getting anything from the ambush rather than at the fiery deaths of the people in the cars and bus.

Some of the testimonies of these girls, directly echo those of former boy soldiers. "The majority of us [those who carried out these attacks] were children. The boys had guns and they smoked marijuana mixed with bullet powder. That is why they were able to be so ruthless and kill so many people. When I think of that I become very depressed."[79] This statement positions all children who served the militia as victims as well as perpetrators, although it distinguishes the boys who killed under the influence of drugs from the unarmed girls who accompanied them. This young woman's description of the whole experience is suffused with sadness and regret as she identifies herself with the boy soldiers.

The term *soldier* is normally employed to identify those who receive formal military training and are considered part of the military institution. This definition certainly applies to professional or national armies with a strong institutional culture. It also applies to combatants who fight other combatants. In armed conflicts such as the ones we are witnessing today, in which the prime targets are defenseless civilians who are killed or abducted and forced to take part in military activities, the boundaries between soldiers and civilians become blurred as civilians engage in warfare and perform military roles.[80] The blurring of the lines between captive girls and combatants is especially visible in these young women's accounts of attacking villages and ambushing convoys. The girls were captives, but by this stage in their captivity, they acted in concert with their captors to victimize others.

Again, the question of agency arises. The debate on women's agency in war is shaped by two basic arguments. One contends that women have no possibility of exercising their personal agency in the context of war because of the constraints imposed on them. The other postulates that women have agency in every situation and use deliberate strategies to exercise it.[81]

Can we consider these young women as mere victims, or were they also agents in the war? The circumstances of their abduction, captivity, and sexual violation made them victims. However, their accounts of military operations in which they participated suggest that they were also perpetrators. Unlike boy soldiers, captive girls did not carry weapons, so they acted under duress without an equivalent means of self-defense. They were always accompanied by armed soldiers. After their violent initiation of physical and sexual subordination to the soldiers, however, they did not—unlike some former boy soldiers—emphasize the immediate coercion under which they operated when participating in raids. Perhaps they did not need to, since other people were aware they had no guns, had been sexually abused, and were exploited for their labor. Former boy soldiers, on the other hand, had to defend themselves against (internal and external) accusations of complicity.

In their testimonies, these young women use collective terms to refer to those who committed atrocities during the war: "we attacked," "we assaulted," "we killed," "I participated," "I took part." They explicitly included themselves in these RENAMO militia groups. What kind of agency, therefore, could and did they exercise?

In order to survive years in captivity, young women had no choice but to become part of the military apparatus that surrounded them. Their abduction cut them off completely from their families and villages. For many, the hope of one day returning home faded as time went by. RENAMO continued to kill and abduct people, and many captive girls learned that their relatives had been murdered. The present was all they had. They had to carry on with their lives in the conditions given in the military camps. To avoid being more seriously injured or even killed, they had to please their abductors by performing their duties as best as they could. One possible strategy was pairing themselves with powerful soldiers who could offer some protection and who would share the spoils of their looting.

In this context, girls and young women, like boy soldiers, exercise what I called a "tactical agency," following De Certeau's distinction between strategies and tactics.[82] A tactical agency is sporadic and constrained, but it helps people cope with immediate circumstances of their lives. This adaptive response enables these girls and young women to make modest gains and avoid further injury and harms. Like the boys, girls found themselves in an interstitial position between civilian and combatant, as well as victim and perpetrator. They can be located in the paradoxical terrain between childhood and adult womanhood. The very term *girl soldier* is certainly an oxymoron, and the elements of these contradictory terms are evident in these women's testimonies.

However, contrary to the boy's accounts presented in Chapter 3, these young women's testimonies do not include descriptions of "little worlds of their own" on the periphery and in the interstices of their daily military life. Some girls mentioned that they missed their homes and families and felt a sense of profound isolation. Their abductors would punish those who openly reminisced about their former lives in the villages. They were not permitted to speak about the past and were forced to give up their former identity. However their testimonies do not reveal any imaginary spaces they managed to build around themselves in order to survive in such conditions. This silence might have to do with the difficulty of getting women to talk about their war experiences at all. But silences, as Das reminded us, are also a significant form of agency. While the tactical agency of boy soldiers seldom exempted them from committing atrocities, the tactical agency of captive girls seldom prevented them from suffering and witnessing atrocities. Clearly, more extensive research is needed in order to develop a better understanding of the subjective experiences and agency of young women in war.

Domestic Work and Labor Exploitation

Apart from being sexually abused and performing military tasks, the daily activities of young women held captive in the RENAMO military camps involved numerous domestic chores. They cleaned the camp, cooked and made beer for the commanders, carried or transferred ammunition from one camp to another, and walked long distances to look for water, firewood, and wild fruit. Young women mentioned that carrying heavy loads, whether looted goods or ammunition, was one of the tasks assigned mainly to women. Muianga's study in southern Mozambique mentions that most women visited several camps in their missions to deliver or collect ammunition and supplies. During the year she spent as a RENAMO captive, Victoria visited eight military camps. The trips were made on foot, and the distances between some of the camps were very long. Victoria recalls having walked with heavy loads for more than six days. She and the other women started the journeys at four in the morning and rested only at sunset.[83] Mrs. Cuamba said that her daughter, who was abducted at the age of seven, had not grown properly; because during her captivity, she had to walk long distances carrying heavy loads, which interfered with her physical development.[84]

In Angola, girls reported traveling between military camps to transfer supplies and teach others to dance. They also had to do domestic work and had little time to rest. Dancing and singing the whole night through was a major activity in the camps.

I went to four bases to teach the others to dance and sing. But whenever we traveled to teach the others we carried the chiefs' backpacks. During the time that we spent in the bases we could sleep. At night, after we cooked dinner, we danced and sang. When the day was breaking, we went to the chief's house and then we took a nap. About 5 a.m. we had to wake up and resume dancing and singing. They did not let us sleep because they feared that the government would come and attack during the night. . . . And if we were sleeping, who would wake us up to carry all the materials and food? That is why they did not let us sleep at night.[85]

Marcela's story typifies the multiple losses that young women suffered during the war.[86] When the UNITA troops arrived in Zanga, Marcela, her mother, and many other villagers tried to escape to Kajimbungo, but they were ambushed by UNITA soldiers, who killed many in the group. She witnessed her mother's murder. Marcela was spared because one of the soldiers decided to take her with him to the military camp. She lived with him and his family as a captive servant; she had to do all the domestic chores, work in the field, and get water and firewood. She hardly had any time to rest or relax, much less play. Like Mrs. Cuamba's daughter, Marcela's physical development was seriously impaired by hard work, malnutrition, and trauma. Although she is sixteen, she looks like a twelve-year-old.

Girls and young women were sent on long expeditions to get water, firewood, and food for the camp. They were responsible for cooking food for the soldiers and sometimes for their fellow captives.

When we got to the camp they sent us out to get water and firewood . . . then they gave us maize meal to cook for them and for the rest of us. Cooking was one of our main tasks in the camp. We had to go out and find the food to cook. It was very hard. . . . [87]

In the camp sometimes they would ask us to fetch water and drink water in human skulls. We, the girls cooked meals for the soldiers . . . sometimes we cooked with no salt because it was very scarce in our camp.[88]

I remember once walking for a whole day until we got to a water source and then had to walk back carrying water for the camp. . . . we could not get back empty handed . . . the guards would force us to continue.[89]

There was not a lot of food in the camps. When the soldiers brought in cattle we had to prepare the meat for them to eat and we had only the skin to flavor our maize meal. . . . Some of us worked in the *machamba* [field] to try and get some food to eat . . . but then we had to run to another location because the of the government troops.[90]

Working the land was another one of the women's jobs in the camps. Other accounts mention the cleaning of the camps as a common domestic task assigned to the young women.

The exploitation of their labor was a major feature in the lives of the captive women. Girls and young women in the camps played multifaceted roles: they were sexual slaves and were often raped and abused by soldiers, became pregnant against their will, and gave birth to unwanted children; they walked for days carrying heavy loads of ammunition and other military supplies from one camp to another; they cooked meals for soldiers and other captives; they cleaned the camps; they guarded the camps; they were deployed on combat missions to carry equipment and looted goods; they fought in combat; they were wives and sexual slaves to be abused at the soldiers' will.

Displacement and Dismemberment

Young women who were abducted to live in the military camps were not the only female victims of war. Others were affected by the war while they remained in their towns and villages. Many young women were killed in military attacks; were blown up by landmines; witnessed the killing and relatives of friends; saw their homes and villages being burned; and were deprived of education, healthcare, and the basic necessities of life. This last section presents the testimonies of these girls and discusses the impact of war on girls behind the front lines.

In Angola, the experiences and perspectives of girls and young women who had lost family members, been displaced by the fighting, or lost limbs to landmines were documented much more fully than the voices of those who had been held captive by military forces. The stories of all these children share some important features. Becoming forcibly separated from family and home, witnessing horrors, and undergoing traumatic injury all took an enormous toll on children. This section highlights the voices and viewpoints of girls and young women. Boys who avoided the military but shared these girls' fates as civilians told very similar tales.

Many children were affected by the war in their homes and villages, suffering from ambushes and attacks, losing several relatives and friends, and being deprived of the basic necessities of life. The insecurity of daily life under the constant threat of deadly and unpredictable military attacks, coupled with the impossibility of producing food in wartime and the collapse of educational and health services, led to a massive displacement of people. Children were forced to abandon their own homes and villages and flee to towns, neighboring provinces, and adjacent countries, sometimes with their parents but often without them.

Marcela lost both her parents during the war. Her father was killed before she and her mother were captured. She witnessed the murder of her mother by UNITA soldiers during their abduction and the killing of many other innocent civilians. Marcela mentioned that during the war many dead bodies were not buried; UNITA troops only performed burials for their colleagues.[91]

Flor, a sixteen-year-old girl from Kilengues in Huila province, lived in a government orphanage when she was interviewed. During the war, Flor, her grandmother, and her three younger sisters had to walk for days fleeing from military attacks.

When the war came my father told us to go with the people who were fleeing the village. He decided to stay to take care of our things. . . . We walked and walked . . . all day walking, hungry and thirsty. . . . I felt sorry for my little sisters and my grandmother, who had to carry the younger one on her back. . . . I was also afraid that we might be caught by them [the soldiers]. In the evening we arrived in Lola, but that wasn't our final destination. My legs were swollen. . . . We walked during the night until we got to Bibala. In the morning my legs were very sore, I couldn't take the pain any more, and my grandmother took me to the hospital. There they gave me an injection and I fell asleep. When I woke up my legs had been amputated. I cried a lot. . . . My legs. . . . why did they do this to me? I was very sad.[92]

Flor still thinks a lot about what happened to her during the war. Both her parents died. But she wants to return to Kilengues, her home village, to see her house and their things and make sure that her father is really dead. Flor said that when she grows up she wants to be a teacher or perhaps a medical doctor so she can cure her younger sisters.

Girls and young women were victims of antipersonnel weapons. Landmine victims carry a permanent reminder of the war with them every day of their lives, for this is a reality that is inscribed in their bodies, and from which they cannot escape or hide.[93] Lena's story illustrates this problem:

I stepped into a landmine when we [my mother and I] went looking for food to eat. . . . When I stepped into it I did not hear any noise or feel anything. I just saw myself lying on the ground and a lot of blood coming out of my leg. When I started to shout and cry my mother also started to cry. . . . My uncle took me to hospital. At the hospital I didn't see anything. I just remember waking up to see that my leg had been amputated.[94]

Lena became very traumatized and sad about losing her leg, and she felt deeply the loss of her sister and uncle, who were killed during the war. She still has bad dreams:

Yesterday I dreamed of the war . . . that I was here in Kuito and that the war came and we started to run. Then my prosthesis fell and I hopped. . . . my mother left me behind. . . . I was talking and crying in my sleep. Then my mother woke me up and held me tight.

Lena's fear of abandonment haunts her sleep. Her sense of body integrity has been damaged, and she lacks confidence in her ability to cope with conditions of wartime. Lena was one of the lucky few children who got the chance to undergo treatment and get a prosthesis in Germany. Back home, she receives support from an organization that sponsors a project to help disabled war victims.

Rosa, a seventeen-year-old landmine victim, lost her parents during the war in the province of Biè. She was living with her mother's sister in Huambo when she lost her leg in October 1996. She recalls the experience:

I woke up in the morning and went out of our yard. There is a footpath which goes up to our neighbor Maria. I wanted to get firewood to prepare breakfast. Then I just heard it explode and found myself lying on the ground. My leg was cut off and my arm and chest injured. I cried out and then people came to rescue me and take me to the hospital.[95]

Rosa was treated at the Huambo provincial hospital, where she spent about eleven months. She has been visiting an orthopedic center and is waiting for her wounds to heal so that she can have a prosthesis. Her account, like Lena's, stresses the psychological as well as physical shock of the exploding landmine. Both speak of observing their injured bodies as if they were objects. This depersonalization is overcome only as they recount crying out and having others rush to their aid. For both Lena and Rosa, their own injuries followed the war-related deaths of other close family members.

These two landmine victims were fortunate in receiving good medical care. Even those who receive initial treatment may not get the continuing care they need, however; prostheses for growing children and adolescents need to be adjusted or replaced every six months.[96] The majority of child victims of landmines have simply had their injured limbs amputated; doctors completed what the landmines began. These children hop and crawl around their neighborhoods and villages trying to accomplish their daily tasks. Landmine victims carry a permanent reminder of the war. It is inscribed in their bodies, and they cannot escape from it, hide it, or forget it by leaving these memories behind. The traumatic experience of having been maimed by a landmine is difficult enough for adult soldiers; it is much worse for children, whose bodies and futures have been suddenly and brutally truncated.

Conclusion

The experiences of girls and young women in contexts of civil war are complex and multifaceted. The emphasis on rape and sexual violence, although valid and important, has tended to obscure the multiplicity of experiences young women live in war contexts. By examining their lives in wartime in a more holistic and contextual way, the chapter has shown that girls play complex roles in war as fighters, companions, "wives," domestic workers, witnesses of violence, orphans, and victims of landmines.

Rape and sexual violence were important aspects of the lives of these women during the war. However, other cases demonstrate that some young women managed to create more meaningful liaisons with soldiers and fellow captives. The long periods in captivity created closer social interactions that might have been conducive to the development of more complex and intimate relationships not necessarily based on violence and abuse but on mutual support and companionship. Some young women even returned home after the war with husbands with whom they had lived in the camps.

Although many young women undertook military training and handled weapons, evidence available in Mozambique and Angola shows that few of them took part in direct combat on the front lines. This does not mean that they were noncombatants; rather, it shows that within the military institution, the notion that direct combat is a man's business is still prevalent. Young women took part in military missions to carry ammunition, supplies, and the spoils of war. They were trained and armed, and they guarded the camps. The agency of these young women is contradictory, as they are simultaneously civilians and soldiers; victims and perpetrators.

Domestic labor exploitation also constitutes an important experience, which touched the majority of young female captives. They told of cleaning, cooking, and carrying heavy loads of ammunition, supplies, water, firewood, and foodstuffs. This labor exploitation, coupled with deprivation, impaired their physical development. Violence, terror, and abuse left emotional scars. Another consequence of the war is the widespread incidence of sexually transmitted diseases, especially HIV/AIDS, which will be discussed in chapter six.

War has changed the lives of these young women and their communities beyond these direct effects of captivity and combat. In Mozambique, older people say that young people do not conform to old rules: courtship, virginity, marriage. Will these notions stay intact after all this *bouleversement* caused by war? How are they changing? What happens when girls, presumably raped by or married to a soldier in the past, are

ready to settle down? What will happen to children fathered by unknown soldiers? Who names them and takes care of them? What kinship
and spiritual connections do they have with their father's families? Further research will help shed light on these questions by examining what
became of these young women many years after the war.

Chapter 5
Healing Child Soldiers and Their Communities

Marcos was stationed in the RENAMO camp of Ngungwè in southern Mozambique for many years where he trained and became a RENAMO soldier.[1] He attacked and looted many villages, killing and robbing innocent civilians. Following the 1992 peace accord between the government and RENAMO, Marcos was reunified with his relatives, who had not received any news of his whereabouts for more than five years. A few days after his return, the family organized a cleansing ritual for Marcos. According to his mother, the ritual was important to purify him from the bad deeds of the war, appease the spirits of those he might have killed, and open up a new and cleaner environment in his life. The ritual took place at a crossroads about one kilometer away from their house. A local healer was invited by the family to officiate at the proceedings. The healer started by invoking the powers of the family's ancestral spirits to help cleanse and purify the boy of his war deeds. She then treated Marcos with herbal remedies. Seated facing east, Marcos was made to inhale the smoke of some herbal remedies and then to drink an herbal infusion specially prepared by the healer. Next, wearing only a pair of shorts, he was bathed with water treated with the powder of various herbal remedies. Family, relatives, and neighbors were present and joined in singing and praying along with the healer. This treatment was aimed at symbolically sealing his past by cleansing his body internally and externally of all the "dirt" accumulated during the war and leaving it at the crossroads away from him and his family. The crossroads had symbolic significance: the dirt from the war would be dispersed in many different directions. Marcos and his relatives were supposed to face only in the direction of their home. They had to move forward to face the future. After this ceremony at the crossroads, Marcos, his family, and the healer walked home for a family meal. A goat was slaughtered, and traditional beer was prepared. The healer offered some food and beer to the ancestral spirits of the family and then invited everybody to share the meal.

In the aftermath of the war in Mozambique and Angola, these kinds of ritual performances are quite frequent in rural areas as people try to deal with the social wounds of war and reconstitute their lives. War-affected populations in these countries, especially in the countryside, draw from a wide range of cultural beliefs and practices to lay war traumas to rest and open the way to reconciliation and peace. This chapter focuses on the mechanisms and processes used by local populations to heal children who have been in the front lines, as well as entire war-affected communities.

In Mozambique and Angola, war is conceptualized in opposition to society as a space without norms or as a place where social norms are routinely violated. People are trained to kill and harm others and rewarded for breaking social codes. Those individuals who have been exposed to war are not easily accepted back into society, for they are considered polluted.[2] This pollution is believed to arise from contact with death and bloodshed. Individuals who have been exposed to war, who killed or saw people being killed, are regarded as polluted. The "wrong-doings of the war" are a dangerous form of disorder. Those people who were caught up in it are contaminated by the spirits of the dead and are potential contaminators of the social body.

A traditional chief (*soba*) in Uige, Angola, described the problem:

[an individual] can become insane because there [in the war] many things happened; seeing the blood of others; carrying dead bodies; killing. . . . When he [the soldier] comes back to the village . . . those things haunt him in his sleep, he dreams the things that took place in the war.[3]

These societies have long-established rituals for treating the disturbances that arise from participation in war. *Soba* Santos from Malange, Angola, explained:

If a person goes to fight a war, he becomes another person, because he learns how to kill other people, even his own mother and father. . . . During that time he only thinks of killing. . . . When he returns he has to be treated to become his own self again.[4]

The traditional treatment for a returned soldier who is "not himself" because he has violated fundamental social norms encompasses the physical, familial, and spiritual domains: purifying his body, quieting his demons, and reincorporating him into the community. Mr. Adam of Malange described what had happened when his soldier son returned:

After fighting the war the *kazumbi* (spirits of the dead) can afflict you. . . . My son came back from the FAA (government army) in 1991 and he was not well;

he was very disturbed and even attacked me. . . . He was unable to look at any kind of blood because that reminded him of the war. . . . I took him for traditional treatment.[5]

Parents understand the disturbed behavior exhibited by sons who have returned from war as a result of their combat experiences.

Their relationships with their relatives, with nature, and with the spirits had been disrupted, disordered, and even reversed during the war; child soldiers were forced to kill their own parents, to shed human blood wantonly rather than slaughtering animals to sustain life, to drink human blood to keep remorse away, and to dishonor the spirits of those whose deaths they had caused. Active intervention by a spiritual healer was needed to repair this whole set of relationships: in this case, the young man's attachment to his father, his contact with blood in slaughtering and eating the meat of animals, and his connections with the spiritual world.

The angry spirits of those killed during the war pose a threat to those who were directly involved in combat and, through them, to the families and communities they rejoin after demobilization. Individuals who fought in wars or lived in military camps are seen as vehicles through which the unquiet spirits of the war dead can enter and afflict entire communities. Such spirits are believed to contaminate and threaten not only the individual soldier but also his family, relatives, and neighbors. After a war, when soldiers and refugees return home, cleansing or purification rituals are a fundamental condition for individual and collective healing and protection. They are also important means of conflict resolution, reconciliation, and social reintegration of war-affected persons.

Communities that have been affected by civil war are also understood as disordered and in need of rituals for cleansing and reconciliation. Community rituals often focus on quieting the spirits of the war dead who were not buried with proper rituals and on venerating the spirits of the ancestors who guarantee health and protection to kin-groups and villages. Burials and rituals to honor ancestral spirits that were not performed during the chaos of wartime need to be completed in order to restore social peace.

The spirits of the dead play a central role in the life of many people, especially in the rural areas of Mozambique and Angola.[6] People regard the supreme being or creator as a remote deity, having no direct relationship with persons, families, and communities.[7] People relate directly to the ancestral spirits with whom they share a combined existence and interact in everyday life. The ancestral spirits are believed to be able to intervene in the life of human beings in society. They protect and guide communities. They promote the fertility of the land and of women, ensuring the reproductive continuation of the family, good agricultural production, and good hunting. They help maintain peaceful relations among members of the group. They protect people against misfortune, disease, ecological dangers, and evil, especially witchcraft and sorcery which can cause illness. In short, the spirits care for the well-being of families and communities.

However, the ancestral spirits can withdraw their protection, which makes people vulnerable to misfortune and to the evil intentions of others, and they can also cause maladies to show their displeasure or anger with their descendants. They are believed to protect and give health and wealth to those who respect the social norms of the group and to punish those who are antisocial, who violate accepted norms, or who disrespect the social order. Maintaining the proper ritual relationship with ancestral spirits and burying the community's dead with prescribed rites are crucial to the fruitful or even safe conduct of daily life.

The enormity of the violation of social norms and spiritual life that civil war entails is revealed in the profound contradiction between the ways in which children normally relate to the dead and the ways in which they come in contact with death in wartime. The documentation of burial rituals in peacetime is fullest for Angola. Children are not allowed to participate in burials because they are regarded as especially vulnerable to affliction by the spirits of the dead, including their own relatives. The close contact with the world of death inherent in such rites of transition was commonly understood as too dangerous for children. Only when one or both of their parents die are children allowed to take part in the proceedings. In Kuíto and Malange, the children pass under the coffin of the parents at a particular moment in the ceremony. They are permitted to say a few words, to express their sadness, and to ask for their parents' forgiveness for any wrongdoing or problem they may have caused them in the past. These actions, exhibited with a deep sense of remorse, ensure that they will not be tormented by the unquiet spirits of their dead parents.

When anyone else dies, children are carefully shielded from the proceedings. They are hidden away and ritually protected to avoid being affected by malevolent forces. An adult is always present to take care of the children and ensure that all the necessary rules for protecting them are observed.[8] Only after the deceased elders have been safely installed in the ancestral hut or burying place can children and youths participate in the ceremonies to honour their spirits. This Angolan practice reminds us that burial ceremonies, while essential, are rites of transition that invoke all the dangers of liminality, and that, in the universe inhabited by Angolans, children below the age of initiation are regarded as especially vulnerable to the forces that may be unleashed at such moments.

Children's participation in war is a grave, dangerous, and ongoing violation of their society's most fundamental distinctions between the worlds of life and death and the boundaries between young persons and the spirits of the dead.

In southern Mozambique, the unquiet spirits of those who did not have a proper burial are called *Mpfhukwa*. These unsettled spirits, unable to take their proper positions in the world of the ancestors, are bitter and angry. They can cause harm to their killers, afflicting those responsible for their death with illness or even murdering them in revenge. The kin of their killers are also vulnerable, as the angry spirits make them pay for their relatives' behavior. Those who pass by the places where they died are endangered; whoever crosses their path may be waylaid, assaulted, afflicted with life-threatening illness, or murdered outright. In Angola, this set of beliefs is also common. Burial rituals for the dead are considered to be of utmost importance to ensure peace and well-being. People say that both the soldiers who killed people and the civilians who witnessed these killings are particularly vulnerable to insanity, which can be caused by the spirits of the dead. Places where people died without burial rituals are dangerous to everyone who might pass there.

In Mozambique and Angola, families and communities heal the social wounds of war in the postwar period through ritual performance. Procedures for the cleansing and reintegration of those affected by war draw from the whole repertoire of traditional healing and spiritual practices. Some rituals for returned soldiers resemble rites of passage, in which the person making the transition from the military to the village is purified of pollution and given a new place in the family and community. Others treat the ills that afflict demobilized child soldiers and their relatives. Many former combatants manifest forms of illness that Westerners would regard as symptoms of mental illness, including flashbacks and nightmares about traumatic events, panic attacks, difficulty in controlling aggressive impulses, and impaired concentration and judgment. Former child soldiers expressed fear, guilt, anxiety, and depression, although many showed enormous resilience.

Healing presents a holistic approach to health, addressing the physical, psychological, and social dimensions of the affliction in order to treat the whole person. The social imbalance in a patient's life is generally reflected in the physical body, and all these dimensions are taken into consideration to restore the patient's health. The corollary is that healing is achieved through a double strategy: divination, which diagnoses the social causes of the patient's affliction and prescribes the rituals to repair it; and healing, which addresses the suppression of the bodily and mental symptoms through the use of herbal remedies.

Spiritual practitioners, called *kimbanda* in Angola and *nyanga* (singular) or *tinyanga* (plural) in southern Mozambique, serve as intermediaries between the world of the living and that of the ancestral spirits. Acting as mediums, they are possessed by the dead person's spirit or, functioning under spiritual inspiration, they communicate the spirit's message to the living. People consult diviners to diagnose and treat disturbances in family relationships and the social body that are manifested in symptoms of illness. They also seek recourse to diviners for protection from the hazards of life, to discover the causes of problems in the family, or to ascertain why domestic animals are dying and agricultural production is not going well. Above all, people seek the powers of the ancestral world to find out the reasons behind such untoward events and how to restore balance in their lives.

When Mozambicans and Angolans seek assistance for an afflicted person, the individual is not treated as a singular entity but as part of a family and community. During the divination séance, the diviner carries out a careful examination of the state of the patient's social relationships, including the living, the spiritual world, and nature. The diagnostic consultation includes a dialogue between diviner and patient, and often with the patient's relatives. This reciprocal learning process generates what one analyst has characterized as a process of "transference and counter-transference" of information that brings them together.[9] The close relationship between practitioner and patient enhances the cultural bonds between them and promotes the effectiveness of the prescribed remedies. This form of traditional healing can be extremely effective in dealing with what Westerners term mental illness, including such phenomena as disturbing dreams and hallucinations.

Treatments by traditional healers involve the administration of herbal remedies through ingestion, inhalation, and bathing. The herbal pharmacopoeia can be presented in a powdered or paste form or can consist of fresh and dried leaves and roots. Remedies can be boiled in water or burned in order to produce steam or smoke for inhalation. The use of these remedies involves a very strong symbolic component. These treatments are used to cure children who witnessed death and bloodshed; who were victims of landmines; and who became disturbed by instability, displacement, and the loss of loved ones. There are specific rituals for orphans who are taken in by foster families; rituals are performed to help the child settle into his or her new family and to appease the spirits of the child's deceased parents.

In these countries, not everyone goes through cleansing or purification rituals or rituals to appease the spirits of the dead. Such practices are more common in rural than in urban settings. The availability of healthcare alternatives and the religious and political affiliations of the people also determine the decisions they make concerning treatment of war trauma and related afflictions. Some churches combine traditional rituals with Christian messages in a syncretistic manner. Patients and their families often move across the boundaries of medical systems in search of the most effective treatment for a variety of illnesses. People commonly take recourse at both the hospital and the traditional healer or the prophet of a religious denomination. In some cases, people start with one and then move on to another; in other cases, they use several forms of healing simultaneously. Mozambicans and Angolans adopt a pluralistic approach to healing. Indigenous approaches to healing and reconciliation are most often used for demobilized child soldiers and other war-affected persons in rural communities.

Cleansing Rituals for Returning Child Soldiers

Rituals for former child soldiers deal with what happened to these children during the war. An acknowledgment of the atrocities they committed or witnessed and a definite break with that past are articulated through ritual performance. Traditional healing for war-affected children in Angola and Mozambique consists principally of purification or cleansing rituals, attended by family members and the broader community. During these rituals, the child is purged of the contamination of war and death, as well as of sin and guilt, and is protected against the avenging spirits of the people the child soldier may have killed. These ceremonies are replete with ritual and symbolism. The details are distinctive to the particular ethnolinguistic group, but their themes are common to all groups in Mozambique and Angola.

When Pitango, of Cambandua in Angola, returned home at the age of eighteen, his family organized a ritual for him.[10] The ritual took place the day Pitango arrived, before he was allowed to socialize with relatives and friends. His body was washed with cassava meal. A chicken was killed during the proceedings and its blood was placed on his forehead. Then his mother took some palm oil and rubbed it on Pitango's hands and feet. During this ritual, the ancestral spirits of the family were repeatedly called in to protect the young man who was back from war and had to start a new life. The prayers were offered by his elder relatives whose generational position brought them closest to the ancestors. Pitango mentioned that the elders of his family explained to him that the performance of this ritual was necessary so that the spirits of those killed in the war would not harm him. Pitango told the CCF team that because he did not kill anybody during the war he did not need to go through a ritual performed by a *kimbanda* (healer).[11]

Paulo was only nine years old when he was abducted by RENAMO forces during an attack on his village in southern Mozambique. He was ordered to carry a bag of maize meal and walk for four days to the military camp of Chinhanguanine. He stayed there about eight months, but he managed to escape from the camp just weeks before he was due to start military training. When he finally arrived home, his relatives took him to the *ndomba*, the house of the ancestral spirits. There he was presented to the ancestors of the family. The boy's grandfather addressed the spirits, informing them that his grandchild had returned alive and thanking the spirits for their protection.

A few days, later the family invited a *nyanga* (healer) to help them perform a cleansing ritual for Paulo. The boy's father described it:

We took him to the bush about two kilometers away from our house. There we built a small hut covered with dry grass in which we put him, still dressed in the dirty clothes he came back with from the RENAMO camp. Inside the hut he was undressed. Then we set fire to the hut and Paulo was helped out by an adult relative. The hut, the clothes, and everything else that he had brought from the camp were burned in the fire. Paulo then had to inhale the smoke of some herbal remedies and was bathed with water treated with medicine to cleanse his body internally and externally. Finally, we made him drink some medicine and gave him *ku thlavela* [vaccination] to give him strength and protect him.[12]

The spiritual practitioner and his adult relatives took the boy to the hut they had built in the bush. The burning of the boy's clothes, everything else that he had brought from the military camp, and the hut itself symbolized the rupture with the past. A chicken was sacrificed for the spirits of the dead, and the blood was spread around the ritual place. The chicken was then cooked and offered to the spirits as a sacrificial meal. The medicine that the boy inhaled and drank cleansed his body and spirit. Finally, the spiritual healer made some incisions in the boy's body and filled them with a paste made from herbal remedies, a practice called *ku thlavela* (vaccination). During this public ritual, relatives and neighbors were present; some assisted the practitioner while others watched, singing and clapping.

The ceremonies for Pitango and Paulo have significant similarities, even though the former took place in Angola and the latter in Mozambique. Rituals for returning soldiers address the pollution that they bring to their homes and villages. Former child soldiers must be cleansed in order to be able to socialize freely with relatives and friends. Pitango was washed with cassava meal, chicken blood, and palm oil on the day of his arrival. Paulo's cleansing ceremony was performed by a specialist healer a few days after he returned. Returning soldiers must also be reintroduced to the spirits of their ancestors. Pitango was presented to the ancestral spirits by his elder relatives, who asked those spirits to protect him from the avenging spirits of any dead he might have encountered during the war. Paulo was taken to the hut of the ancestors first, so his oldest relative could thank them for returning this child alive from the militia who had kidnapped him. Although nine-year-old Paulo was less likely than seventeen-year-old Pitango to have been involved in combat, his family took measures to prevent his being afflicted by spirits of the dead. Perhaps his age made him more vulnerable, even though it had also delayed his military training.

Traditional chiefs (*sobas*), healers and diviners (*kimbandas*), and elders (*seculos*) in Angola described and explained the rituals used in their regions to purify and reintegrate returning soldiers. A *kimbanda* in Uige, Angola, explained the procedure for welcoming home a former boy soldier.

When the child or young man returns home, he is made to wait on the outskirts of the village. The oldest woman from the village throws maize flour at the boy and anoints his entire body with a chicken. He is only able to enter the village after this ritual is complete. After the ritual, he is allowed to greet his family in the village. Once the greeting is over, he must kill a chicken, which is subsequently cooked and served to the family. For the first eight days after the homecoming, he is not allowed to sleep in his own bed, only on a rush mat on the floor. During this time, he is taken to the river and water is poured on his head and he is given manioc to eat. As he leaves the site of the ritual, he must not look behind him.[13]

According to this procedure, the returning child soldier is kept out of the village before ritual cleansing. He cannot greet people, interact with relatives and friends, or sleep in his bed until the purification rituals are completed. Children may be asked about their war experiences as part of treatment, but verbalization is not a fundamental condition for healing. The ceremony aims at symbolically cleansing the polluted child and enabling him to forget the trauma he has undergone, to put the war experience behind him. Here, as in other cases, the returned soldier is forbidden to look back, symbolizing a complete break with the past. Food taboos and other kinds of ritual restrictions apply. In Uige, the cleansed person must avoid fish and fowl for a month or two and be reintroduced to these foods gradually by the healer who officiated at the ceremony.

The Okupiolissa ritual from Huila, Angola, illustrates the active participation of the community in the process of cleansing returning boy soldiers from impurities and protecting them from unquiet spirits. People are usually excited and pleased at the homecoming. Women prepare themselves for a greeting ceremony. Some of the flour used to paint the women's foreheads is thrown at the boy, and a respected older woman of the village throws a gourd filled with ashes at his feet. At the same time, clean water is thrown over him as a means of purification. The women of the village dance around the boy, gesturing with hands and arms to ward off undesirable spirits or influences. With both hands, they each touch him from head to foot to cleanse him of impurities. The dance is known as Ululando-w-w-w. When the ritual is complete, the boy is taken into his village, and the villagers celebrate his return. A party is held in his home where only traditional beverages are served. The boy must be formally presented to the chiefs by his parents. He sits beside the chiefs, drinking and talking to them, an act marking his change of status in the village.[14]

In Huambo, Angola, when a soldier reenters the community, he cannot enter the house before stepping on the first egg of a chicken (*elembui*) that is placed in the doorway. The broken egg symbolizes the break with the past and the expulsion of any spirits of the dead that might haunt the former soldier.[15] Another ritual procedure involves killing a chicken and having the soldier jump over the animal while it is still shaking. Then he is showered with water before entering the family house.[16] Sometimes a pot of water is broken between the soldier's legs. This act is usually performed by the mother, who says " '*Onhassa*' for the spirits to go away and for him to become as pure as the water thrown at his feet."[17]

In the province of Moxico, according to Soba M. S., returning soldiers are welcomed home with a festive celebration; relatives and villagers throw *fuba* maize meal on his head and face as a sign of gratitude to the spiritual deities for having protected him. Only if the soldiers show signs of disturbance are they treated with a healing ritual.[18] The same is true in some areas of Biè province. A retired teacher told me that when his nephew returned from the war, the family held a welcoming celebration, slaughtering animals and offering a sacrificial meal to the ancestors in gratitude for their having brought him back alive. The youth had *fuba* maize meal thrown on his head and palm oil rubbed onto his hands. The retired teacher explained:

Those who killed unjustly . . . the spirits of the dead person possess them; they become mentally disturbed. When that happens, it is necessary to do traditional treatment, *ku thoka*, so that the illness goes away. . . . My nephew seems to be all right. So far we haven't noticed any strange behavior, but we will be watching him carefully, and if necessary look for a *kimbanda* to treat him.[19]

There are, then, two distinct moments in the reception of demobilized soldiers: an act of welcoming, which often involves the purification of the former boy soldier and a ritual separation from the past; and a ritual of healing, which often involves cleansing and protection. These moments may be separate or combined in one procedure.

The ritual for returning soldiers among the Bakongo in Uige, Angola, ensures that they are fully purified before they enter the village. According to Seculo (elder) Kazunzu, "In the past when a young man returned from the war, before getting into the family house he was taken to the river. In the river an elderly person treats him with water and the leaves of a tree called *mululua*."[20] Seculo Loloca elaborated: "The treatment in the river always takes place at dawn. . . . In the middle of the river the soldier has to drink medicine—*lulua, ngola,* and *cassale*—and the liquid extracted from the *mululua* leaves is splashed on the body. . . . When he gets out of the river the soldier cannot look back until he gets to the village."[21]

Angolan ritual complexes for greeting and cleansing returning boy soldiers, like those used in Mozambique, are what anthropologists call "rites of passage" or "transition."[22] The boy undergoes a symbolic change of status from someone who has existed in a realm where the violation of fundamental social norms was sanctioned—where killing and other atrocities were not only permitted but required—to someone who must now live in a peaceful realm where his actions must conform to social norms. Until the transition is completed through ritual performance, the boy is considered to be in a dangerous state, a marginal state that anthropologists call "liminal." What makes liminality dangerous is not merely its ambiguity but its instability; a person in a liminal state does not occupy a recognized social category, and his and her relationships with others are subject to sudden change and reversal.[23] For this reason, a boy cannot return to his family or hut, sleep in his bed, or perhaps even enter his village, until the rituals have been completed. Once the former soldier has been cleansed, he can rejoin the community and formally take his new place among relatives, villagers, and chiefs.

Central elements in these rituals of purification and reintegration come from the larger ritual complex for honoring the ancestors, called *mhamba* (singular) or *timhamba* (plural) in southern Mozambique. Rituals to venerate the ancestral spirits are conducted by the elders of the family. Only when healing is also necessary does a ritual require a spiritual medium or specialized healer. Rituals honoring the ancestors commonly involve the sacrifice of an animal, in times of abundance a cow or a goat, but in these cases a chicken. The blood is spread around the ritual place, and the meat is incorporated in a sacrificial meal offered to the ancestors and shared by the entire family. Meal and flour may also be offered to the spirits; in healing rituals, they are smeared on the child as well. Traditional beer may be served to the spirits and to all the participants. The festivities that mark the successful completion of the ceremony include dancing and singing, and may involve local chiefs as well as family members.

With this ritual complex in mind, we can see why chickens are sacrificed and symbolic meals are eaten in the rituals that welcome child soldiers back into the family and present them to the ancestral spirits. The next example is especially rich because it involves a traditional healer and her nephew, who had fought with UNITA.

Nzinga is a fifty-five-year-old *nyanga* in Malanje, Angola. When her nineteen-year-old nephew Pedro returned after more than seven years fighting with the rebel militia, she performed a ritual for him. When I asked about it, she said:

I could not let him stay without the cleansing treatment. He needed it because there [in the war] he might have done bad things like kill, beat and rob people . . . without the treatment the spirits of the dead would harm him. I do not know what happened there, he said he did not do anything . . . young people sometimes lie . . . I decided to go for full treatment because otherwise he could become crazy or even die.[24]

As a spiritual practitioner, Nzinga was in a position to give him a full treatment. Although her nephew said he had not killed anyone, she knew he might have reasons to conceal his past conduct; even if he had not committed murder, he had certainly witnessed atrocities. In her view, Pedro needed healing and protection from the afflictions that often ail those who have undergone such horrific experiences.

What Nzinga called the "full treatment" is generally performed by traditional healers. The ritual lasted four days and took place in and near her house. It required a chicken, a special mat, medicine, and some wine or traditional beer. Nzinga put her nephew Pedro in a place of seclusion and ritual treatment called *mwanza*, with a *huando* mat for him to sleep on. She placed some powdered medicine (*ditondo* and *dikezo*) under the mat and in his food and drink. Pedro had to stay inside the *mwanza* for three days. At dawn on the fourth day, he was taken to the river to be washed. He was oriented so that he faced upstream, symbolically turning toward the future while the polluted past streamed away behind him. The actual and symbolic dirt of the war was washed from his body. Afterward, he was not allowed to look back, symbolizing a total break with the dirty war. Back home, Nzinga opened an egg, put some sugar and powdered medicine inside, and threw it away, saying, "You malevolent spirits, here is what you want . . . leave us now." The chicken and drinks were prepared with medicine, and Pedro ate and drank them throughout the duration of his treatment. During the ritual, family members contributed food and drink, which they also shared during the proceedings.

In Malange, returning soldiers commonly received this type of healing, even if they showed no sign of disturbance. One adult man explained:

All young soldiers have to go through the *mwanza* treatment according to our tradition. In the *mwanza* he does not talk to anyone apart from the *kimbanda* who is treating him. The *kimbanda* prepares his food and talks to him about what happened during the war . . . This is our kind of therapy.[25]

People involved in programs to promote the readjustment of demobilized soldiers understand the parallels and intersections between rituals based on local knowledge and Western forms of psychotherapy for traumatized persons. Still, the isolation in the *mwanza* was only one phase in the treatment of war-affected persons in Angola. Returning soldiers were treated as members of their kin groups and villages.

In all these rituals, returning soldiers are purified before they are reintegrated into the family and community. A key element is symbolically breaking with the past: proclaiming the beginning of a new life; burning the hut and the clothes brought from the war; pouring water over the former soldier or washing the body in the river so that the dirt of the war goes away; and not looking back. Many rituals employ chickens; the blood is used for ritual cleansing, and the meat is used in the sacrificial meal shared with the ancestors and surviving relatives. Maize flour and cassava meal are also used for cleansing purposes. Most healing rituals involve herbal remedies to cleanse the body internally, by inhaling and drinking, and externally, by bathing and rubbing.

Some children had undergone rituals to protect them as they entered military service or the rebel militia. As discussed in chapter 2, some commanders were given medicine to protect them in battle. This practice was common in Mozambique and Angola, where several former child soldiers recalled the intervention of *kimbanda* (healers or spiritual practitioners) in the military camps.

In southern Mozambique, Amèlia, a *nyanga*, said that when her son Titos went to join the Portuguese colonial army in the 1960s, she performed a protective ritual for him before he had to present himself as a conscript.[26] She treated her son with a series of herbal remedies aimed at protecting him against the dangers of the war. First, in order to make him courageous and strong, he was vaccinated (*ku thlavela*) by having small incisions made on his body, which were filled with a medical paste obtained from a blend of different plants. Then Titos drank a solution made from several remedies and bathed himself with water mixed with medicine. Finally, Amèlia prepared him a talisman (*nhlulo*), which he carried around the waist for the duration of his military service.[27]

When Titos came home after fighting in the colonial war, he went through a purification ritual that contains elements found in cleansing rituals for unprotected soldiers as well as elements from the protection rituals he had previously undergone. His mother, Amèlia, conducted this ritual with the help of family elders. His clothes were burned outside, and he entered a special grass hut where he spent his first night home. He inhaled the smoke of a remedy called *mbasso*, a paste made from the combination of different plants and vegetable oils, which was blended with some dry grass from the hut. Then he had to bathe himself with water treated with a remedy called *hlambu*, a powder made with the leaves and roots of different plants. After his bath, he was taken to the family *ndomba* (the hut of the spirits), where he was welcomed and blessed by the ancestral spirits.[28] The similarities between Amèlia's treatment of her son Titos and Nzinga's treatment of her nephew Pedro are striking, even though one occurred in Mozambique and the other in Angola.

As in most traditional Mozambican and Angolan healing practices, the Cartesian dichotomy that separates body and mind in Western epistemology is not recognized in these cases. Individuals are seen and treated as whole persons, with integrated body and mind, and as part and parcel of a collective body rather than as isolated or autonomous individuals. Because their wrongdoings can affect their families and villages as well, the community is drawn in; purification and reintegration go hand in hand. Family members—including both the living and the dead—are directly involved in the cleansing and healing process. The ancestors are believed to have a powerful role in protecting their relatives against evil and misfortune. Pitango's family reintroduced him to the ancestors and invoked their protection. Paulo's relatives took him to the hut of the ancestors and thanked them for his safe return. Nzinga put Pedro in the place of the ancestors for the duration of his ritual treatment. Amèlia took Titos to the hut of the ancestral spirits after he had been cleansed.

Few accounts of rituals performed to treat former soldiers suffering from serious war-related mental disorders are available because in African and other cultures, relatives and healers seek to prevent such afflictions and to protect the privacy of persons whose minds and actions became disordered enough to need the treatment of a specialist. An informant in Moxico recounted such a ceremony in general terms.

The patient is taken to the bush by the *kimbanda* and stands on the top of a *mupanga* [small sand hill] with the shape of a crocodile made for the occasion. On the side of the crocodile's head the *kimbanda* places a pot with herbal remedies in boiling water, and on the side of the tail a pot containing cold water. In the midst of singing and drumming, the *kimbanda* splashes alternately hot and cold water from the pots onto the patient's body. . . . In this treatment the use of hot water is aimed at the expulsion of the malevolent spirits and the cold water at calming down the patient.[29]

In cases such as this, when the diviner has diagnosed spirit possession as the cause of a former soldier's insanity, the ritual aims at driving the evil spirits from the body and restoring the patient to his former self. The treatment in the bush is followed by a ceremony in the home in which relatives and friends participate.

Kimbandas and *tinyanga* are not the only spiritual practitioners to whom Angolans and Mozambicans appeal for assistance when returned soldiers suffer from war-related afflictions. Leaders and prophets of independent churches and established religious denominations organize religious services and special rituals for returned soldiers. People in need of healing utilize whatever help is available, simultaneously or in succession.

Nineteen-year-old Gil of Huambo, Angola, who had fought with the government army, had a traditional welcoming ceremony. He was met on the edge of the village by his mother and all his relatives. As he said:

[My family] acted according to the tradition. . . . My aunt took a live chicken and she rubbed it all over my body, as if she was dusting it, and then she rubbed palm oil on my hands and some ashes on my forehead. After that she threw *fuba* maize meal all over my body.[30]

However, that ceremony did not prevent him from suffering afflictions. He went to hospital but was not cured, which suggested that his difficulties might respond better to spiritual than to biomedical treatment.

On advice, Gil saw a prophet, an elderly woman affiliated with an independent church. The prophet requested rice, oil, salt, firewood, a few candles, and matches for the treatment, which took place in church. First, the rice was cooked with the oil and salt and offered to the gods. The plate of food was left overnight inside the church. If it remained untouched the next morning, that would be a sign that the gods had rejected the offering and the petitioner could not be cured. Fortunately, Gil's offering was accepted, so the prophet began her treatment. She gave him medicine to drink, to bathe in, and to use to protect his home. She held regular prayer sessions for him, placing her hands on his chest while praying. No payment was required. Gil recovered and joined the church, giving up smoking and drinking in order to maintain the good health that had been restored.[31]

Dacosta's cleansing ritual also took place in the local Zionist church.[32] His father was the Zionist bishop in the island where they lived in southern Mozambique. The day he got home—through the Red Cross reunification program for unaccompanied minors—the whole family went to church to pray and welcome him. Later, a Zionist ritual was organized in the church. The family got two pigeons, oil, maize flour, candles, salt, firewood, and matches. The flour was spread around the altar and the candles lit and placed on the altar. The church was packed with family, friends, and members of the congregation for the special service dedicated to Dacosta. The bishop made the prayers and the congregation, forming a circle around him and Dacosta, prayed and sang along. Then a fire was lit in the middle of the circle next to the bishop and his son. The bishop killed one of the pigeons and sprinkled the blood on his son's body (Dacosta had no shirt on). The dead pigeon mixed with the oil and salt was let to burn to ashes in the fire. Meanwhile, the bishop took the other live pigeon and placed it on his son's head and, while praying, he let the bird fly free. This symbolized Dacosta's freedom from the bad things he might have done in the war. The bird's blood was also used to cleanse him. Part of the ashes of the burnt pigeon was sprinkled on the young man's body, and the rest was taken home to be mixed in his bathing water for a few days. Then, Dacosta put on a shirt and was greeted by the whole congregation, which formally welcomed him back.

These independent churches, unlike mainstream churches, bring about divine healing through the power of the Holy Spirit, but they manage illness and misfortune in similar ways as traditional healers. The main feature of the Zionist healing rituals is the cleansing and exorcism of malevolent forces. Zionist priests and prophets are often possessed by the spiritual agencies, as was the case with Dacosta's father.[33]

The similarities between the rituals performed by local healers and the healing procedures undertaken by healing churches demonstrate the religious syncretism involved. What differs is not the concept of the healing process but rather the place of the treatment (crossroads, river, home, or church). There are differences of emphasis and some additional features, but the underlying belief system is basically the same. For Gil, the church treatment led to his affiliation with a new religious community—affiliation not based on kinship or locality but on shared spiritual practices. In the case of Dacosta, the religious treatment strengthened ties with his family and congregation, bringing him back to his roots, as he had grown up in a Zionist family.

Sometimes returned young combatants are not comfortable immersing themselves in these cultural and religious traditions. Some see such actions as a return to the old ways—a world of tradition and gerontocracy—and aspire to a more modern outlook on life. However, in the context of their villages and communities of origin, they are often confronted with the need to be pardoned and accepted back in order to belong, especially in light of their participation in the war. Social stigma and intolerance might drive them to conform to local practices. This happened to Zita, a young man we met in 1995 in Macia, southern Mozambique. Zita refused various attempts made by his mother and grandmother (his father had died during the war) to have him undergo a cleansing treatment with a healer or in a Zionist church. Zita also refused to accept the authority of his stepfather. Many months after his return, his mother claimed that although he was physically healthy, he was suffering from insomnia and nightmares and rejected the authority of the elders. Zita often got himself into lots of trouble, not only at home but also in the village. He was accused of stealing, breaking into the car of a tourist in the nearby beach of Bilene, and many other misdemeanors that prompted people to stigmatize him and call him *matsanga* and "armed bandit"—perjurative terms used to refer to RENAMO soldiers. The family put more pressure on Zita and finally got him to undergo treatment with a local healer. Zita's treatment was very similar to the one undertaken by Marcos. He was treated with herbal medicines away from his home where, as the healer said, "the bad spirits that afflicted him" were exorcised. Then the family got together at home for a ritual meal to thank the ancestors. Zita's mother told me that following the ritual, his behavior changed for the better, and she was pleased.

When girls and young women were reunited with their relatives after the war, they too went through cleansing and purification rituals performed by elderly women, traditional healers, and priests from local Zionist churches. These rituals are very similar to the ones performed for boy soldiers. When Ntombi returned from the military camp of Muroni in southern Mozambique, her family took her to the Zionist church for a cleansing ritual performed by the bishop (Dacosta's father). The ritual was very similar to the one performed for Dacosta, but in her case, because her body had been violated through rape and other forms of sexual abuse, she had to drink some herbal remedies to purge her body. The bishop who performed the ritual pointed out the following:

We have cleansed many young men and women that came from the camps. . . . The rituals are very important to cleanse them from the dirt of the war. We don't want them to live with that dirt because it can affect their lives negatively . . . we cleanse them inside and outside . . . they have to leave behind the bad things of the war . . . we don't want them to live like they did in the military camps.[34]

Other girls underwent ritual treatments by local healers or were helped by elderly women; some had a combination of these therapeutic strategies. Ana had nightmares, and her family was worried about her sanity. They looked for a healer in Xinavane, a nearby district. The healer called on the spirits of Ana's father's family first and then on the spirits of her mother's ancestors to help in her purification. Ana inhaled the smoke of herbal remedies called *basso* for three days. She drank herbal solutions and was washed with water treated with a medicinal powder. After the three-day treatment, Ana took home some of these remedies to drink and add to her bathing water for several

weeks. Simultaneously, her family organized prayers for her at the local Zionist church.

These rituals do not focus exclusively on the physical body; they are
also intended to deal with the emotional and psychological problems
that affect the young women. Thus, the whole symbolic array of the spirits, family traditions, and prayers to God are brought into the ritual.

In Angola, a number of treatments aim at solving afflictions presented by children who did not fight or kill anyone, but who witnessed
killings or bombardments or were victims of landmines or military attacks. Veronica, a ten-year-old girl from Lubango in Angola, showed
signs of distress after she survived an attack in 1992 in which her mother
and brother died. She was rescued from underneath dead bodies by her
father many hours after the massacre. The family decided to organize a
ritual to help ease her problems. Veronica's grandparents remarked,
"[B]ecause we were displaced and away from our village we did not have
the means to do things the proper way. A goat was required for the treatment but we didn't have one . . . we used plants, the roots of the
muhongo and *enhati* trees. . . ." The roots of these trees were boiled in water, and Veronica drank the reduced solution. The leaves of the trees
were used to prepare a cleansing steam bath for her whole body. Covered under a blanket with her grandmother, Veronica was instructed to
inhale the steam while sweating.

These kinds of treatments help children disturbed by displacement,
instability, and the loss of loved ones. Specific rituals are performed for
orphans who are taken into foster families to help the child settle into
the new family and to appease the spirits of the deceased parents.

These cleansing, protective, and healing rituals—wherever in the two
countries they are conducted, and despite their rich variety—do not involve verbal exteriorization of the traumatic experience of war. Marrato's study of war-affected people in Mozambique shows that recalling
the traumatic experience through verbal externalization was not part of
the process of coming to terms with it. People would rather not talk
about the past; they were directed not to look back but to start afresh after ritual procedures, which do not necessarily involve verbal expression
of the affliction, had been performed.[35]

Viewed from this perspective, the well-meaning attempts of psychotherapists to help local people deal with war trauma may, in fact,
cause more harm than help. Healing is achieved through nonverbal,
symbolic procedures that are understood by those participating in them.
Clothes and other objects brought from or symbolizing the past are
burned or washed away, impressing on the individual and the group a
complete break from wartime experience and the beginning of a new
life. Recounting and remembering the traumatic experience would be

like opening a door, inviting the harmful spirits to enter families and communities.

The performance of these rituals and the politics that preceded them extend beyond the particular individuals who are returning home. They involve the collective body. The family and friends are drawn into the ritual, and the ancestral spirits are invoked to mediate and ensure a good outcome. These cases show how the living have to acknowledge the dead—both their ancestors and the war dead—in order to carry on with their lives. The rituals are aimed at seeking forgiveness, appeasing the souls of the dead, and preventing any future afflictions from the spirits of the dead in retaliation for what happened to them during the war. In these ways, the links between the personal and communal present and the destruction and death that permeates the past are severed, freeing young people to reenter the social world of peace.

These rituals should not be seen as ends in themselves. They constitute just the beginning of a healing process, which can be long. Here, the involvement and support of the family and community in the healing process becomes crucial.

Community Rituals to Create Safe Places

The pollution that war brings is an extreme case of the more general sort of pollution that results from exposure to other social groups and environments. In rural communities of Angola and Mozambique, most people believe that persons who cross group boundaries, such as migrant workers, are particularly exposed to social contamination. They are especially likely to become victims of witchcraft and sorcery, to pick up unknown spirits, and to become ill in a strange environment. Ecological conditions, too, may be a source of pollution.[36] Civil war involves crossing established boundaries between social groups, transgressing distinctions between categories such as children and soldiers, and trespassing into the territory of others. Even those who did not participate directly in warfare are affected by these kinds of contamination.

In her study of war and violence in Mozambique, Nordstrom stresses that war-related violence should be understood as extending well beyond the military attacks, landmines, and other direct situations of armed conflict. Violence is embedded in daily life, involving poverty, hunger, nakedness, displacement, and loss of dignity.[37] In line with this definition, we can say that most people in the aftermath of the civil wars in Mozambique and Angola are still living under violent and potentially traumatic circumstances. Many refugees and displaced people returned to completely devastated villages where the houses and agricultural fields were burned, where schools, hospitals, factories, roads, and railway lines were destroyed. Many people continue to live without the basic conditions required for a livelihood; without food and clean water; proper clothing and shelter; jobs and education. The situation in Angola was exacerbated by the resumption of civil war after two short periods of truce. Twice civilians were again plunged into full-scale armed conflict, and many young demobilized soldiers were re-recruited into the military. This cycle of violence made peace seem more tentative and uncertain to Angolans. The death in 2002 of Jonas Savimbi, UNITA's leader, finally brought an end to war in Angola.

Honoring the Ancestral Spirits

People in Mozambique and Angola honor the ancestral spirits in order to secure their protection. In circumstances of war, when the protection of spirits is even more necessary than usual, many people were prevented from conducting these rituals regularly or at all because they were displaced. When people died, it was extremely difficult or even impossible for surviving family members to bury the dead and conduct the proper rituals. After the war, the enormous numbers of dead without proper burials and of ancestral spirits who had been neglected posed serious problems that people had to address to continue their lives in safety and security.

In Angola, civilians whom we interviewed conducted burial rituals, often called *óbitos* (a word taken from Portuguese), for their kin who had been killed during the war even though they had been unable to do so at the appropriate time. As Seculo Kapata of Moxico put it, "We perform burial rituals so that the spirits of the dead continue to be linked to the living without problems."[38] The spirits of the dead had to be settled and honored so that they would provide protection rather than sending affliction. This link began with the burial rituals. Many survivors had to conduct these rituals belatedly.

Seculo Samba, an elderly Angolan from Biè, was prompted by his dead father's spirit to hold a proper ritual.

During the war, my father was killed. I did not perform the *óbito* (burial ritual) because I thought that in times of war there is no need for that. But, during the night I was unable to sleep. . . . I dreamed of my father telling me that "I am dead but I haven't reached the place of the dead; you have to perform my *óbito* because I can see the way to the place where other dead people are but I have no way to get there." Afterwards I performed the *óbito* rituals, and I have never dreamed of my father again.[39]

The dead father needed the prescribed burial rituals in order to reach his proper position in the world of the spirits. The dead man's son had believed that the war made burial rituals unnecessary—or, perhaps, he believed them impossible in the absence of a dead body. So the man's unquiet spirit visited his son to let him know what was needed. An elderly *kimbanda* (healer) from Bié explained that when someone dies, it is imperative to perform the *óbito*. Without them, access to the spiritual world can be blocked. The unburied dead have to catch the attention of their relatives, through illness or dreams, and ask them for a proper burial.[40]

The illness of surviving family members prompted some relatives to seek the services of diviners. Soba Lohali of Bié told us:

My mother was killed during the war, and because at that time there was no way of performing the *óbito*, we did not do anything. After some time, my daughter became very ill, and ordinary traditional treatment did not cure her illness. Later a *kimbanda* [spirit medium] told us that the spirit of my mother had possessed my daughter because after she died we did not do anything. After performing the *óbito*, the child's illness disappeared.[41]

According to the diviner, the child's illness was the result of possession by her grandmother's unquiet spirit. Performing the burial rituals that had been impossible amid the chaos of war allowed the dead woman's spirit to rest and cured her granddaughter.

In times of war, those who did perform burial rituals often had to do so in the absence of the dead body. Most people received the news of their relative's death by word of mouth. The relative had died away from home, and the body had not been brought back to the family. The people who performed the burial rituals under such circumstances believed that the spirits of the dead would join their kin for the ceremony. As *Seculo* Kapata of Moxico commented, "[E]ven when the person dies far away from home [and the dead body is not present] the spirit comes with the wind."[42] Another adult Angolan, Mr. Marimba, pointed out that even those who "died away from home need a burial ceremony. When they die far away their soul stays there unsettled. With the performance of the burial the soul comes with the wind and settles down."[43] Surviving relatives performed burial rituals in the absence of a dead body in the belief that the spirit would come "with the wind" and be quieted, taking its place among the ancestors, rather than remaining restless and troubling either their relatives or people who lived in the place they died.

In some situations, families that had received no news from their relatives for a long period would hear about their deaths through those who escaped from military camps or attacks. In these circumstances, some families would choose for the performance of the burial ritual without the body. In case the relative turned out to be alive and returned home, the ritual had to be undone by another ritual before the person could resume social interaction with relatives and friends. I heard of such cases in both Mozambique and Angola.

Rituals to honor ancestral spirits in Mozambique closely resemble those in Angola. Analyzing the ritual complex he observed in Mozambique in the early twentieth century, Junod gave the following definition of the *mhamba*: "*Mhamba* is the object, the act or the person used to establish the link between the ancestral spirits and their descendants."[44] In my observation, *mhamba* is a ritual and, therefore, a set of beliefs and practices that unite members of a community to pay respect to their ancestral spirits. The *mhamba* is not just the object, the isolated act, or the person but rather the combination of these elements. It has action, dynamics, and a profound symbolic value that is intelligible for the members of that community.

Timhamba rituals (plural for *mhamba*) take place at dawn in the family cemetery or near the *gandzelo*, the sacred tree of the spirits. First an animal is sacrificed. In times of peace and prosperity, the ox was the most common sacrificial beast, but because of the widespread poverty caused by war, people make do with a goat or even a chicken. The animal's neck is pierced with an *assegai*. Piercing the goat's jugular vein or carotid artery makes the blood spurt out and allows the animal to die quickly. The animal's blood has to be spread all over the ritual place. The meat is then prepared into a meal to be offered to the spirits and also consumed by the members of the family.

The person presiding over the ritual, generally the senior family member, speaks to the ancestors. He invokes the names of all the family's deceased ancestors, starting with the *hahani* or *kosezana*, the elder sister of the paternal grandfather, unless the spirits have indicated differently. The officiant then informs the ancestral spirits about the state of the family, thanks them for their protection and guidance, and asks them to continue to look after the family. Other members of the family are allowed to express their feelings and offer their prayers to the ancestors at this moment.

Then each participant in the ritual must eat a small portion of the sacrificial meal that remains after being shared with the ancestors. The children are the first to be served. They are given the front legs of the ox because these are *mpakama*, the ramifications or the arms of the family. The *vakonwana*, the sons-in-law, eat the back legs, the best meat of the animal, as a sign of respect and consideration, for they have paid the *lobolo*, bridewealth, to the family. The *nkosikhazi*, the daughters-in-law, have the *nhlana*, the rump, for they are the ones who reproduce the group and nurse the children, carrying them on their backs. The remaining parts are consumed by the other participants. In addition to the sacrificial meal, more food and drinks are available to the members of the family to celebrate the occasion. At the end of the meal and throughout the day, drums are played and people sing and dance. It is a festive occasion for the whole family united by their ancestral spirits.[45]

Timhamba rituals entail collective healing and reestablishment of balance. The bloody sacrifice which characterizes these rituals also emphasizes reciprocity toward the ancestral spirits to whom the individual owes his possessions, food, and life itself. The purpose of the *timhamba* is both communication and communion with the dead. Communication comes through addressing them verbally to seek protection, healing, and guidance. Communion is achieved through sharing the same sacrificial animals in a meal, which is consumed by both the spirits and the living.

In Angola, the hierarchy among the ancestral spirits reproduces that existing among the living. The most important spirits are those of the elders, who in life held positions of seniority; the spirits of dead children or youth do not have the same status as those of senior members of the spirit world. The *ainê-cadet* relationship between older and younger generations is transposed to the spiritual world; in other words, the spiritual world is a continuation of the living world. Even after death, the elders continue to guide and control their descendants.

According to Soba (chief) Chissico from Biè, "[o]ur power lies in the hands of our dead *seculos* (elders)." Soba Chilombo added, "We have our own natural power, but this power needs to be enhanced by that of our ancestors."[46] The spirits are responsible for promoting health, good fortune, and well-being of individuals and entire communities. However, as Seculo Kalema emphasized, "The ancestral spirits can help you, but they can also harm you . . . if they feel neglected they can punish people by provoking illness or can even cause death.[47] Kalema explained that there are different types of spirits (*hambas*), some more dangerous than others; among the Tchokwè, the spirits that cause death and female sterility are called *ngombo, thambe*, and *nhanga*. Informants from Moxico reported that misfortunes in business, hunting and fishing, infertility and repeated miscarriages are often attributed to the unhappiness of the ancestral spirits.[48]

In order to deserve the blessing and protection of these spiritual entities, people have to venerate them through prayer and ritual performance. As *Seculo* Selundo put it, the living must "show respect towards the dead." One of the ways of honoring them, according to *Seculo* Selundo, is to build a hut in the family yard for the *olosandu* (the name given to the spirits among the Ovimbundu) of the family. Regular offerings are to be placed in the hut, especially the food and drink that the ancestors preferred when alive. Bread, sugar, and *caxi* (traditional beer) are the most common offerings.[49]

People believe that the spirits provide protection if one takes good care of them. Their protection is especially important during wartime, according to *Soba* Camarada of Huambo:

The dead are always with us. During the war we walked day and night through the bush, we crossed rivers and nothing happened to us precisely because our ancestors were watching over us. So, for that reason, when a relative dies we have to take good care of the grave, to make him or her happy to help us.[50]

Those who do not comply with these social obligations lack protection and become vulnerable to evil forces. Seculo Congo from Uige emphasized that

We have to respect our dead. . . . We should obey those of us who have already gone. In case of difficulty one should pray for them and say "*nuakuetu, nua-fuakala na yenda ku na yenda*," you our ancestors wherever you are, please tell me why my life is not good, why my family is not well.[51]

This prayer will only be acknowledged if the spirits are satisfied with the petitioner's social behavior.

Communities and families venerate and worship the ancestral spirits through special rituals to propitiate them. In southern Mozambique, *ku pahla* is a verb which means "to venerate" or "to honor" the ancestral spirits. *Ku pahla* is a permanent way of paying respect to one's ancestors, performed on various occasions such as births, before harvesting, during a meal, and before a long trip. The performance of *ku pahla* gives individuals and groups a sense of security and stability, which they need in order to carry on with their lives. This permanent liaison between the living and the dead gives meaning to the existence of both the spirits and the community.

When displaced people are preparing to return to their communities after the war, the first rituals to be performed are the *timhamba*, to venerate the ancestral spirits buried in the family cemetery and symbolized by the *gandzelo*, the "tree of the ancestral shades." These rituals aim to restore the liaison between individuals and their ancestors and enables the family to receive the guidance and the protection of the spirits as they rebuild their lives. Refugees and displaced people expressed regret at having abandoned their ancestral spirits when they left their land, and they organized a big *mhamba* on their return. Some people had gone home after the ceasefire to check on the situation in their village and prepare the conditions for the return of the whole family. During that short stay, they performed *ku pahla* to honour the dead.

Xitoquisana, who left his home in Mukodwene, Inhambane province,

Mozambique in 1987 after being tortured by RENAMO soldiers, said that in January 1993 he went back to Mukodwene:

I went to see the place and gave it a good clean. Next June [in two months time] I will return again, but this time to make a *mhamba*. I will go with my family and I will take everything for the ceremony: goats, chicken, maize meal, etc. We are going to present ourselves to our ancestors and thank them for their protection, because most of us managed to survive the war. We will move back home for good probably at the end of the year as we want to make sure that the war is really over.[52]

Xitoquisana planned to return to Mukodwene permanently when he felt assured that peace would last. In the meantime, the family would go home to conduct the *mhamba* ceremony to give thanks for their survival and prepare for their return.

Damião, a government soldier from Zibondzane in Manjacaze, had brought his family—mother, brothers, and sisters—to live with him in Massaka because of the escalation of RENAMO attacks in Zibondzane. When we interviewed him during the process of demobilization, he said that they would not rush back, as he wanted to see what would happen after the elections.

I would rather wait here. Nevertheless, we will go home for visits and prepare the fields. Also, the elders in the family are organising a *mhamba* for next month. *Timhamba* are a tradition in our family; my grandfather had always organised *ku pahla* ceremonies.[53]

He, too, was going back with his family to their home in order to attend a *mhamba* ceremony in preparation for their eventual return.

Carlos, a refugee from Chibuto, Gaza province, Mozambique, said that he wanted to take his family home as soon as possible even though he planned to stay in town because he had a good job which he wanted to keep. He mentioned that in August he and his relatives would go to Chibuto to perform a big *mhamba* for their ancestors. The *nyanga* of the family, who had survived the war and was back in the village, would be called to officiate at the ritual.[54]

These accounts attest to the centrality of rituals that venerate the ancestral spirits in people's lives. The first action people take, even before returning for good, is to reestablish their relationship with the dead ancestors, which has been seriously impaired by the war. The reestablishment of that relationship becomes a strategy for social healing, reconciliation, and reconstruction. Although some people might neglect to venerate their ancestral spirits on a regular basis when everything in their lives goes well, most turn immediately to the spirits for help in times of crisis and affliction.

Settling the Unquiet Spirits of the Dead

An individual had to maintain a link with deceased elders. On the other hand, disassociation from the spirits of the war dead who were not kin and were killed by members of one's own group was crucial for preserving well-being.

In Mozambique, the civil war between the government and RENAMO rebels is believed to have produced many "spirits of bitterness," which can cause mental problems or death if not properly appeased. People unanimously stated that rituals for appeasing these spirits had to be performed in the places where battles occurred and many people died. These rituals are vital to calm the spirits and place them in their proper positions in the spiritual world. Such rituals are generally performed by traditional practitioners, because they have the ability to seize and exorcise (or appease) these angry spirits. The goal is to make the village and related areas safe for the living.

Mipfhukwa spirits are particularly important after a war when soldiers and civilians have not been appropriately buried. In fact, the Mipfhukwa phenomenon is often referred to as a result of warfare. Some of my elder informants recalled that after the Nguni wars in southern Mozambique in the nineteenth century, the spirits of the Nguni and Ndau warriors who had been killed in this region, far away from their homes, and were not properly buried had afflicted and killed many local Tsonga families.[55] The Ndau spirits are regarded as the most dangerous. Most informants believe that the Ndau spirits are very powerful and that the Mpfhukwa phenomenon is originally Ndau.

Mpfhukwa is a capacity that is acquired through the powers conferred by a plant. According to the Ndau tradition, every Ndau person drinks a solution made from this plant a few weeks after his or her birth. This medicine is believed to make people stronger, and after they are dead, it empowers them to take revenge on their killers. The connection between the civil war in Mozambique and the problem of Mpfhukwa spirits has a particular historical connection, since the RENAMO rebels had a strong base of support in Ndau (although that changed during the last years of the war). Since there has been increased interpenetration between the Tsonga, the Nguni, and the Ndau groups, the secret of Mpfhukwa is no longer exclusively Ndau. For that reason, many people fear that the re-emergence of Mipfhukwa spirits will be greater and stronger than in the past.

The angry spirits of people who were killed far from home can make the places where they died dangerous for others. One especially striking case comes from southern Mozambique in April 1993. Fabião Sitoe from Manhiça said that traditional healers and diviners from Munguine in the district of Manhiça, about 100 kilometers north of Maputo, were called to perform a ritual on the road that links the locality of Munguine to Manhiça. The ritual was needed because no one could use the road after dark to get to Manhiça. Some people reported that as they approached the place they felt something beating on them. Others heard voices sending them back. Still others became blind and could not see their way to Manhiça. These assaults, detours, and afflictions made people suspect that something was seriously wrong along the road, and so they requested the help of spiritual practitioners.

After analyzing the situation, the *tinyanga* decided to perform a ritual of divination to diagnose the problem. The ritual was performed at dawn in the presence of local chiefs, local government authorities, and the people of Munguine. The diviners performed *ku femba* ("to catch or seize the spirit") and identified the spirit as a RENAMO commander killed there during the war. Then the spirit spoke through a medium and acknowledged that he had been harassing local people because he wanted to go back to his own place and have a proper burial. The spirit requested some money and *capulanas* (pieces of locally produced fabric) to take with him as he departed for his home in Ndauland. Munguine residents agreed to contribute money to the spirit and to buy the *capulanas*. The chiefs and the government also contributed. A week later, the spirit was caught again. A ritual took place in which the spirit was symbolically placed in the *capulanas* and tied together with the money. Some herbal remedies provided by the healers were also placed in the *capulanas* to prevent the return of the spirit. Then the whole bundle was buried far away from Munguine. According to the local people, since then no more problems have occurred along that road. Quieting the angry spirit of the rebel commander made the road safe for local residents to use.[56]

Another example of Mpfhukwa was widely discussed in the media in Mozambique. According to an article in the *Mediafax*[57] in May 1996, in the district of Govuro (Sofala province), a battalion of Maconde[58] soldiers who had killed the former *régulo* (chief) Laquene Nguluve from Vuca (also in that district) was suffering from retaliation by Nguluve's spirit. According to Carvalho's reports, this Ndau chief had been killed ten years earlier by soldiers who suspected that he was supporting RENAMO in the war against the government. In two months, six members of that battalion died under strange circumstances, and the commander who ordered the killing had a mental breakdown. Divination revealed that the spirit wanted a Maconde child to be killed with the same gun used to kill him. The Maconde pleaded with the spirit to accept as a settlement three goats, a bottle of brandy, and a virgin Maconde girl to take care of the hut of the spirit.[59] Apparently, the spirit rejected the offer, and people feared he would continue to kill the soldiers. Interviewed by a journalist, the current chief of Vuca and brother of the deceased stated, "[o]ur spirits [the Ndau] are stronger than the Maconde spirits. . . . The spirit of my brother knows what he wants. I asked him to save the boy and accept their offerings but he refused, saying that he will finish that group who killed him unjustly." The situation became a matter of public concern.

Ritual performance was successful in appeasing the angry spirit that blocked the road from Munguine to Manhiça, but the second case was more problematic. The fact that the Mpfhukwa spirit demanded the death of an innocent child complicated the matter. The intervention of the *tinyanga* was intended to mediate this sort of situation by establishing a liaison between the living and the dead. In this case, however, the group believed responsible for killing the RENAMO commander rejected his demands, and his surviving relative did not intercede successfully. The Mpfhukwa spirit threatened to continue his retaliation against the entire group that he regarded as responsible for his death. Social peace was not restored. It took the involvement of governmental authorities in the Govuro district, the Association of Traditional Healers, and the Association of Former Combatants to achieve a successful mediation of this conflict.[60]

In Angola, too, rituals were believed necessary to heal places where many deaths had occurred during the long civil war. Indeed, they were perceived as necessary to the restoration of peace itself. Soba Kavingangi of Biè explained: "With this war many people died and did not have proper burials; their heads are in the bush. . . . The souls of those who died and were not buried are wandering around and will not let us have peace. The war will continue here because the spirits are angry."[61] This chief's prediction was, in fact, proved accurate. In his view, the social and spiritual disorder caused by the war, which left dead bodies in the bush and unleashed unquiet spirits, had become self-perpetuating. Only the proper performance of rituals designed to restore normal relationships between the living and the dead would bring lasting peace.

The town of Kuíto, situated in the plateau of Biè in the central region of Angola, was severely affected by the 1992–94 war, which erupted when UNITA lost the general elections to the MPLA. Thousands of people lost their lives in that urban war. Many of them died on the plateau as they tried to escape from military attacks or look for food across military fire lines.[62] Until July 1997, many bodies remained on the plateau because landmines prevented people from reaching the place to identify the dead and organize burial rituals. Many people in Kuíto believe that life will not go well unless something is done to appease the dead and place them in the world of the spirits. Kutximuila and Aurora, two female healers from Kuíto, stated that the government should organize a big ceremony to honour the dead of the plateau.[63] Their views were shared by Soba Capumba, the traditional chief of the area: "The government must think of having collective ceremonies to bury the bones of those killed in the war. . . . Here in Kuíto many people died and no ceremonies were performed to appease their souls. Their souls are wandering about and can afflict anyone."[64] Soba Kavingangi from Biè went so far as to say that: "[I]t would be possible to collect all the bones that are still lying in town and in the bush and bury them with an *obito*. But for that we need the government's approval; we cannot do it without their approval."[65]

People in Huambo call these community ceremonies to quiet the spirits of the dead *ayele* rituals; they are commonly sponsored by the *soba*, take place once a year, and may last a week.[66] A collective affliction requires a collective remedy.

In southern Mozambique at certain points along the National Route One, which links the capital to the north of the country, some communities performed rituals to appease the spirits of the dead. During the war, travellers along this route, which facilitated the circulation of goods between the north and south, were frequently ambushed for looting, and many massacres and killings occurred. The populations along the route feared that the spirits of the dead killed in these attacks could harm them if not properly appeased. Some people mentioned to me in Manhiça, after the war ended in 1992, that when people started using this route more freely, many car accidents happened in places where innocent civilians had been killed during the war. People saw these car accidents as the actions of unquiet spirits. Therefore, they believed that these spirits had to be appeased and placed in their proper positions in the spiritual world, before peace would be possible.[67]

These rituals are aimed at addressing, not the illness of one person, but the afflictions of an entire community that is being haunted by the spirits of the dead and the troubles caused by the war. In Munguine, the spirit of the dead RENAMO soldier blocked the road and made traveling to Manhiça impossible. Along the National Route One, the actions of unsettled spirits caused car accidents and other misfortunes. In Kuíto, the fear of retaliation from the spirits of the unburied dead of the plateau and landmines made it inaccessible. Community rituals to restore peace and stability are generally carried out by village leaders and traditional practitioners who look after the interests of the community as a whole and have specialized knowledge of how to guarantee its welfare.

In the aftermath of war, people from the Angolan areas of Huambo and Biè perform a ritual called *okusiakala o'ndalao yokalye*, which can be translated as "let's light a new fire." According to local residents, this ritual is performed after crises of great magnitude, such as natural disasters and wars. On the day of the ritual, every household extinguishes its fires. The traditional chief, assisted by spiritual practitioners, lights a new fire, sparked by the friction of two stones, in the center of the village. The people of the village witness and participate in the ceremony. A portion of this huge new fire is distributed to every household, so that all new fires have a common origin. The symbolism is simple but powerful: extinguishing the past, making a new start, a fresh beginning and a rebirth of hope.[68]

Conclusion

The problems from which children and other war-affected populations suffer and the rituals performed to cleanse and heal them illustrate the complexities of healing, reintegration, and reconciliation after a devastating war. War-affected populations have to start from scratch to try to rebuild their lives, make sense of their present, and regain their dignity. In postwar conditions, people have to deal with a myriad of situations that fall far outside of what is believed to be the regular state of affairs: families were torn apart; sons killed their fathers; child soldiers were forced to raid their own villages; mothers had to deal with sons who fought on different sides. Under these circumstances, the processes of healing and social rebuilding are very delicate, and reconciliation and healing are often articulated by reference to traditional beliefs in the power of spiritual agencies.

Individuals and communities come together after a war by employing their notions of health, illness, and healing. The role of the spirits of the dead in postwar healing and reintegration processes is powerful. Pollution that arises from death and bloodshed in war can harm families and communities. Polluted individuals are potential contaminators of the social body. Cleansing rituals are vital for society's protection against the evils of war and for freeing individuals from spiritual retaliation that can lead to mental illness or death. Healing is accomplished through intricate acts with symbolic as well as physical significance.

I have argued throughout the chapter that there are many perspectives on healing war trauma and facilitating postwar reconciliation. Cultural beliefs and practices are important to help people redefine their lives after a devastating war. As Swartz pointed out, "[w]e all make meaning of our lives in the light of our own experiences and those of the people around us."[69] The majority of the Mozambicans and Angolans most directly affected by these wars are from rural settings. Thus, any attempts to help them have to take their worldviews and systems of meaning into account. Local understandings of war trauma, healing, and community cohesion are vital when dealing with populations affected by conflict and political violence. Research undertaken in Mozambique and Angola suggests that, at the local level, families as well as traditional chiefs and healers are already taking responsibility for healing the social wounds of war. They are not waiting for government authorities to provide them with trained psychologists, psychotherapists, and other medical practitioners to help deal with their problems. They are using the means available to them to restore peace and stability to their communities.

Chapter 6
Looking to the Future and Learning from the Past

This final chapter examines the prospects for rehabilitation and reintegration of young people affected by armed conflict and considers national and international policies that might prevent the involvement of children in postcolonial civil wars. What resources are available to facilitate their transition into "normal" life? What are the strengths and limitations of the programs implemented to support them? How do the fundamental causes and devastating consequences of these conflicts affect the prospects these young people have for becoming full and active members of society? What are the problems and possibilities of national and international policies designed to prevent the recruitment and abduction of children to serve as soldiers and to serve soldiers? The chapter presents a critical analysis of programs developed by national and international agencies to address the difficulties that young former soldiers and captives experience in post-conflict situations and to protect children from war. How effective and sustainable are such efforts in the particular cultural, socioeconomic, and political contexts in which these programs are undertaken? Young people's perceptions of their past experiences and their perspectives on the future are central to this discussion. What are their thoughts about their experiences? How do they assess their present situations? What do they find most troubling or frustrating as they struggle to construct new lives as young adults in peacetime? How do they envisage their future? What are their aspirations for their own children?

The chapter is organized in five sections. The first two sections describe the processes of demobilization and the programs put in place to facilitate the reintegration of child combatants and other war-affected children into their communities and society. Here we listen to the voices and viewpoints of young men who were recruited or coerced into the military as boys and of young women who were captured and held by militias as girls. How have their distinct, yet shared wartime experiences shaped the problems and prospects of young men and women in peacetime? How do these youths make sense of their lives? What happens when demobilized young men realize what they have missed, as they learn to live with what they have done and seen? How do young women freed from captivity see their prospects for marriage, especially when they have children fathered by their captors? The third section considers the healing and therapeutic strategies used to help youth overcome trauma and other forms of distress caused by their involvement in armed conflict in relation to Western and African notions of health and the healing of social and psychological disorders. This section also situates these approaches within the perspective of the affected communities.

The chapter then shifts from ways of addressing the consequences of the involvement of children in armed conflict to ways of preventing the problem. It evaluates the effectiveness of international humanitarian law designed to prevent the participation of children in armed conflicts. I consider both the actual circumstances that prevail during irregular civil wars and the relation of international conventions to the norms and value systems of African and other non-Western societies. The assumptions that underlie Western approaches to childhood and the protection of children from armed conflict are inapplicable to the social structures and cultural patterns that define the positions of young people in peacetime, let alone amid armed conflicts. Beyond the needs for demobilization and healing, the final section focuses on the need to address the structural causes of the phenomenon of the participation of children in war.

Demobilization and Social Reintegration of Boy Soldiers

Demobilization programs intended to assist former soldiers in the transition home are more immediately designed to contain, disarm, and demobilize rebel forces. These programs often excluded soldiers under the legal age for military recruitment. They focused exclusively on males, leaving out girls and young women who had been held captive in the service of military forces. These transitional aid programs assumed that demobilized soldiers could reenter intact families and communities, but many had lost kin, and their villages and neighborhoods were unable to absorb them. Equally serious, many boys who had been recruited at a young age and spent years in the military had entirely missed the initiation, schooling, and job training that ordinarily takes place during those years. Many demobilized young men had no route into adult status, but were, nonetheless, required to be independent. The capacity of kin groups and communities to make productive places for returning soldiers had been deeply compromised by the general conditions of protracted warfare.

The process of demobilization of combatants in Mozambique was formally initiated in 1994. Data provided by the technical unit of the UN Mission in Mozambique (ONUMOZ) indicates that 27 percent (about 25,498) of the soldiers presented for demobilization were younger than eighteen at that time.[1] Child combatants younger than fifteen, even after fighting the war for many years, could not be considered soldiers under international law, according to the Geneva Conventions. Ironically, the same Geneva Conventions could not be enforced to preclude these young combatants from being recruited into the military in the first place. Underage combatants who were taken to containment centers or sought out the facilities established under demobilization schemes were not given the same package of benefits—a sum of money, foodstuffs, and working materials—as regular soldiers. They were instead referred to non-governmental organizations, such as the International Committee for the Red Cross and the Save the Children Alliance, which established programs to support them and other war-affected children.

Intervention programs to support war-affected children—both combatants and noncombatants—started before the ceasefire in 1992 to accommodate children who fled from military camps and other displaced, unaccompanied children. The Children and War Project (CWP) was established in 1988 by the Save the Children Federation USA to support the national program of Documentation, Tracing, and Reunification (DTR) implemented by the State Secretariat for Social Welfare, the Ministries of Health and Education, international agencies, and other non-governmental organizations. The DTR was the most important instrument for implementing the Mozambican government's 1985 policy for providing assistance to children affected by war. The policy emphasized community involvement and promoted the reintegration of unaccompanied children into their families and communities. The CWP undertook the documentation, tracing, and family reunification of unaccompanied children found in military camps at the end of the war and was staffed entirely by Mozambicans. The process consisted of six stages: (1) identifying the unaccompanied child, (2) registering biographical information and taking a Polaroid photo of the child, (3) searching for members of the child's family through widespread dissemination of the photo and biographical information by posters and radio, (4) once the family was located, confirming the child's and the family's wishes to be reunited, (5) reuniting the family, and (6) following up with home visits and other activities aimed at facilitating the reintegration of the child into the family and community.

The CWP contributed directly to the reunification of more than 12,000 unaccompanied children with their relatives and helped make possible thousands of other family reunifications between 1988 and 1995. Before 1992, most of the reunified children had fled from military camps. Fleeing RENAMO combatants, both children and adults benefited from an amnesty law passed by the government in 1987.

In the capital, Maputo, the government of Mozambique established the Lhanguene Rehabilitation Centre to accommodate the child combatants who benefited from the amnesty law. The first group of forty-two boy soldiers (between six and sixteen years of age) that came from the RENAMO camps in 1987 was placed at Lhanguene. All had been abducted from their families by RENAMO, taken to base camps, trained as combatants and, in many instances, forced to kill other human beings. These boys eventually escaped or were liberated from rebel strongholds. After brief stays in detention prisons, the government placed them in the Maputo Center, where Save the Children USA was asked to provide psychological and social assistance. The goal was to evaluate the young combatants' psychological situation in order to develop appropriate strategies for support and family reunification. The CWP put together a team of two national teachers and one social worker, a Cuban educator, and an American psychologist to develop the psychosocial program and work with the children.

According to Neil Boothby, one of the team's most striking initial observations was the range of behaviors the boys exhibited after arrival at the center.[2] Some appeared listless and numbed, unable or unwilling to talk or to engage in organized activities. Others were talkative, anxious, and active. A number of younger boys interacted with the center's adult caregivers; many older ones avoided contact or communication with them altogether. Some did not interact with peers; others engaged openly with one another; a few older boys bullied younger ones; and some engaged in fights and high-risk behavior. As program staff spent more time with these boys, they learned that their child soldering experiences differed as well. The length of time spent in base camps ranged from months to years, and their functional roles varied from cooks, cleaners, and porters to spies, combatants, and even leaders of combatants.

The Lhanguene program did not achieve the intended and expected results, because most of the children did not open up to talk about their experiences in the military and apparently were not comfortable verbalizing their emotions and feelings with the psychologists brought in to help them. Located in the heart of the capital, the center completely removed the boys from their communities and cultural environments. The fact that they were asked to talk about their painful memories of the war as a way of healing alienated them further. Neither their social isolation nor the process of verbally reliving their most horrific experiences was helpful in enabling them make the transition into peacetime society. Indigenous methods of healing take exactly the opposite approach, reconnecting returned soldiers to their families, communities, and ancestral spirits and enabling them to leave the past behind them.

Moreover, the decision to place these boys in the Lhanguene Center went against the Ministry of Health and Department of Social Welfare (DNAS) policy on noninstitutionalization of war-affected children in need of care and placement. Once the Lhanguene experience was considered a debacle, one of the main goals of the CWP was to work toward the return of the boys to their families and communities. As part of a nationwide tracing and reunification effort, forty-one of the forty-two Lhanguene children were eventually reunited with their families and communities in three provinces.

Family reunifications in times of war, although limited in number, were very costly, as they had to be done by airplane or helicopter. They represented a risk for everyone involved; planes could be shot at anytime, and military incursions could suddenly occur in the place of reunification. The majority of the reunifications took place after the ceasefire, when massive numbers of displaced populations started moving back to their places of origin and tried to locate lost relatives. The CWP dealt with two categories of children: the unaccompanied children released from RENAMO-controlled areas and military camps who had no military training and were not soldiers (including cooks, servants, abused girls, spies, and carriers of ammunition and looted goods); and child combatants.

The reunification process for child combatants began in 1994 concurrent with the formal demilitarization and demobilization process for combatants conducted by the ONUMOZ. Soldiers who went through it benefited from compensation. Child combatants under the age of fifteen, who were to be involved in programs by humanitarian agencies such as the CWP, were not happy with their exclusion from the formal demilitarization and demobilization process.

Angered by the decision, a group of RENAMO child combatants under the age of fifteen awaiting demobilization in one of the cantonment areas staged a mutiny in RENAMO's headquarters in Maputo and besieged RENAMO leaders. They demanded the same benefits that their fellow soldiers over fifteen were getting and refused to be treated like children. These young RENAMO combatants claimed compensation and benefits for the time they had spent fighting the war:

They promised us many things . . . they said that when the war was over they would give us money because we were good fighters . . . now they are taking everything for themselves and leaving us out . . . we were better fighters than many of them.[3]

They refused to set the RENAMO leadership free before their demands were met. During these riots, the Children and War Project and the International Committee for the Red Cross were called in to mediate the conflict. These organizations offered to provide a small package of goods—basic foodstuffs, a blanket, and clothing—to serve as partial compensation, which helped calm the young soldiers. Responding to the distinctive needs of these former boy soldiers, these agencies reunified them with their relatives or placed them in foster care and tried to provide some post-reunification support whenever possible.

While the tracing and the reunification of children with their families was successfully accomplished by the Children and War Program, providing effective follow-up support and assistance to them once back in the villages was a bigger challenge. Most children were reintegrated into communities so severely devastated by war that all the inhabitants had to rebuild their lives from scratch. Parents or close relatives of many former combatants had been killed; homes had been burned, schools and hospitals had been destroyed; friends and neighbors had disappeared. In these circumstances, reunification with family, relatives, and covillagers did not represent the end of the children's predicament. The real issues regarding reintegration arose after children were back in their communities. They needed to return to school, obtain vocational training, and get access to healthcare; sometimes they needed regular food, clothing, and shelter. The reintegration kit provided by the NGOs did not last more than a week, as the children most likely shared it with relatives and friends who welcomed them back. Service provision could not be solely directed to children reintegrated by the CWP, as the entire war-affected community needed the same assistance. The NGOs' limited capacity to handle the problem became apparent. Tensions soon arose with government institutions, as in the case of the community schools being absorbed into the educational system mentioned in Chapter 1. Given the lack of publicly provided services, most children had to find solutions for their problems themselves. While some were successful, others migrated to urban areas in search of employment and ended up as street children. Others drifted into gangs and criminal groups.

In Angola, policies for dealing with former child soldiers did not repeat Mozambique's initial error of creating a treatment center, but family reunification and reintegration programs encountered similar problems. In the demobilization process conducted after the 1996 ceasefire, rebel militia members were assembled in cantonment areas and were supposed to be returned to their areas of origin within six months. In this process, at least 9,133 soldiers under the age of fifteen were demobilized and reunified with their families or returned to their communities. Given the disruptions produced in the country by the prolonged civil war, a massive effort was necessary to locate surviving members of the immediate or extended families of children and to bring the children and their families back together. When family reunifications were not possible, institutionalized care or foster parenting was available. Several non-governmental organizations were involved in the process and organized support programs for war-affected children. As in Mozambique, children under the age of fifteen received care and support outside formal demobilization processes and through NGO programs. Christian Children's Fund (CCF) in Angola started the Reintegration of Underage Soldiers (RUS) program in 1996. The RUS program focused on the provision of care and support for young combatants coming out of the cantonment areas and in need of reintegration into their communities of origin. To provide for the children's immediate needs, a demobilization package consisting of a sum of money in Angolan Kwanzas and a kit with clothing and basic foodstuffs was given to every demobilized young soldier at the time of the reunification. The RUS program was very similar to the one organized by Children and War Project in Mozambique, but smaller in scale. Instead of embarking on a description of the program's architecture, I will focus on testimonies of children who took part in these demobilization, reunification, and reintegration processes.

Sula, a young former soldier from Camgumbe, described his experience:

I was in a cantonment area for about one year waiting to be demobilized. The day of my demobilization I was taken by car from Malange to Luanda, where I spent one day. Then I flew to Luena, where I waited four days for my family to come and get me. I went to my uncle's house and I took with me 35 million Kwanzas, two blankets, two cardigans, two hoes, two cooking pots, five plates, three bags of maize, 25 kilograms of dried beans, and 25 kilograms of salt.[4]

Astro from Karilongue, Huambo, explained the difficulty of trusting program officials:

I was in Huila when the Blue Berets [UN peacekeepers] took us to our cantonment area in Vila Nova. In the cantonment areas we often gave fake names and sometimes lied about our areas of origin because we were afraid of being rerecruited. I received three bags of maize, a pair of trousers, a shirt, a pair of shoes, and 39 million Kwanzas. From the cantonment area I was taken to the church of S. Pedro, and it was a catechist [church member] who reunited me with my family.[5]

Astro's fear that war might resume and former soldiers might again be drawn into UNITA was well founded. The ways in which boys had learned to survive in the militia—by indirection and deception, including lying about their own identities—also made the process of returning to their homes and families difficult. For Astro, only a church member who had no relationship with either the government or the rebel militia could be trusted to escort him home.

Pitango, the boy from Cambandua in Biè who had volunteered to serve in the government forces when he was fifteen because his family was suffering from hunger and UNITA attacks, was seventeen at demobilization. He described the process:

In August 1996 the Brigadier [commander] called all the young soldiers and told us that we should get ready to go to Luanda to be demobilized . . . we went to Gabela for two weeks and then to Grafanil in Luanda. After two months our demobilization came. That day we were 320 young soldiers to be demobilized. The International Organization for Migration took us to a transit centre.[6]

"When demobilization came I was very happy; because I am young I wanted to go home and study," he told the CCF team. Pitango was in the demobilization center of Grafanil in Luanda from December 1996 to January 1997. The International Organization for Migration took him to their transit centre in Kunje, where his brother and sister-in-law came to get him to take him to his aunt's house. Pitango said that he was well received by his family, who killed a chicken and organized a small party for him.[7]

Many of these youths expressed mixed feelings—joys, fears, and uncertainties—about returning to their communities of origin and starting new lives from scratch. Many justifiably feared being re-recruited into the military forces. Demobilized rebel militia members were particularly reluctant to return to the areas where UNITA remained strong because they had heard that UNITA still wanted them. Others feared rejection by their communities because of the role they had played during the war. Those who had—willingly or unwillingly—fought with UNITA but came from areas that supported the MPLA government were especially apprehensive. Former boy soldiers were joyful at leaving behind the violence and terror they had endured and return to their parents, relatives, and friends. Yet they worried about whether their relatives would be found alive and whether their villages or homes had been bombed or burned.

The statements that former boy soldiers gave to CCF staff members are eloquent testimony to the ways in which these concerns were intertwined. Soma, a nineteen-year-old from Huambo, expressed despair:

In the village some people despise the ex-soldiers who belonged to UNITA; they say that they will denounce us to the government. . . . I live in fear. . . . I fear the war might start again. . . . When I think of all that, I think it is better if I die because I have suffered a lot. Many in my family died in the war and some disappeared.[8]

Soma felt guilty at having survived when so many of his relatives did not, and he feared that others held him responsible for their losses. The punishment they might inflict on him echoed his feeling that he might as well die, since he had suffered so much. Soma's wartime experiences had cut him adrift from the moral and emotional moorings that give meaning to existence.

João, a twenty-year-old from Huambo, worried most about other people's reactions to him:

Some people in my village look down at me because I was part of the UNITA army. That makes me very sad and sometimes I don't sleep well. . . . The people in the village don't respect the ex-soldiers from UNITA.[9]

João's uncertainly about whether he deserved of respect made him sad and uneasy. Mario, who was nineteen years old and came from the same province as both Soma and João, was anxious about his own safety:

Some people don't like to see me at all because I was a UNITA soldier. They hate me because they say UNITA came here and killed the people and robbed their possessions. . . . That makes me fear that something might happen to me.[10]

For former soldiers like these, reintegration into their communities was problematic.

Miguel, a sixteen-year-old from Uige, was consumed by his own feelings of anger and remorse:

I don't have much appetite. When I am sitting by myself I think a lot about the war and sometimes I feel like taking a knife and hurting or killing somebody to see blood . . . now the only thing that helps me to forget is to drink.[11]

Miguel's statement expresses an obsession with the sight of blood and the experience of hurting. Although during the war he had inflicted injuries on others, after the peace, he feared his own aggressive impulses but seemed more likely to hurt himself than others. No wonder he tried to drown his memories and impulses in alcohol.

Demobilized boy soldiers expressed considerable anxiety about what they would do after the war. Most had no training, no skills, and no formal education. Civilian life was a whole new stage in their lives, full of joy from breaking with the past but also full of fears and uncertainties about the present and the future.

In both Mozambique and Angola, many young soldiers were initiated into the military when they had not yet entered their teens. When they returned home after the war, they were seventeen or eighteen, and some were in their early twenties. For many families, boy children went away, but young men came back. These were not young men like their fathers and grandfathers had been; they had missed the training and initiation into adult male roles that their communities normally offer and had, instead, transgressed the boundaries of acceptable adult male behavior. Reintegrating these returned soldiers was a formidable challenge.

Former boy soldiers were acutely conscious of the truncated futures they faced as a result of their military involvement. Mario, a nineteen-year-old from Huambo, said regretfully:

I lost my time in the military and now I don't manage to study to learn a profession. . . . Working the land without fertilizers won't produce anything. Also here in the village there is nothing to do to amuse us. The only soccer ball we had broke a long time ago. . . . When I think of all this, my heart beats and becomes sore and I am unable to sleep at night. . . . For the future . . . I want to be a good farmer, because I already lost hope of being able to study, and because I don't want to lose hope completely in my life, I would rather live, work the land, help my mother and try to get a wife.[12]

Mario worried more about what he had missed than about what happened during the war. Nineteen and fatherless, he was coming to terms with a possible future in farming and directing his aspirations toward family life.

Eighteen-year-old Fonseca was making a new life in Kuíto, his home town, after fighting with the government army—by his account, serving in the communications unit. Fonseca was enrolled in a skill training center in Kuíto. He wanted to get a truck driver's license and become a mechanic, but he reported that his plans were in some disarray.

I am in big trouble. Three of my girlfriends are expecting my babies. Each of their families wants me to marry them, but I have no means to marry anybody. . . . I want to study, but that happened, so I don't know what to do. If I could I would have fifteen children, but I wouldn't want any of them to be a soldier.[13]

The path to maturity that Fonseca might have followed in peacetime had been utterly disrupted. His time in the militia had postponed his education, and he incurred parental responsibilities before being prepared to fulfill them.

João, a twenty-year-old demobilized Angolan soldier, also longed for what he had lost because of the war.

If I could I would have told those who gave orders to start the war to talk among themselves and stop the war. Because of the war I cannot be a truck driver. I needed to have studied, but I lost my time in the war. When I came back I learned that my father died. Now I cannot study; I have to work to help my mother and my younger siblings.[14]

For João, as for Mario, the war-related death of his father was as destructive to his future prospects as his own years spent in the military.

Social reintegration is a serious problem for noncombatant children affected by conflict, as well as for former soldiers. Landmine victims and soldiers who incurred disabling injuries face the most difficult futures. Twelve-year-old Manuel, from Malange, Angola, lives in a government orphanage. He was playing under a mango tree at his grandmother's house when he stepped on a landmine. One leg was instantly cut from his body, and the second had to be amputated later in the hospital. Manuel was among the fortunate ones; he was sent to Luanda and then to Germany, where he received appropriate medical care. Yet he remains indelibly marked, both physically and psychologically, by his experience.

I still remember the landmine exploding on me. . . . I cry when I am on my own. . . . Sometimes I talk about it with my friend Jacob [also in the orphanage]. He helps me to wash the dishes and to have my bath. Jacob tells me not to think about it because I become very sad.

Manuel attends a primary school and is now in the third grade. A caregiver at the orphanage described him as a very nice child who is doing well at school. However, she mentioned that he argues sometimes very aggressively with other children, and he feels very sad about not being able to play football with the others.[15]

Pedrito, a twelve-year-old from Moxico, lost one leg after stepping on a landmine when he was nine years old. His father, who was with him at the time, told us the story:

It was in June 1995 that it happened. . . . We were at a white man's farm in Cassongo. I was walking with Mr Noé and my son was following us . . . we were a few yards in front when we heard the noise. When Mr Noé and I looked back it was my son who had fallen into the trap.

Pedrito was immediately taken to hospital, where his leg was amputated. At the local hospital, there were no remedies to treat him, so his father got them through the help of Mr. Noé, who owned the farm where he worked. Pedrito mentioned that the food in the hospital was very bad; his mother sent him food from home whenever she could, even though she had little to spare. His father or brother would occasionally stay with him at the hospital to help him wash and change. Pedrito is a very sad child. His family is very poor. He said he has no friends because the other children call him "cripple, cripple"; he plays only with his brother. Pedrito still had his family to support him, but he faced a difficult future.[16]

Children who lost their parents faced difficult times even if they had not been injured. Gabriel, a fourteen-year-old from Huambo, went to live with his aunt after both his parents were killed during the war. He did not get along well with his aunt's husband, so he moved to his older brother's place. In the morning he attends school, and in the afternoons he sells cigarettes to make some money to buy food and clothes. He says that life is very hard without his parents.

> I really have to do any type of work and earn money to eat. My life was much better when my mother was with us. . . . We had food to eat; I didn't need to sell or beg to eat. Now everything is very difficult. Since my parents died I am suffering a lot. Before I had time to play, but now I can't because otherwise we will go to bed with empty stomachs.[17]

Gabriel told us that he likes to study, but he lacks the school materials he needs, such as books and pencils. He becomes very sad when he is unable to sleep at night because he did not manage to secure any food that day. He misses his parents a lot.

Postwar Reintegration for Girls and Young Women

The fate of girls and young women who were kidnapped and held captive in military camps depended on the ability of their families to take them back. Like demobilized boy soldiers, they faced daunting problems. Many had lost their parents and other relatives during the war. Their homes and villages had been destroyed. Their educations had been truncated, and few opportunities for training were now available. Chronic poverty and unemployment had only been exacerbated by protracted civil conflict. In addition to the difficulties that were common to men and women, younger women faced gender-specific problems: their sexual reputations and marital prospects had been seriously compromised by their captivity and, in some cases, by their maternity. Their experience of sexual violation was more difficult for them to overcome, in part because it was an open secret—recognized by everyone but seldom discussed or dealt with directly. The survivors of captivity in military camps bore traces of their war experience as indelible, although not always as visible, as the victims of landmines. The shame that they have endured and the stigma that has branded them blight their futures, dimming their prospects for marriage as well as social reintegration.

In Mozambique, where it was possible to study the experiences of young women who had been held captive in military camps, clearly, their families and community were making a concerted effort to reintegrate them into local society. When these young women were reunited with their relatives after the war, they went through cleansing and purification rituals performed by traditional healers and by priests from local

Zionist churches. These rituals were the same as those performed for former boy soldiers; they reaffirmed family cohesion and support and signified social acceptance for returned girls. The rituals were also intended to address the emotional and psychological problems these young women experience.

Cleansing rituals are just the beginning of a healing process that can take a long time. On the island of Josina Machel, Reconstruindo a Esperança, a national NGO that provided assistance to war-affected children through skills training and creation of livelihoods and employment opportunities, was also providing counseling sessions for the girls by making available the services of two young Mozambican psychologists. The fact that the counselors were young women themselves perhaps made the therapeutic relationship easier. These counseling sessions took place concurrent with the treatments and rituals performed by local healers and religious leaders. David Ntimane, the Zionist Bishop who performed rituals for many people in the island, described these purification rituals as necessary to restore war-affected children and their families to wholeness and enable them to "start a new life." This Zionist minister echoed indigenous beliefs regarding the importance of ritual purification and of making a complete break with the past. Zionist churches have a strong influence in the island, and many war-affected people went through cleansing rituals performed by these churches. The Zionist rituals are similar to those performed by traditional healers, drawing on local beliefs in the power of ancestral spirits but synthesizing those with Christian religious ideologies.

Despite the performance of healing rituals, both former captive girls themselves and the adults who are concerned about their welfare expressed worries about the continuing effects of war. The state of sexual relationships on the island seems particularly problematic. As referred to in Chapter 4, the mother of a girl who was kidnapped and raped by RENAMO soldiers lamented:

Because there aren't many men in the island, girls give themselves to men very easily. Most of these men do not have serious intentions. They just want to sleep with them, but do not want to marry them. They say they are "second hand" because they were RENAMO soldiers' "wives." They just use and abuse them.[18]

In this mother's view, the instrumental, short-term viewpoint that soldiers adopted in the military camps has been adopted by the rest of society after the peace. The sexual abuse that girls suffered has diminished their potential value as brides and impaired bargaining power in negotiations between the sexes. A twenty-year-old voiced similar sentiments:

Men only want to take advantage of girls like me—who were forced to be "wives" of soldiers during the war. Therefore, for us it is very difficult to marry. . . . My childhood was destroyed by the war, and now my adult life is suffering the consequences of the war.[19]

Those who have children conceived in the military camps are in the most difficult position. These young unmarried mothers have no means by which to support themselves and their children. Many live with their own mothers and contribute to the support of numerous siblings. Some try desperately to find a man who will marry them and take care of them and their children. However, with the current situation on the island, that search is very difficult. Some young women who brought one child home from the military camp had another child after they returned to Josina Machel. They explained to me that men repeatedly promised to marry them when they found a job, had made enough money in Maputo or in South Africa. Women remained at home on the island after the men departed. Over the months and years, when they failed to return, the promises of marriage evaporated.

In one of my visits to the clinic on Josina Machel, Teresa Mazive, the nurse, mentioned that the island has a very high incidence of sexually transmitted diseases (STDs). Those most affected include young people of both sexes and the wives of migrant workers. Many come to the clinic for treatment, but others prefer to go to traditional healers. Mazive believes that the incidence of HIV/AIDS in the island must also be high, given the association of HIV transmission with STDs. But the clinic had no means of diagnosing HIV infection. No HIV/AIDS tests had yet been carried out in the island by May 1999. The high incidence of STDs is believed to result from male labor migration to South Africa and the towns and from the sexual abuses and promiscuity that occurred during the war and, worrisomely, continue afterwards.

Watching these young women go about their daily routines six years after the ceasefire and four years after the first general elections in Mozambique, an ordinary observer would never imagine that their lives are filled with such devastating and dramatic experiences of terror and survival. In spite of all they have suffered, these young women are tremendously resilient. Postwar conditions remain difficult: they live in dire poverty, without jobs or proper education. The resilience of these young people calls into question orthodox views of child development, which assume that children and youth are especially vulnerable under circumstances of adversity. Young people in Africa have proved to be especially able to accommodate dissonance, adversity, and change, and more capable of personal resilience than many adults.[20]

As these young women themselves assured me, if they managed to survive the war they can certainly find ways of coping with the present. The project of the NGO Reconstruindo a Esperança keeps many of them busy in productive activities for part of the day. They receive a token sum from the NGO to help with daily subsistence. Through the NGO, too, they buy some products, especially locally produced goods, inexpensively. Many young women work on their family's land. To earn cash, they buy and resell goods, such as snacks, juice drinks, and cigarettes. Some travel to a nearby town and buy these goods to bring back to the island. Others receive goods from boyfriends in South Africa and resell them. Few of them can fully rely on family support. Indeed, if they live with their mothers and other siblings, they often make the main contribution to the family income.

To make ends meet, these young women have rotating savings and loan schemes among themselves called *xitique*. About ten girls get together in a *xitique* group. At the end of each month, each participant puts in the same small amount of money. The total is then given to one of them on a rotation basis. So, if ten members each contribute 1,000 Meticais, the combined total will be 10,000 Meticais. Each member receives this sum every ten months. This system enables young women to accumulate money for more substantial expenditures. Those women who have boyfriends in South Africa may also receive clothing and shoes from them. Young women on Josina Machel like modern clothing, which they wear to church on Sunday or when they travel to Xinavane, Xai-Xai, or Maputo. During the week, they dress in local *capulanas*, pieces of fabric they tie around the waist. Modern goods get to the island through Maputo and other small towns nearby, as well as through Johannesburg and Nelspruit in South Africa (the towns closest to the Mozambican border).

Some young women in Josina Machel have decided not to stay at home and wait for remittances from their boyfriends; they are also migrating illegally to South Africa in search of a better life. Some of these women, like some men, are caught and deported. Those who manage to stay in South Africa often end up in very poorly paid jobs or even in prostitution. South African media report that prostitution rings use young migrants from Mozambique and other countries in the region. These reports suggest that girls recruited in Mozambique are promised proper jobs in South Africa and then coerced into prostitution once they are far from home. Those who remain on the island hope that one day they, too, will travel to South Africa or Maputo and be able to afford all the goods of the modern world. Through television and films, as well as through news from migrants, they are aware of the bounty and autonomy the wider world promises.

Healing Children's Social Wounds of War

Postwar healing and reintegration of war-affected children and youth are major concerns, for these young people constitute the next generation, the producers, the parents, and the leaders of tomorrow. Those individuals who welcome them back to local communities seek to ensure that they are fully rehabilitated and prepared to assume their adult social roles. Building on the discussions initiated in Chapter 5, this section contrasts the Western psychological approaches with local, indigenous approaches to healing war trauma and social distress. It describes the variety of difficulties related to reconciliation and social reintegration of war-affected children, especially of former boy soldiers, whom others regard as perpetrators, and of young women abused by soldiers, whose reputations are now damaged.

Psychological approaches have been used to understand the impact of political violence on the mental health of these children, which is most often diagnosed as psychological trauma.[21] As White correctly asked, "[w]hat is 'mental' about 'mental health'?"[22] What Westerners call "mental health" is culturally defined: the way in which people express, embody, and give meaning to their afflictions are tied to specific social and cultural contexts. Culture plays a central role in social and emotional well-being and in the diagnosis and treatment of disorders and distress, including those arising from wartime experiences of violence and loss.[23] The manner in which people manage their afflictions is inextricably connected to their understanding of how such afflictions originate. These shared conceptions of the causes and manifestations of distress must be taken into account when devising appropriate therapeutic strategies for the alleviation and elimination of such afflictions. In this perspective, Western biomedical and psychotherapeutic notions of distress and trauma cannot be employed effectively in the African context because they do not embrace local cultural beliefs and worldviews. In southern Mozambique and in Angola, community-based support, the family, and especially traditional approaches to healing play a crucial and constructive role in the rehabilitation of war-affected young people. In rural communities, especially at times of personal and wider societal crisis, these institutions are the fundamental means through which healing occurs and order can be reestablished.

Dominant paradigms shaping aid policies and international interventions during and after conflicts in Africa have been informed by Western biomedical notions of health and illness. But Western understandings of distress and trauma and Western approaches to diagnosis and treatment cannot properly or effectively be applied to societies that have different ontologies of health and illness. The Western biomedical tradition is deeply shaped by the fundamental logic articulated by Descartes: body and mind are perceived to be distinguishable and separate entities. Although early twentieth-century psychoanalysis, the late twentieth-century field of psychosomatic medicine, and recent medical efforts to incorporate alternative therapies all struggle to overcome this dichotomy, medical care and psychotherapy remain deeply marked by the Cartesian dualism. Generally, the causes of illness are located either in the body or in the mind. Mental illness, too, remains a residual category in dominant approaches to treatment. When medical tests reveal no physiological abnormalities or when physiologically based medical treatments fail, people may be redefined as mentally rather than physically ill. If a diagnostician perceives that both body and mind are involved in a patient's illness, the situation is quite awkward, since neither biomedicine nor psychoanalysis has a coherent model of how body and mind interact. If coordinated treatment can be managed at all, psychiatrists prescribe powerful psychoactive drugs while psychotherapists do counselling.

Furthermore, dominant Western psychotherapeutic models locate the causes of psychosocial distress within the individual and design responses which are primarily based on individual therapy.[24] In psychotherapy in general, and in counselling after traumatic events in particular, recovery is achieved through helping the individual come to terms with his or her experience. Treatment focuses on the patient's intrapsychic world and is performed in private sessions aimed at "talking out" or "talking through" the patient's problems, externalizing feelings on a one-to-one basis. As White and Marsella pointed out, "the use of 'talk therapy' aimed at altering individual behavior through the individual's 'insight' into his or her personality is firmly rooted in a conception of the person as a distinct and independent individual capable of self-transformation in relative isolation from particular social contexts."[25] Family psychotherapists have realized that the distress manifested by one family member may reflect disturbances in the whole set of relationships involved. These practitioner devise methods of drawing significant others into the treatment in parallel and joint ways, but the model of talk therapy and the goal of curing individual distress in isolation from social context prevail even in those cases. These approaches have been relatively successful and culturally acceptable in European-American contexts because they are rooted in local, ancient religious traditions, such as the institution of the confessional in the Catholic Church. They developed within Western culture and are in harmony with its ontological presuppositions. Modern psychological therapy has become such an integral part of popular consciousness that it is now accepted as common sense.[26]

European and American efforts to assist war-affected young people in African nations in the wake of civil wars have drawn specifically on the concept of post-traumatic stress disorder (PTSD), a diagnosis now applied to survivors of violence in a variety of contexts. PTSD is now applied to persons who experienced physical violence and sexual abuse as children in domestic situations and in other contexts where the care and protection of children is assumed. However, the concept constitutes a new discourse of trauma and its psychological sequelae that was developed during the 1980s in the United States, emerging especially from efforts to comprehend and address the problems experienced by American veterans of the Vietnam War.[27] These former soldiers were plagued by a variety of symptoms of psychological distress, including flashbacks, panic attacks, and anxiety. Most experienced and coped with these symptoms, which were interpreted as memories of traumatic events they had undergone in combat, as interruptions of the normal lives they had resumed on their return—thus the prefix "post."[28] PTSD was defined as a syndrome in otherwise healthy persons that arose from their exposure to traumatic events that could not be assimilated into the psyche and integrated into their sense of self. Talk therapy, in small or large groups and usually with other veterans who had similar experiences and afflictions, was the primary form of treatment. The goal was to enable the affected individuals to integrate these memories into the present to the extent possible and, if the memories remained inassimilable, to assist veterans in coping with the terrifying eruptions into their daily lives.

Some mental health professionals have studied the relevance of this new model of postwar psychological disorders to non-Western societies.[29] One fundamental difference is clear right at the start: American soldiers returned home to a society that had not been the setting for military conflict, and they endeavored to resume the ordinary lives that their military service had interrupted. Conditions in Mozambique and Angola were entirely different. In societies riven by civil war, no home was untouched by conflict and no life resumed normally. In many African countries, as well as in parts of Southeast Asia and Latin America, the majority of adults, youth, and especially children have lived their entire lives under conditions of armed conflict. For these people, violence and the trauma it involves are not *post* but rather immediate and continuing facts of daily life.

Western approaches to treatment are, thus, not necessarily applicable in non-Western contexts or cultures. Summerfield points out that Cambodians do not share or talk about their feelings and memories about the trauma of the Pol Pot years with foreigners. He also mentions that Mozambican and Ethiopian refugees describe forgetting about the traumatic past as means of coping with it.[30] Boyden and

Gibbs have shown that in Cambodia such therapy failed to address trauma effectively. They offer two explanations: it did not account for the place that ancestral spirits, malevolent spirits, and other forces were perceived to have in causing distress and in the process of healing afflictions; and it undermined family and community efforts to provide support and care.[31]

Recalling traumatic experiences through verbal externalization does not constitute a necessary condition for coming to terms with the traumatic past, and people would avoid verbalizing it for blocking access to malevolent forces.[32] The pollution of the past is washed away from the body; its physical remains are burned. After performing symbolic and medicinal ritual procedures, people were admonished not to look back and assisted in starting afresh. Indeed, recalling and recounting the traumatic events that war-affected people had witnessed might reopen the door to malevolent forces. In Mozambique and Angola, any international interventions must be compatible with and supportive of local knowledge about trauma and healing.

African societies are based on forms of "common sense" that differ from those prevailing in the West. These cultures have their own routes to understanding and healing war-related afflictions. Such approaches are based on distinctive and ancient forms of religious belief, spiritual expression, and healing practices. In such settings, individual psychotherapy conducted by a medical expert may be ineffective or even counterproductive. These African societies are based on a holistic cosmological model. The Cartesian dichotomy does not apply because mind and body are perceived to be integrated; an affliction in the body involves the mind, and vice versa. Nor does Western philosophical and practical individualism pertain. Persons are not perceived as isolated, autonomous atoms who enter into discrete relationships with various others; transact economic exchanges in a commodified marketplace; and are citizens or subjects of a remote and depersonalized nation-state. Persons are constituted by their relationships with kin and community; social norms are taught and enforced by known and nearby authorities; local markets remain face-to-face places where producers exchange goods and services; and local government is not just a set of regularized, formal legal and political arrangements.

Anthropological studies of African societies reveal the social and cultural construction of persons and communities that has become less visible but, nonetheless, remains very powerful in Western societies. In these African cultures, the order that European-Americans often see as universal and locate in the abstract laws of physics and mathematics is understood in more direct and local terms. Here, too, the organization of life in human groups is conducted within visible relationships among persons rather than seen as defined and mediated by legal structures and state systems. These African societies remain close to their ancient cultural and religious traditions. They certainly are more varied than Western societies, differing from one ethnolinguistic group and regional location to another. These societies understand their world in particularistic terms, but they recognize their own pluralism. This pluralism, too, makes Western models of social relationships and of health and illness inapplicable in these African contexts.

People perceive health as a natural state for all human beings. To be unhealthy denotes abnormality, showing that something is out of its normal place and that harmony is jeopardized. Indeed, the modern Western terminology of disease is entirely inappropriate in this context, for it suggests a pathological state of the body, its invasion by foreign microbes or by proliferating cancer cells run amok. Only its archaic meaning, as *dis-ease*, connoting discomfort and discord, has any resonance with African notions of illness. In an African context, health is approached as a life process rather than just a physical process, and it acquires broader dimensions than Western concepts of health and illness. Health is defined by the harmonious relationships between human beings and the surrounding environment, between individuals and the spiritual world, among individuals, and within the community. Furthermore, community includes both the natural and spiritual worlds. Rather than being narrowly defined and clearly delimited realms, the personal, the social, the spiritual, and the natural are united within a larger cosmological universe.[33]

Thus, rain should fall at its ordinary time, crops should grow, people should not fall sick, and children should not die. If this harmonious state is disturbed, the cause is understood as the intervention of malevolent spirits of some kind: those controlled by *valoyi* (the term for witches and sorcerers in Mozambique), the ancestral spirits punishing their descendants for improper behavior,[34] the unquiet spirits of war dead, or other spiritual forces. If the relationships between human beings and their ancestral spirits, between them and the environment, and among themselves are balanced and harmonious, health ensues. However, if these relationships are disrupted in any way, the well-being of the whole community is jeopardized. A complex set of rules and practices governs the maintenance of well-being and fecundity in the community, and a more elaborate repertoire of diagnostic and healing procedures is available to restore well-being when ill-health or other signs of difficulty suggest that harmony and balance have been disturbed.

Ill-health is, therefore, considered to be primarily a social phenomenon that alters the normal course of the individual's life and may or may not manifest itself initially in the physical body. Fainzang's study of concepts of health in Burkina Faso suggests that ill-health constitutes an event that marks an alteration in the normal course of life of individuals and groups. Divination is the method employed to diagnose the social life because it relies not on the physical manifestations of the affliction but rather on its social origins.[35] Traditional healing takes a holistic approach, involving both the social and the physical dimensions of the malady in order to treat the person as a whole. Here there is an overall integration between body and mind. The patient's health is restored through divination, which diagnoses the social causes of the patient's affliction, and through healing, which addresses the suppression of symptoms through ritual and medicine.

The afflicted person is never treated as a singular individual, but rather as part of a community. During the divination séance, the diviner always looks at the state of the patient's social relationships in the community—relationships with the living and with the spiritual world—to make a diagnosis. The diviner-patient dialogue developed during the consultation represents a reciprocal learning process in which, as Jackson puts it, a process of transference and counter transference of information brings them together.[36] In this context, the relationship between practitioner and patient is very close and enhances the cultural bonds between them. In this way, traditional healing can be extremely effective to heal trauma and other social disorders caused by war.

Purification and protective rituals as discussed in Chapter 5 are aimed at liberating the individual from pollution and restoring his or her identity as a member of the group. Persons who are polluted by their close encounters with death constitute a threat to the community. They are temporarily excluded when they return from the antinomian space of war to the family and village. They go through a period of separation in which they do not belong to the social body and cannot enjoy social interaction. These ritual proceedings reflect what Van Gennep identified as three phases of the ritual process: separation, seclusion, and reintegration.[37] Only after ritual procedures are complete are they reincorporated into society, the phase that Turner calls "communitas."[38]

In southern Mozambique and Angola, beliefs about the power of spiritual agencies in the lives of families and communities are strongly embedded in everyday action. By means of the ancestral spiritual powers, people make sense of themselves and restore balance and peace to their society. In rural communities especially, spiritual agencies form an integral part of the wider system of meanings. Although spiritual powers are clearly a stabilizing factor in social relations, they are by no means a static or automatic regulator of human endeavour and identity. On the contrary, their capacity for allowing individual and collective changes of identity explains precisely much of this ritual system's ontological force and persistence. The ancestral spirits do not represent the dead hand of the past; they are living spirits who engage with and support people as they confront devastating and entirely new situations. The spirits do not simply punish their descendants for social transgressions or protect them from the evil intentions of others. They can be invoked to guide persons as they move from one social position to another, from soldier or captive to a peaceful family and community; to cure them from afflictions caused by their experiences of committing and witnessing antisocial and terrifying acts; and to protect them as they move into uncertain futures and face problems that their societies have never before encountered. As the title of my book on this subject suggests, these are "living spirits" and "modern traditions."[39] Spiritual beliefs and practices remain vital forces in the lives of contemporary Mozambicans and Angolans, offering them support as they seek to heal their decimated families, repair disrupted social bonds, and restore ecological balance in their environment.

Indigenous worldviews and systems of meaning are the basis upon which understandings of social distress, war trauma, and healing are built. In order to deal effectively with the problems of war trauma in such contexts as Mozambique and Angola, it is important to consider the ways in which the affected populations understand, embody, and ascribe significance to their war-related afflictions. Traditional healing systems possess elaborate and complex explanations for these kinds of disorders and the mechanisms to heal them. These forms of understanding and healing social afflictions caused by war are fundamental in processes of postwar healing; rehabilitation; and reconciliation, both individual and collective. Ignoring or antagonizing traditional healing systems as superstitious or backward is not productive and will ultimately be ineffective. Some analysts have pointed to particular indigenous healing practices that can be unsafe and have deleterious effects, but the important consideration is the overall concept and philosophy that guide these local views and practices, which differ from Western rationality. These systems are holistic and establish close interconnections between mind and body, the mundane and the transcendent, the individual and group. The existence of erroneous practices here and there does not constitute grounds for eliminating and discrediting a whole system. Traditional healing systems are alive and function effectively in these social contexts. Thus, in order to be effective, the healing strategies to deal with the problems faced by children affected by war in Africa need to take into account, and be inscribed within, these healing systems and world views.

Preventing Children's Participation in War

The international community has agreed to a number of conventions and protocols prohibiting the military recruitment of children under the age of eighteen. However, as shown in Chapter 2, these agreements have been ineffective in protecting children in situations of armed conflict. Two fundamental reasons for their ineffectiveness are clear. First, the restrictions on military actions that are stipulated by these conventions cannot be enforced during civil wars with irregular military forces and attenuated state structures. Indeed, the coercive recruitment of underage male soldiers and the abduction and captivity of girls are defining features of militias in postcolonial conflicts; these violations of international law are part and parcel of the violence that obliterates distinctions between combatants and noncombatants and makes civilians the primary targets of military action. Second, the definition of childhood used in these treaties is idealistic and inappropriate to the social and economic conditions of these societies, even in peacetime. Notions of childhood and the processes that mark the transition from childhood into adulthood are socially constructed and vary from one society to another and are based on the specific social and economic conditions.

In both Angola and Mozambique, the extreme social crises of protracted civil war compelled a displacement of responsibilities from adults to children. Many children assumed roles that in normal circumstances would be filled by adults—and not only by participating in armed conflict. Children and youths were required to support themselves and younger siblings, to protect themselves and others against violence, and to devise survival strategies under conditions of displacement. Boys who became soldiers assumed combat roles normally filled by men who had completed initiation into adulthood. Girls who were held as the forced wives or sexual slaves of soldiers incurred the burdens of maternity without the supports of marriage or kin. The dramatic shifting of roles and rules—that children witnessed murders, came into close contact with dead bodies, became killers, and committed horrific atrocities—is intrinsically linked to the breakdown of state structures, of ordered relationships between adults and children, and of moral norms defining acceptable and unacceptable acts, as well as the boundaries between life and death. The phenomenon of child soldiers and captive girls is, thus, one dimension of the total societal crisis that is both cause and consequence of civil war. The absence or nonobservance of normative frameworks and value systems can "give rise to an 'ethical vacuum'—a setting in which international standards are ignored with impunity and where normative and value systems have lost their sway."[40] What kind of economic, political, and social conditions underlie the eruption of these violent conflicts? What makes this massive participation of children in armed conflicts possible, even seemingly unavoidable? How can children be protected from war? Such basic questions must be asked and answered in order to bring about change.

It is important to identify norms and values that could lead to the prevention of war and the protection of children caught up in it. International humanitarian law has been unable to secure the protection of human rights in times of war; the case of children is but one example of this more general problem. Even when the age limit for recruitment was fifteen, children as young as eight continued to be systematically coerced into military activities. Raising the legal minimum age for recruitment has done very little, if anything, to improve this situation. Effective enforcement of every child's right to protection from direct involvement in armed conflict requires, at the very least, the dissemination of information about these conventions, knowledge and understanding of children's rights, and the translation of rights and norms into local worldviews and meaning systems in order to make them recognizable and locally sanctioned. As Olara Otunnu pointed out:

The most damaging loss a society can suffer is the collapse of its value system. Values matter, even in time of war. In most societies distinctions between acceptable and unacceptable practices were maintained, with taboos and injunctions proscribing the targeting of civilian populations, especially children and women.[41]

Maintaining societal values in the midst of uncivil war is difficult but not necessarily impossible.

The centrally important role that families and communities play in the postwar healing and social reintegration of war-affected children suggests that they could play a stronger role before and during violent conflicts. In Mozambique and Angola, parents and traditional leaders did attempt to protect children. Under the circumstances of war, that often meant encouraging or forcing boys to enlist into one army or the other. Elements of local societies deserve support and strengthening. Protection may be possible if people are aware of children's rights and can understand them within the framework of their own values and norms. Local agents, especially families, community members, and traditional leaders, must be involved in any effective strategy for the protection of children in situations of armed conflict. Trying to shield children in such catastrophic conditions by expecting governments to act is not enough, especially when those governments are themselves under siege. Similarly, complete reliance on international agencies and organizations that try to impose international rights and norms established outside the local context, without looking at local understandings and without framing their goals within local ideologies, is woefully ineffective. This book argues for a bottom-up rather than a top-down approach, enlisting greater community participation in protecting children from conflict and in enforcing their human rights.

Addressing the Structural Causes of Child Soldiering

Community-based cleansing and healing rituals seem to be effective in dealing with the emotional and social problems of war-affected children, helping them to come to terms with their war experiences and facilitating their reintegration into family and community life. However, such practices on their own cannot sustain long-lasting results, especially for young former soldiers who do not have yet a clear direction in their lives. While these rituals brought them psychological and emotional relief, the fact that they do not have jobs, are not going to school, and have no skills makes them vulnerable to a myriad of problems. Many could not attend school because they had to support themselves, while those who did go to school had to attend with children half their age. In these circumstances, programs for healing war-affected children and youth must be complemented by job creation and skills training programs. A general alleviation of poverty is urgently needed in order to offer these young people some prospect of a better future. If youths are not given a chance to improve their lives, they will easily be absorbed into violence, whether urban gangs, illicit business dealings, or rebel militias in new civil wars.

During these wars, many young men became vulnerable to recruitment because of a lack of economic, political, and social opportunities in the countryside. Ethnic alliances and a general disenchantment with the postcolonial state over its rejection of traditional authorities and cultural values motivated some chiefs to help recruit boys into the rebel forces. Some boys and young men volunteered to join either the government or the rebels as soldiers. For many, the possession of an instrument of coercion was their only mean of gaining access to food and gave them a sense of power. These developments are intrinsically linked to the general collapse of social and economic structures in these societies.

The failures in social and economic development programs and the disruptions caused by globalization, war, and disease promoted an environment of basic instability and global conflict that exacerbated generational disconnections and dramatically impaired the capacity of households and communities to nurture and protect children. A the social norms and values that protected children weakened

Africans became more vulnerable. One of the consequences of these developments is the commodification of children. The revaluation of children's labor has induced an increase in their exploitation in low-paying, dead-end employment as well as in child soldiering.[42]

Taking into account that more than half of Africa's population is under the age of eighteen, clearly, the burden of poverty and economic underdevelopment falls heavily on the young. Today unprecedented numbers of children and youth in Africa—and around the world—are undereducated, malnourished, unemployed, and marginalized from major social, economic, and political processes.[43] Many children and youth in Africa are finding it difficult to pursue academic and vocational education and livelihoods that would enable them to become economically independent and make an orderly transition into adulthood. Adding to this already gloomy picture is the AIDS epidemic that is ravaging the developing world, particularly sub-Saharan Africa, creating a pool of orphans who will have to fend for themselves. In the hardest-hit countries in Africa, more than forty-three million children will have lost one or both parents to AIDS by the year 2010. Children without parents miss the traditional transfer of social and cultural norms and values from the older generation. Young people who are not firmly anchored in families and communities and who lack sponsors and guidance into adulthood are particularly vulnerable to recruitment into irregular militias and other forms of criminal or destructive activity. So, too, are war-affected young people in war-ravaged communities and countries.

In the aftermath of the war, many demobilized and reintegrated youth continue to be as vulnerable as they were before joining the military. The socioeconomic situation has worsened in the rural areas from where most of them have come; war brought not only displacement but also a massive destruction of social and economic infrastructure, including housing, health clinics, and schools. After the war, extreme poverty and difficult environmental conditions continue to prevail. Young former soldiers and captive girls return to villages and communities physically devastated by the war and with profound social wounds. These are the dilemmas that face youth and children of war in the postcolonial state.

The issue of child soldiers and captive girls must be addressed by weaving together the threads of both terror and survival heard in their testimonies. Beyond healing in the immediate aftermath of war, lasting results will only be achieved if the world is committed to address the structural causes of this problem, undertaking poverty reduction and economic development and facilitating political participation and social stability.

Conclusion

While children's participation in war does not constitute an entirely new phenomenon, it has expanded quantitatively and been transformed qualitatively because of changes in the nature of warfare that occurred during the second half of the twentieth century, especially in postcolonial nation-states torn by political conflict. Contemporary armed conflicts are marked by violence that indiscriminately kills, violates, abducts, and terrorizes civilian populations and brings children to the forefront of military activity. Young people become both targets and instruments of violence. Technological advances in the design of small arms make weapons lighter and easier to manipulate, and, thus, more readily usable by children. Proliferating production and distribution networks make such arms more readily available to irregular militias. At the same time, changing conceptions of childhood and child protection, coupled with the development of a global consciousness of human rights and the sanctity of human life, has made the phenomenon of child participation in war unacceptable in today's world. Elders in Africa lament the utter breakdown in orderly traditions that families and communities use to guide children into adulthood. Young men lament having "lost their time." These perceptions must be understood by the international community as evidence of the violation of the human rights of children.

Although the social, economic, and political conditions that involve children in armed conflicts are widespread, the young people affected by armed conflict do not constitute a homogeneous group. In Mozambique and Angola, boy soldiers and captive girls occupied strikingly different positions, even when both were abducted by force. Younger children had different experiences than older ones. War-affected young people varied in their exposure to particular types of experiences: witnessing murder, committing atrocities, and suffering rape. Rather than placing them together in a single category, recognizing their particular situations and needs is more important. Yet their daily experiences of war and their tales of terror, violence, and survival connect children and youth across warring factions and extend beyond their local and regional communities. Serving as soldiers, laboring for soldiers, and serving soldiers sexually are particularly traumatic, but these young people also share the harms suffered by children who are not coerced into military forces. Children are uprooted from their homes and villages, orphaned, dismembered by landmines, and made refugees. Young people in war-affected regions miss out on education, proper healthcare, and the nurturing care of parents, relatives, and friends.

Children and youth should not all be cast as passive victims of these assaults on themselves, their loved ones, and their communities, how-ever. Young people respond to the exigencies of war with resourceful-ness and—for better and for worse—a substantial degree of adaptability. Warfare transformed young people as it changed the conditions of their lives. Even in the extreme conditions of military camps, some children were able to exercise what I call "tactical agency" (borrowing from De Certeau) to cope with their particular circumstances. Children and youth caught up in civil wars are not empowered political actors; they seldom have the strategic perspective that those who initiate and perpet-uate armed conflict use to justify such acts. Nor do they exercise the au-tonomy that legal responsibility for their own actions would require. On the other hand, they exercise their wits to survive, bargain with their commanders and captors, and find sustenance and even momentary sol-ace amid the chaos and violence that engulf them. They take risks and make compromises in their attempts to save themselves and, on rare oc-casions, to defend others, even though they know that the conditions of irregular warfare mean that random events, rather than their determi-nation or cleverness, make the difference between death, life, and living hell. Those who survive to demobilization and liberation are trauma-tized and profoundly altered by what they have experienced, but they are resilient enough to come to terms with peacetime as they come to terms with the past. Adults at all levels—from local communities to in-ternational agencies—must provide the resources they need and sup-port their endeavors to enter a healthy adulthood. Young people's own energy, adaptability, and resilience can be counted on to make the most of whatever opportunities they are given.

Indigenous community structures and social relationships should be mobilized to play an active role in the protection of children from par-ticipation in armed conflicts. Effective prevention, healing, and reinte-gration strategies for children affected by war must be embedded in local world views and meaning systems in order to be sustainable and achieve optimal results. Complete reliance on governments and inter-national organizations has not been effective. While these institutions can provide material resources, expertise, and coordination, the par-ticipation of local agents is essential to the protection of children. In order to facilitate and support such efforts, we must develop our knowl-edge and understanding of local norms and value systems that may contribute to child protection, as well as disseminate information about international humanitarian law at the local level. International conven-tions need to be well understood within the context of local worldviews and meaning systems so they are recognized, accepted, and enforced on the ground, where protection of children from armed conflict begins and ends.

The examination of local healing strategies demonstrates that biomedicine and psychotherapy are only two of many ways of understanding and healing distress and trauma. Considering that the majority of
the Mozambican and Angolan population affected by war is rural, the
use of indigenous approaches to healing is necessary in order to address
people's perceptions and understanding of their afflictions. Local understandings of war trauma, of healing, and of community cohesion and
stability need to be taken into account when dealing with post-conflict
reconciliation and social reintegration. Traditional healers, religious leaders, the family, and elderly members of the community are already creating their own spaces to heal the social wounds of war. To be more
effective and meaningful, the intervention programs undertaken by the
international community have to make the effort to go beyond Western
psychotherapy and universalizing notions of childhood. They must be
open to new strategies for addressing the problem. It is critical that such
programs pay attention to the context and specificities of the culture.
The active participation and direct engagement of local communities in
the formulation and implementation of these programs is fundamental.
Local communities need to understand and take ownership of these
programs in order to make them sustainable and achieve long-range
goals.

Official and NGO-sponsored programs for the demobilization and social reintegration of boys and girls have been successful in tracing unaccompanied children and reunifying them with family, relatives, or foster
families in their communities, but they still face serious challenges with
regard to provision of support services—education, healthcare, employment, food and proper shelter—in the post-reunification period. War-
affected children often have to sort themselves out alone, especially
those whose close relatives are very poor or were killed during the war.
Some of the children manage to cope with their situation through local
basic support schemes and solidarity networks. Others migrate to urban
areas for employment, where the majority become street children or associate with criminal groups. This pattern shows that, while community
processes of reintegration are important and can help the children
emotionally, poverty and lack of social provisions prevent them from
gaining access to school, healthcare, and employment and becoming
full and active citizens.

The rehabilitation and social reintegration of children affected by
armed conflict should go hand-in-hand with larger strategies of social
development and poverty eradication. In my view, intervention programs
aimed at curbing the problem of children affected by armed conflict
face two major challenges: on the one hand, the challenge of culture,
of understanding the worldviews and value systems that guide people's

actions in the affected areas. On the other hand, the challenge of societal and state structures, of addressing the fundamental institutional and structural causes of armed conflict that continue after ceasefires and peace agreements. The analysis presented here clearly demonstrates the inability of governmental and international programs to deal with the serious problems of poverty and underdevelopment that are at the origin of child soldering and children's victimization by war. The total societal crisis which both results from and, even more important, produces these civil wars is what propels children and youth into military activity and at the same time limits their prospects for a better future. Former combatants and captives do not return to normal life; members of their families and kin-groups have been killed or displaced, their villages and communities destroyed. The local economy is in a familiar sort of shambles, with few resources available to subsistence-oriented producers and many factors inducing or propelling people to migrate to low-wage jobs or prostitution in urban centers, furthering the cycle of underdevelopment and the distortion of social relations. As for the state, political participation is absent or irrelevant, and basic state structures are absent or do not serve most people. What would be required to address the consequences of armed conflict for children is exactly the same as what would be required to prevent their being drawn into such conflicts in the first place.

Indeed, the solutions to the problems suffered by child soldiers and captive girls in postcolonial African civil wars are the very same measures that would prevent the occurrence of such conflicts. Addressing the total societal crisis in such states requires fundamental economic, social, and political transformation, a long-term perspective, and democratic participation in the process of change. The future of Africa's youth depends on finding solutions to poverty and global inequality, and the future of Africa depends on its youth.

Notes

Introduction

1. Robert Gersony, "Summary of Refugee Accounts of Principally Conflict Related Experiences in Mozambique" (Washington, D.C.: Bureau for Refugee Programs, U.S. State Department, 1988); Alex Vines, *Renamo: Terrorism in Mozambique* (Oxford: Center for Southern African Studies, University of York, in association with James Currey, 1991); William Finnegan, *A Complicated War: The Harrowing of Mozambique* (Berkley: University of California Press, 1992); William Minter, *Apartheid's Contras: An Inquiry into the Roots of War in Angola and Mozambique* (London: Zed Books, 1994); Christopher Clapham, ed., *African Guerrillas* (Bloomington: Indiana University Press, 1998); William Reno, *Warlord Politics in African States* (Boulder, Colo.: Lynne Rienner, 1998); Mary Kaldor, *New and Old Wars: Organised Violence in a Global Era* (Cambridge: Polity Press, 1999); Michael Ignatieff, *Virtual War: Kosovo and Beyond* (New York: Henry Hold, 1999); Mats Berdal and David M. Malone, eds., *Greed and Grievance: Economic Agendas in Civil Wars* (Boulder, Colo.: Lynne Rienner, 2000).

2. Cole P. Dodge and Magne Raundalen, eds., *Reaching Children in War: Sudan, Uganda, and Mozambique* (Uppsala, Sweden: Sigma Forlag, 1991); Neil Boothby, Peter Upton, and Abucabar Sultan, "Boy Soldiers of Mozambique," Refugee Children, Refugee Studies Program, Oxford, March, 1992; Ilene Cohn and Guy S. Goodwin-Gill, *Child Soldiers: The Role of Children in Armed Conflict* (Oxford: Oxford University Press, 1994); Human Rights Watch, *Easy Prey: Child Soldiers in Liberia* (New York: Human Rights Watch, September 8, 1994); Oliver Furley, ed., *Conflict in Africa* (London: I. B. Tauris, 1995); Alcinda Honwana and E. Pannizo, "Evaluation of the Children and War Project in Mozambique," Research Report for Save the Children USA and USAID, 1995; Ed Cairns, *Children and Political Violence* (Oxford: Blackwell, 1996); Pamela Reynolds, *Traditional Healers and Childhood in Zimbabwe* (Athens: Ohio University Press, 1996); Paul Richards, *Fighting for the Rainforest: War, Youth and Resoruces in Sierra Leone* (Oxford: James Currey, 1996); Rachel Brett and Margaret McCallin, *Children—the Invisible Soldiers* (Växjö, Sweden: Rädda Barnen, Swedish Save the Children, 1996); Ibrahim Abdullah et al. "Lumpen Youth Culture and Political Violence: Sierra Leone Civil War," *African Development* 22, no. 3/4 (1997):171–216; Andy Dawes and Alcinda Honwana, "Kulturelle Konstruktionen von kindlichem Leid," Medico Report 20, *Schnelle Eingreiftuppe Seele* (Frankfurt: Medico International, 1997), 57–67; Jo Boyden and Sara Gibbs, *Children of War: Responses to*

Psycho-Social Distress in Cambodia (Geneva: United Nations Research Institute for Social Development, 1997); Michael G. Wessells, "Child Soldiers," *Bulletin of the Atomic Scientists* 53, no. 6 (November/December 1997): 32–39; Krijn Peters and Paul Richards, "Fighting with Open Eyes: Young Combatants Talking about War in Sierra Leone," in *Rethinking the Trauma of War*, ed. Patrick J. Bracken and Celia Petty (London: Free Association Books, 1998), 76–111; Alcinda Honwana, "*Okusiakala O'ndalo Yokalye*, Let's Light a New Fire: Local Knowledge in the Post-War Reintegration of War-Affected Children in Angola," Consultancy Report for CCF Angola, 1998; Alcinda Honwana, "Negotiating Post-War Identities: Child Soldiers in Mozambique and Angola," in *Contested Terrains and Constructed Categories: Contemporary Africa in Focus*, ed. George Clement Bond and Nigel C. Gibson (Boulder, Colo.: Westview Press, 2002); Rémy Bazenguissa-Ganga, "The Spread of Political Violence in Congo-Brazzaville," *African Affairs* 98, no. 390 (1999): 37–54.

3. Ahamdou Kourouma, *Allah n'est pas oblige* (Paris: Editions du Seuil, 2000).

4. Gersony, "Summary of Refugee Accounts."

5. Filip DeBoeck, "Borderland Breccia: The Mutant Hero and the Historical Imagination of a Central-African Diamond Frontier," *Journal of Colonialism and Colonial History* 1, no. 2 (2000) (electronic journal). One analyst has characterized these children's situation and actions as those of quasi-child or crypto-adult; see Chris Jenks, *Childhood* (London: Routledge, 1996).

6. M. M. Bakhtin, *The Dialogic Imagination: Four Essays*, ed. Michael Holquist, trans. Caryl Emerson and Michael Holquist (Austin: University of Texas Press, 1983).

7. Homi K. Bhabha, *The Location of Culture* (London: Routledge, 1994).

8. Throughout this book, I use pseudonyms to protect the identity of the children/interviewed.

9. Jean Bethke Elshtain, *Women and War* (Brighton: Harvester, 1987); Meredeth Turshen and Clotilde Twagiramariya, eds., *What Women Do in Wartime: Gender and Conflict in Africa* (London: Zed Books, 1998); Jacklyn Cock, *Colonels and Cadres: War and Gender in South Africa* (Cape Town: Oxford University Press, 1991).

10. Yvonne Keairns, "The Voices of Girl Child Soldiers" (New York and Geneva: Quaker United Nations Office, 2003); Susan McKay and Dyan Mazurana, *Where Are the Girls? Girls in Fighting Forces in Northern Uganda, Sierra Leone and Mozambique: Their Lives during and after War* (Montreal: Rights & Democracy and International Center for Human Rights and Democratic Development, 2004).

11. Alexandra Stiglmayer and Marion Farber, eds., *Mass Rape: The War against Women in Bosnia-Herzegovina* (Lincoln: University of Nebraska Press, 1994).

12. Veena Das, "The Anthropology of Violence and the Speech of the Victims," *Anthropology Today* 3, no. 4 (1987): 11–13.

Chapter 1

1. Alex Vines, *Renamo: Terrorism in Mozambique* (Oxford: Center for Southern African Studies, University of York, in association with James Currey, 1991); William Minter, *Apartheid's Contras: An Inquiry into the Roots of War in Angola and Mozambique*. (London: 2ed Books, 1994).

2. E. Hall, "The Mozambican National Resistance Movement (RENAMO) and the Reestablishment of Peace in Mozambique," paper delivered at a workshop on Security and Cooperation in Post-Apartheid Southern Africa, Maputo, Mozambique, September 1991; Joao Honwana, "The United Nations and

Mozambique: A Sustainable Peace?" *Lumiar Papers,* no. 7 (Lisbon: Instituto de Estudos Estrategicos e Internacionais, 1995).

3. Robert Gersony, "Summary of Mozambican Refugee Accounts of Principally Conflict Related Experiences in Mozambique" (Washington, D.C.: Bureau for Refugee Programs, U.S. State Department, 1988); Vines, *Renamo.*

4. For more on FRELIMO's villagization policies, see Christian Geffray, *La cause des armes au Mozambique: Anthropologie d'une guerre civile* (Paris: Credu-Karthala, 1990).

5. Geffray, *La cause des armes au Mozambique;* Christian Geffray and Mogens Pedersen, "Nampula en guerre," *Politique Africaine* 29 (1988): 28–40.

6. United Nations, *The United Nations and Mozambique, 1992–1995,* Blue Book Series (New York: UN Department of Public Information, 1995).

7. Ibid.

8. Hall, "The Mozambican National Resistance Movement (RENAMO)"; J. Honwana, "The United Nations and Mozambique."

9. Gersony, "Summary of Refugee Accounts."

10. Ibid.

11. Vines, *Renamo;* Minter, *Apartheid's Contras.*

12. Ibid.

13. Minter, *Apartheid's Contras;* United Nations Development Program (UNDP), *Angola Poverty and Human Development Report* (New York: UNDP, 1997). The peace that had come after sixteen years lasted only sixteen months.

14. Minter, *Apartheid's Contras.*

15. UNDP, *Angola Poverty and Human Development Report;* see also Minter *Apartheid's Contras.*

16. UNDP, *Angola Poverty and Human Development.*

17. Alcinda Honwana, "Spiritual Agency and Self-Renewal in Southern Mozambique" (Ph.D. diss., University of London, School of Oriental and African Studies [SOAS], 1996). A version of the dissertation was later published as a book: Alcinda Honwana, *Living Spirits, Modern Traditions: Spirit Possession and the Politics of Culture in Southern Mozambique* (Maputo: Promedia, 2001; Lisbon: Ela Por Ela, 2003). Research for my Ph.D. was funded from 1992 to 1995 by the Commonwealth Secretariat, Special Fund for Mozambique. I also received a SOAS field research award in 1992. The Fundacao Calouste Gulbenkian in Portugal supported my research trip to Lisbon in 1992. The Swiss Cooperation for Development in Mozambique helped to fund my fieldwork in Maputo during 1993. The Ministry of Culture in Mozambique was very helpful throughout this research.

18. Honwana, *Living Spirits.* The activities of this center are discussed in Chapter 6.

19. Alcinda Honwana, "*Okusiakala Ondalo Yokalye,* Let's Light a New Fire: Local knowledge in the Post-War Reintegration of War-Affected Children in Angola," Consultancy Report for CCF Angola, 1988.

20. This evaluation was done in 1997 by Edward Green, anthropologist, and Michael Wessells, psychologist. Their report is "Mid-term Evaluation of the Province-Based War Trauma Training Project: Meeting the Psychosocial Needs of Children in Angola" (Arlington, Va.: USAID Displaced Children and Orphans Fund and War Victims Fund), 54.

21. Ibid., 56.

22. For a more detailed description of the process through which the project was designed and carried out, see Honwana, "*Okusiakala O'ndalo Yokalye,* Let's Light a New Fire."

Chapter 2

1. See Rachel Brett and Margaret McCallin, *Children—the Invisible Soldiers* (Växjö, Sweden: Rädda Barnen, Swedish Save the Children, 1996).
2. G. Dickson, "Prophecy and Rationalism: Joachim of Fiore, Jewish Messianism and the Children's Crusade of 1212," *Florensia* 13–14 (1999–2000): 97–104; Norman P. Zacour, "The Children's Crusade," in *A History of the Crusades*, ed. Kenneth M. Setton, vol. 2: *The Later Crusades, 1189–1311*, ed. Robert Lee Wolff and Harry W. Hazard (Madison: University of Wisconsin Press, 1969), 325–42.
3. T. White Lynn III, *Politics of Chaos: The Organizational Causes of Violence in China's Cultural Revolution* (Princeton: Princeton University Press, 1989), 280–81.
4. UNICEF, *The State of World's Children 1996: Children in War* (New York: UNICEF, 1996).
5. C. Spenser, *A Child's War: Kidnapped by Uganda Rebels, Innocents Are Trained to Kill* (Ottawa: Southam, 1998); Human Rights Watch, *Stolen Children: Abduction and Recruitment in Northern Uganda* (New York: Human Rights Watch, March 2003); Human Rights Watch, *The Scars of Death: Children Abducted by the Lord's Resistance Army in Uganda* (New York: Human Rights Watch, September 1997); Stavros Stavrou, Robert Stewart, and Amanda Stavrou, *The Reintegration of Child Soldiers and Abducted Children: A Case Study of Plaro and Pabbo, Gulu District in Northern Uganda* (South Africa: Pretoria Institute for Security Studies, 2000).
6. Amnesty International, *Democratic Republic of Congo: Children at War* (New York: Amnesty International, September 2003); James Schechter, "Governing Lost Boys: Sudanese Refugees in UNHCR camp in Kenya" (Ph.D. diss., University of Colorado, 2004).
7. Human Rights Watch, *Easy Prey: Child Soldiers in Liberia* (New York: Human Rights Watch, 8 September 1994). See also Mats Utas, "Sweet Battlefields: Youth and the Liberian Civil War" (Ph.D. diss., Uppsala University, Sweden, 2003); Paul Richards, *Fighting for the Rainforest: War, Youth and Resources in Sierra Leone* (Oxford: James Currey, 1996).
8. Ibrahim Abdullah et al., "Lumpen Youth Culture and Political Violence: Sierra Leone Civil War," *African Development* 22, no. 3/4 (1997):171–216; Susan Shepler, "Globalizing Child Soldiers in Sierra Leone," in *Youthscapes: The Popular, the National, the Global*, ed. Sunaina Maria and Elizabeth Soep (Philadelphia: University of Pennsylvania Press, 2004); Krijn Peters, *Re-Examining Voluntarism: Youth Combatants in Sierra Leone* (Pretoria: Institute for Security Studies, April 2004); Paul Richards, "Rebellion in Liberia and Sierra Leone: A Crisis of Youth?" in *Conflict in Africa*, ed. Oliver Furley (London: I. B. Tauris, 1995).
9. H. Ponciano Del Pino, "Family, Culture and 'Revolution': Everyday Life with Sendero Luminoso," in *Shining and Other Paths: War and Society in Peru, 1980-1995*, ed. Steve L. Stern (Durham: Duke University Press, 1998), 158–92.
10. Human Rights Watch, "You Will Learn Not to Cry: Child Combatants in Colombia" (New York: Human Rights Watch, September 2003); Guillermo Gonzalez Uribe, *Los Ninos de la Guerra* (Bogota: Planeta, 2002).
11. UNICEF, *The State of the World's Children 1996*. On Sri Lanka, see also Harendra de Silva, Chris Hobbs, and Helga Hanks, "Conscription of Children in Armed Conflict—A Form of Child Abuse," *Child Abuse Review* 10, no. 2 (March/April 2001); and Rohan Gunaratna, "Tiger Cubs and Childhood Fall as Casualties of War in Sri Lanka," *Jane's Intelligence Review* 10, no. 7 (1998).

12. Muzamil Jaleel 10 Child Newsline, quoted in J. Sutton-Redner, "Children in a World of Violence," *Children in Need Magazine*, 2002.

13. Nahed Habiballah, "Interviews with Mothers of Martyrs of the Aqsa Intifada," *Arab Studies Quarterly* 26, no. 1 (Winter 2004); A. Baker, "The Psychological Impact of the Intifada on Palestinian Children in the Occupied West Bank and Gaza: An Exploratory Study," *American Journal of Orthopsychiatry* 60, no. 4 (1990); Salman Elbedour, "Youth in Crisis: The Well-Being of Middle Eastern Youth and Adolescents During War and Peace," *Journal of Youth and Adolescence* 27, no. 5 (1997): 539–56; Raija-Leena Punamaki, *Children under Conflict: The Attitudes and Emotional Life of Israeli and Palestinian* Children (Tampere: Tampere Peace Research Institute, 1987); Defence for Children International, *Use of Children in the Occupied Palestinian Territories: Perspective on Child Soldiers* (Geneva: Defence for Children International, July 2004).

14. UNICEF, *The State of the World's Children 1996*; Alexandra Stiglmayer and Marion Faber, eds., *Mass Rape: The War Against Women in Bosnia-Herzegovina* (Lincoln: University of Nebraska Press, 1994).

15. Dahlia Gilboa, "Mass Rape: War on Women."

16. Ilene Cohn and Guy S. Goodwin-Gill, *Child Soldiers: The Role of Children in Armed Conflict* (Oxford: Oxford University Press, 1994).

17. Geneva Convention for the Amelioration of the Condition of the Wounded and Sick in Armed Forces in the Field, August 12, 1949, 75 UNTS 31 (First Geneva Convention); Geneva Convention for the Amelioration of the Condition of Wounded, Sick and Shipwrecked Members of Armed Forces at Sea, August 12, 1949, 75 UNTS 85 (Second Geneva Convention); Geneva Convention Relative to the Treatment of Prisoners of War, August 12, 1949, 75 UNTS 135 (Third Geneva Convention); and Geneva Convention Relative to the Protection of Civilian Persons in Time of War, August 12, 1949, 75 UNTS 287 (Fourth Geneva Convention).

18. Karma Nabulsi, "Evolving Conceptions of Civilians and Belligerents: One Hundred Years after the Hague Peace Conferences," in *Civilians in War*, ed. Simon Chesterman (Boulder, Colo.: Lynne Rienner, 2001), 9–24.

19. Karl von Clausewitz, *On War* (London: Penguin Books, 1982); Mary Kaldor, *New and Old Wars: Organised Violence in a Global Era* (Cambridge: Polity Press, 1999); S. N. Kalyvas, " 'New' and 'Old' Wars: A Valid Distinction?" *World Politics* 54 (October 2001): 99–118; Mark Duffield, "Post-modern Conflict: Warlords, Post-adjustment States and Private Protection," *Civil Wars* 1, no.1 (1998): 65–102; David Keen, "The Economic Functions of Violence in Civil Wars," *Adelphi Paper* 320 (London: Oxford University Press for the International Institute for Strategic Studies, 1998).

20. Kaldor, *New and Old Wars*; Michael Ignatieff, *The Warrior's Honor: Ethnic War and the Modern Conscience* (New York: Henry Holt and Company, 1998); Mats Berdal and David M. Malone, eds., *Greed and Grievance: Economic Agendas in Civil Wars* (Boulder, Colo.: Lynne Rienner, 2000).

21. Mary Kaldor, "Beyond Militarism, Arms Races and Arms Control," in *Understanding September 11*, ed. Craig Calhoun, Paul Price, and Ashley Timmer (New York: New Press, 2002), 159–76.

22. Ibid.

23. Kalyvas, " 'New' and 'Old' Wars."

24. Seyla Benhabib, "Unholy Politics: Reclaiming Democratic Virtues After September 11," in *Understanding September 11*, ed. Calhoun, Price, and Timmer, 241–53.

25. See Kalyvas, " 'New' and 'Old' Wars."

26. Simon Chesterman, ed., *Civilians in War* (Boulder, Colo.: Lynne Rienner, 2001).

27. Jacklyn Cock, *Colonels and Cadres: War and Gender in South Africa* (Cape Town: Oxford University Press, 1991).

28. See Utas, "Sweet Battlefields," on women in the civil war in Liberia.

29. Kaldor, *New and Old Wars*; Kaldor, "Beyond Militarism"; and Carolyn Nordstrom, *A Different Kind of War Story* (Philadelphia: University of Pennsylvania Press, 1997).

30. Nordstrom, *A Different Kind of War Story.*

31. Michael Ignatieff, *Virtual War: Kosovo and Beyond* (New York: Henry Holt, 1999), 6.

32. Robert Gersony, "Summary of Refugee Accounts of Principally Conflict Related Experiences in Mozambique" (Washington, D.C.: Bureau for Refugee Programs, U.S. State Department, 1988); William Finnegan, *A Complicated War: The Harrowing of Mozambique* (Berkley: University of California Press, 1992).

33. Human Rights Watch, "Easy Prey."

34. Fernando, a former RENAMO child combatant, was fourteen years old when he told his story, quoted in Eduardo White, *Voices of Blood: Children and War in Mozambique* (Maputo, Mozambique: s.n., 1988).

35. Twenty-year-old former child soldier from Huambo, interviewed by the author in February 1998 in Huambo, Angola.

36. Lora Lumpe, *Running Guns: The Global Black Market in Small Arms* (London: Zed Books, 2000); Small Arms Survey, *Small Arms Survey 2001: Profiling the Problem* (Oxford: Oxford University Press, 2001); Coalition to Stop the Use of Child Soldiers, *Light Weapons: Not Suitable for Children* (London: Coalition to Stop the Use of Child Soldiers, 1998).

37. Paul Davies, "Cambodia and the Landmine Burden—A General Overview," in Paul Davies with Nic Dunlop, *War of the Mines: Cambodia, Landmines and the Impoverishment of a Nation* (London: Pluto Press, 1994); CIET International, *The Social Costs of Landmines in Four Countries: Afghanistan, Bosnia, Cambodia and Mozambique* (New York: CIET International, 1995).

38. Amnesty International, *No More Dying for Diamonds: Save the Children of Sierra Leone* (New York: Amnesty International, undated).

39. On warlords, see William Reno, *Warlord Politics and African States* (London: Lynne Rienner, 1998); Michael Klare, *Resource Wars: The New Landscape of Glo Conflict* (New York: Metropolitan, 2001).

40. Mats Berdal and David M. Malone, eds., *Greed and Grievance: Economic Agendas in Civil Wars* (Boulder, Colo.: Lynne Rienner, 2000).

41. Olara Otunnu, "Innocent Victims: Protecting Children in Times of Armed Conflict," in *United Nations 2000* (London: Agenda Publishing. 2000), 84.

42. Graça Machel, *The Impact of War on Children: A Review since the 1996 United Nations Report on the Impact of Armed Conflict on Children* (New York: Palgrave, 2001); Rachel Brett and Irma Specht, *Young Soldiers: Why They Choose to Fight* (Boulder, Colo.: Lynne Reinner, 2004); Jo Boyden and Joanna de Berry, *Children and Youth on the Frontline: Ethnography, Armed Conflict and Displacement* (New York: Berghahn Books, 2004); Cole P. Dodge and Magne Raundalen, eds., *Reaching Children in War: Sudan, Uganda, and Mozambique* (Uppsala, Sweden: Sigma Forlag, 1991); Rachel Brett and Margaret McCallin, *Children—the Invisible Soldiers* (Växjö, Sweden: Rädda Barnen, Swedish Save the Children, 1996); James Garbarino, Kathleen Kostelny, and Nancy Dubrow, *No Place to Be a Child: Growing Up in a War Zone* (San Francisco: Jossey-Bass, 1991); Alcinda Honwana, "Innocent

and Guilty: Child Soldiers as Interstitial and Tactical Agents," in *Makers and Breakers: Children and Youth in Postcolonial Africa*, ed. Alcinda Honwana and Filip De Boeck (Oxford: James Currey, 2005); Alan Raymond and Susan Raymond, *Children in War* (New York: Simon and Schuster, 2000); Peter W. Singer, *Children at War* (New York: Pantheon Books, 2005); Pamela Reynolds, "Youth and Politics in South Africa, in *Children and the Politics of Culture*, ed. Sharon Stephens (Princeton, N.J.: Princeton University Press, 1995), 218–42.

43. Carolyn Nordstrom, "Girls Behind the (Front) Lines," *Peace Review* 8, no. 3 (September 1996): 151.

44. Additional Protocol I, art. 77(2).

45. Convention on the Rights of the Child, art. 1., UN Doc A/44/49 (1989), available at *http://www.unhchr.ch/html/menu3/b/k2crc.htm* (accessed 22 February 2005). See also Jenny Kuper, *International Law Concerning Child Civilians in Armed Conflict* (New York: Clarendon Press, 1997); Geraldine Van Bueren, *The International Law on the Rights of the Child* (Dodrecht: Martinus Nijhoff, 1995).

46. Ibid., art. 38(2) (emphasis added).

47. African Charter on the Rights and Welfare of the Child, OAU Doc. CAB/LEG/24.9/49 (1990), art. 2.

48. See Cohn and Goodwin-Gill, *Child Soldiers*.

49. Optional Protocol on the Convention of the Rights of the Child concerning involvement of children in armed conflicts, available at *http://www.icrc.org/web/eng/siteeng0.nsf/iwpList520/F1D2C91CCBDBF035C1256B66005B8FA9* (accessed February 25, 2004). See also Filipe Gomez Isa, *La Participacion de los Ninos en los Conflictos Armados: El Protocolo Facultativo a la Convencion sobre los Derechos del Nino* (Bilbao: Universidad de Duesto, 2000).

50. See Furley, *Conflict in Africa*.

51. Radda Barnen, "Children of War," *Newsletter on Child Soldiers* 1 (March 2000). British citizens protested their army's use of seventeen-year-olds in active service in the Gulf War of 1991.

52. "Boy Soldier, Fourteen, Bears Witness to Burma Torture," *Sunday Times* (London), 5 January 2003.

53. Rome Statute of the International Criminal Court, UN Doc. A/CONF/183/9*, available at *http://www.un.org/law/icc/statute/romefra.htm*.

54. ILO Worst Forms of Child Labour Convention (1999), convention no. 182, art. 3(a).

55. Philippe Aries, *Centuries of Childhood: A Social History of Family Life* (New York: Random House, 1962); see also Stephens, *Children and the Politics of Culture*.

56. Boyden and Gibbs, *Children and War*.

57. Michael Freeman, *The Rights and Wrongs of Children* (London: Francis Printer Publishers, 1993).

58. Honwana, "Children of War."

59. Chris Jenks, *Childhood* (London and New York: Routledge, 1996); Virginia Caputo, "Anthropology's Silent 'Others': A Consideration of Some Conceptual and Methodological Issues for the Study of Youth and Children's Cultures," in *Youth Cultures: A Cross-Cultural Perspective*, ed. Vered Amit-Talai and Helena Wulff (London: Routledge, 1995); Allison James, *Childhood Identities: Self and Social Relationships in the Experience of Childhood* (Edinburgh: Edinburgh University Press, 1993).

60. Amit-Talai and Wulff, *Youth Cultures*.

61. C. John Sommerville, *The Rise and Fall of Childhood* (Beverly Hills: Sage, 1982); Jo Boyden, "Childhood and Policy Makers: A Comparative Perspective on the Globalisation of Childhood," in *Constructing and Reconstructing*

Childhood: Contemporary Issues in the Sociological Study of Childhood, ed. Allison James and Allan Prout, (London: Falmer Press, 1990).

62. James and Prout, *Constructing and Reconstructing Childhood*.

63. Harry Hendrick, Children, *Childhood and English Society, 1880–1990* (Cambridge: Cambridge University Press, 1997).

64. Honwana, "*Okusiakala O'ndalo Yokalye*, Let's Light a New Fire."

65. Antonio Sonama, from Uige, Angola, interviewed by the CCF team.

66. Ronald Grimes, *Deeply into the Bone: Reinventing the Rights of Passage* (Berkeley: University of California Press, 2000).

67. Marie Louise Bastin, "Mungonge: initiation masculine des adultes chez les Tshokwe (Angola)," *Baessler Archiv* 32, no. 2 (1984): 361–403; Filip De Boeck, "Of Bushbucks without Horns: Male and Female Initiation among the Aluun of Southwest Zaïre," *Journal des africanistes* 61, no. 1 (1991): 37–71.

68. *Seculo* Kapata, interviewed by the CCF team in Kuito, 1997. The honorific *seculo* means elderly person in Umbundu.

69. *Seculo* Afonso mentioned this to me in Kuito in February 1998.

70. Antonio Sonama, Uige, interviewed by the CCF team.

71. Rachel Brett, "A Time for Peace: A Time to Act," *Peace and Conflict: Journal of Peace Psychology* 6, no. 1 (2000): 89.

72. Robert Kaplan, "The Coming Anarchy," *Atlantic Monthly* 273, no. 2 (February 1994): 44–76.

73. Richards, *Fighting for the Rainforest*; William Reno, *Corruption and State Politics in Sierra Leone* (Cambridge: Cambridge University Press, 1995).

74. Oliver Furley, "Child Soldiers in Africa," in *Conflict in Africa*, ed. Furley; Human Rights Watch, *Easy Prey*.

75. Arjun Appadurai, *Modernity at Large: Cultural Dimensions of Globalization* (Minneapolis: University of Minnesota Press, 1996); Akhil Gupta and James Ferguson, "Culture, Power, Place: Ethnography at the End of an Era," in *Culture, Power, Place: Explorations in Cultural Anthropology*, ed. Akhil Gupta and James Ferguson (London: Duke University Press, 1997); Nordstrom, *A Different Kind of War Story*.

76. Arjun Appadurai, "Global Ethnoscapes: Notes on Queries for a Transnational Anrthropology," in *Recapturing Anthropology*, ed. Richard Fox (Santa Fe, N.M.: School of American Research Press, 1991), 191–210.

77. Nordstrom, *A Different Kind of War Story*, 37.

78. Richards, *Fighting for the Rainforest*.

79. Christian Geffray and Mögens Pedersen, "Nampula en guerre," *Politique Africaine* 29 (1988): 28–40; Christian Geffray, *La cause des armes au Mozambique: Anthropologie d'une guerre civile* (Paris: Credu-Karthala, 1990); Furley, *Conflict in Africa*; Ishmail Rashid, "Bush Path to Destruction: The Origin and Character of the Revolutionary United Front (RUF/SL)," *Africa Development* 22, no. 3/4 (1997): 19–44; Boyden and Gibbs, *Children of War*; Abdullah and Bangura, "Lumpen Youth"; Ibrahim Abdullah and Patrick Muana, "The Revolutionary Front of Sierra Leone," in *African Guerrillas*, ed. Christopher Clapham (London: James Currey 1998), 172–94; Richards, *Fighting for the Rainforest*.

80. T. W. Bennet, *Using Children in Armed Conflict: A Legitimate African Tradition?* (Essex: Institute for Security Studies, 2002).

81. Olara Otunnu, Special Representative of the UN Secretary-General for Children and Armed Conflict, quoted by Singer in *Children at War*, 10.

82. Ibid.

83. Julia E. Maxted, "Children and Armed Conflict in Africa," *Social Identities* 9, no. 1 (March 2003): 51–73. See also Paul Collier, *Economic Causes of Civil Conflict*

and Their Implications for Policy (Washington, D.C.: World Bank, 2000); Singer, *Children at War;* Ali Al-Kenz, "Youth and Violence," in *Africa's New People, Policies and Institutions,* ed. Stephen Ellis (The Hague: DGIS [Ministry of Foreign Affairs], 1996), 42–57.

Chapter 3

1. Marula is not his real name. I use a pseudonym to protect his identity.

2. Marula was twenty years old when I interviewed him in September 1995 in Chibuto, Gaza province, Mozambique. Marula said that in the beginning he was very afraid of the war, but he had no alternative to adjusting to it, and over time he learned to live that life.

3. Fernando, from Tchokwè district in Mozambique, was fourteen years old when he told his story; quoted in Eduardo White, *Voices of Blood: Children and War in Mozambique* (Maputo, Mozambique: s.n., 1988), 14–15.

4. Michel De Certeau, *The Practice of Everyday Life,* trans. Steven Rendall (Berkeley: University of California Press, 1984).

5. Andrè Matsangaíssa, RENAMO's first leader, died in combat with government forces in Gorongosa, Sofala province, in 1979. His followers are commonly known as the *matsangas.* His successor was Afonso Dhlakama. See Alex Vines, *Renamo: Terrorism in Mozambique* (Oxford: Center for Southern African Studies, University of York, in association with James Currey, 1991).

6. Robert Gersony, "Summary of Refugee Accounts of Principally Conflict Related Experiences in Mozambique" (Washington, D.C.: Bureau for Refugee Programs, U.S. State Department, 1988); Vines, *Renamo;* William Finnegan, *A Complicated War: The Harrowing of Mozambique* (Berkley: University of California Press, 1992); William Minter, *Apartheid's Contras: An Inquiry into the Roots of War in Angola and Mozambique* (London: Zed Books, 1994).

7. Sara Gibbs, "Post-War Reconstruction in Mozambique: Re-Framing Children's Experience of Trauma and Healing," *Disasters* 18, no. 3 (September 1994): 268–76; Alcinda Honwana, "*Okusiakala O'ndalo Yokalye,* Let's Light a New Fire: Local Knowledge in the Post-War Reintegration of War-Affected Children in Angola," Consultancy Report for CCF Angola, 1998.

8. Jo Boyden, "Childhood and the Policy Makers. A Comparative Perspective on the Globalisation of Childhood," in *Constructing and Reconstructing Childhood: Contemporary Issues in the Sociological Study of Childhood,* ed. Allison James and Allan Prout, (London: Falmer Press, 1990); A. Dawes, "Helping, Coping and 'Cultural Healing'," *Recovery: Research and Co-operation on Violence, Education and Rehabilitation of Young People* 1, no. 5 (1996); Allison James, *Childhood Identities: Self and Social Relationships in the Experience of Childhood* (Edinburgh: Edinburgh University Press, 1993); Pamela Reynolds, *Traditional Healers and Childhood in Zimbabwe* (Athens: Ohio University Press, 1996); Jo Boyden and Sara Gibbs, *Children of War: Responses to Psycho-Social Distress in Cambodia* (Geneva: United Nations Research Institute for Social Development, 1997).

9. Barbara Roberts, "The Death of Macho-think: Feminist Research and the Transformation of Peace Studies," *Women's Studies International Forum* 7 (1984): 195–200; Jacklyn Cock, *Colonels and Cadres: War and Gender in South Africa* (Cape Town: Oxford University Press, 1991).

10. Cock, *Colonels and Cadres,* 58.

11. Kutximuila, a well-known female healer from Kuito, Biè province, Angola, interviewed by author and Carlinda Monteiro in July 1997.

12. Ibid.

13. Fernando, quoted in White, *Voices of Blood*, 14.

14. Tisoma, a former child soldier from Huambo, Angola, interviewed by author, February 1998.

15. Zita, then aged seventeen, interviewed by author in September 1995 in Macia, Mozambique. Zita belonged to a group that was in charge of stealing food and other goods from the population. He was also often assigned the task of guarding civilians in the camp.

16. Maria, a seventeen-year-old girl, interviewed by author in Josina Machel Island, Manhiça, southern Mozambique, May 1999. Very little is usually said about the roles girls play as combatants, cooks, and domestic workers, and the sexual abuse they suffered. The next chapter focuses exclusively on the situation of girls.

17. Astro, then seventeen, interviewed by the CCF team in Huambo, Angola, March 1998. Astro stated that he was never involved in direct combat. He was trained to operate with landmines; his group would plant landmines in enemy territory and clean paths of any possible landmines.

18. Ernesto told his story in White, *Voices of Blood*, 29.

19. Balto, then aged eighteen, interviewed by author and Carlinda Monteiro, Huambo, Angola, February 1998.

20. Honwana, "*Okusiakala O'ndalo Yokalye*, Let's Light a New Fire."

21. Lopes, a former child soldier from UNITA, interviewed by author in July 1997 at the International Organization for Migration (IOM) Transit Centre, in Viana (near Luanda), Angola. In this interview, Lopes was with Sam, his friend and also a former child soldier; Sam was less talkative and often just nodded while Lopes told us his war stories.

22. Domingo, aged nineteen, interviewed by author in Malange, February 1998. I also had a chance to talk with his mother and sister-in-law, with whom he lived for a while. Domingo had been demobilized and had managed to secure a job. He was attending classes at night and had just paid bridewealth for his girlfriend, who moved in with him.

23. Dunga, a seventeen-year-old former soldier from Malange, Angola, interviewed by author in Lombe, February 1998. When I met Dunga, he was still struggling with nightmares about the war; he mentioned dreaming of being kidnapped again to fight and of holding an AK-47 machine gun and killing everybody around him. He was undergoing treatment by a local healer.

24. Ben, a young former soldier from Malange, Angola, served as a UNITA soldier and was demobilized in 1997. Interviewed by author in Malange, February 1998.

25. Mrs. Andrade, interviewed by author and Carlinda Monteiro in Malange, Angola, February 1998.

26. For Nelson's story, see Bóia Efraime Júnior, "The Psychic Reconstruction of Former Child Soldiers," *Children, War, and Persecution—Rebuilding Hope: Proceedings of the Congress in Maputo, Mozambique, 1–4 December 1996* (Mozambique: s.n., 1996), 62–63.

27. Alcinda Honwana, "Negotiating Post-War Identities: Child Soldiers in Mozambique and Angola," in *Contested Terrains and Constructed Categories: Contemporary Africa in Focus*, ed. George Clement Bond and Nigel C. Gibson (Boulder, Colo.: Westview Press, 2002); Paul Richards, *Fighting for the Rainforest: War, Youth and Resources in Sierra Leone* (Oxford: James Currey, 1996); Oliver Furley, "Child Soldiers in Africa," in *Conflict in Africa*, ed. Oliver Furley (London: I. B. Tauris, 1995).

28. Christian Geffray, *La cause des armes au Mozambique: Anthropologie d'une guerre civile* (Paris: Credu-Karthala, 1990); Vines, *Renamo*; Minter, *Africa's Contras*.

29. Pitango is a former child soldier who fought alongside the FAA, the government army, rather than the insurgent UNITA. He was eighteen when interviewed in Cambandua, Biè, Angola, by members of the CCF team in March 1998. He was demobilized in 1997 from the demobilization center of Grafanil in Luanda. In 1998, he had enrolled for evening classes at a nearby secondary school.

30. Fonseca, interviewed in Kuito by the CCF team in January 1998. He was thirteen when he joined the military and seventeen at the time of this interview. His military training took place in Kuito, and he was then sent to fight in the province of Kwanza Sul.

31. Geffray, *La cause des armes au Mozambique*; Honwana, "*Okusiakala O'ndalo Yokalye*, Let's Light a New Fire"; Honwana, "Negotiating Post-War Identities."

32. Pitango, a nineteen-year-old former child soldier from Biè, Angola, interviewed by members of the CCF team in March 1998.

33. Mats Utas, "The Agency of Victims: Women and War in Liberia," *in Makers and Breakers: Children and Youth in Postcolonial Africa*, ed. Alcinda Honwana and Filipe De Boeck (Oxford: James Currey, forthcoming 2005); Furley, "Child Soldiers in Africa"; Honwana, "Negotiating Post-War Identities."

34. Roberts, "The Death of Macho-think," quoted in Cock, *Colonels and Cadres*, 56.

35. Cock, *Colonels and Cadres*; Ilene Cohn and Guy S. Goodwin-Gill, *Child Soldiers: The Role of Children in Armed Conflict* (Oxford: Oxford University Press, 1994).

36. Paul Antze and Michael Lambek, eds., *Tense Past: Cultural Essays in Trauma and Memory* (New York: Routledge, 1996).

37. Smokeless powder is the most commonly used powder in bullet rifles. It is composed of nitrocellulose and nitroglycerine compounds and binders. Smokeless powders are generally classified by application based on their burning rate and properties. There are handgun powders, shotgun powders, and rifle powders. However, there is considerable crossover. Many shotgun powders are also useful pistol powders and vice-versa. When inhaled or ingested, smokeless powder can have moderate toxic effects. See Chuck Hawks, "Guns and Shooting Online," www.chuckhawks.com; US National Research Council Committee on Smokeless and Black Powder, "Black and Smokeless Powders: Technologies for Finding Bombs and the Bomb Makers" (report, 1998).

38. Honwana, "*Okusiakala O'ndalo Yokalye*, Let's Light a New Fire"; Honwana, "Negotiating Post-War Identities."

39. Fernando's story quoted in White, *Voices of Blood*, 14.

40. I interviewed Paulo's father, Boaventura, in Maputo Urban District Number Five in April 1993 at his house. I also met Paulo and other family members.

41. Pedro, a twenty-year-old former UNITA soldier from Malange, Angola, interviewed by author and Carlinda Monteiro in February 1998. We also had a chance to interview Pedro's aunt Nzinga, a well-known healer, who helped Pedro deal with the traumas of war.

42. Josè, an eighteen-year-old former UNITA soldier from Lombe, Malange, Angola, interviewed by the CCF team in June 1997. He spent six years as a soldier. His brother was also abducted and died after a failed attempt to escape from the camp.

43. Dunga, former UNITA soldier, interviewed by author, Lombe, Malange, Angola, February 1998. In military terms the "parade" was a large, open space where troops were drilled in formation and assemblies were held.

44. Pitango, interviewed in Cambandua, Biè, Angola, by members of the CCF team in March 1998.

45. I interviewed Noel and his father at their home in Nhamatanda, Mozambique, in September 1995. Fourteen-year-old Noel was a very talkative boy who would talk about his military deeds with friends and neighbors. His father didn't like him sharing war stories because he feared that people could be angry at him for what he did.

46. These methods of destroying old identities and imposing new ones are familiar from the history of the trans-Atlantic enslavement of West Africans. Although the two experiences are separated by several centuries, their resemblance is not coincidental. In many African societies, names constitute social relations and obligations. See Honwana, "*Okusiakala O'ndalo Yokalye*, Let's Light a New Fire"; Honwana, "Negotiating Post-War Identities."

47. Dunga, a former UNITA soldier from Lombe, Malange, Angola, interviewed by author in Lombe, February 1998. At the time of the interview, he was seventeen years old.

48. Domingo, interviewed by author in Malange in February 1998.

49. Josè, a young former UNITA soldier from Malange, Angola, interviewed by the CCF team in June 1997.

50. Eduardo, a former young soldier from the government army, interviewed by the CCF team in 1998. Eduardo is from Kuito in Angola and was eighteen at the time of this interview.

51. Lopes, former UNITA soldier from Malange, interviewed by author, IOM transit center in Viana, Angola, July 1997.

52. Of course, these traditional rituals are enacted not in the context of death but rather in the context of ritual bloodshed. See Alcinda Honwana, "Spiritual Agency and Self-Renewal in Southern Mozambique" (Ph.D. diss., University of London, School of Oriental and African Studies [SOAS], 1996). A version of the dissertation was later published as a book: Alcinda Honwana, *Living Spirits, Modern Traditions: Spirit Possession and the Politics of Culture in Southern Mozambique* (Maputo: Promedia, 2001; Lisbon: Ela Por Ela, 2003).

53. By adapting these cultural forms, UNITA attempted to strengthen the alliance with its support base. UNITA portrayed its rival, the MPLA, as an urban-based, mainly creole, movement with only marginal ties to the masses.

54. Vines, *Renamo*, 95–96.

55. Homi K. Bhabha, *The Location of Culture* (London: Routledge, 1994).

56. Marcos, a twenty-year-old former soldier from Mozambique who fought alongside RENAMO troops, interviewed by author in Chibuto in September 1995. Marcos was about twelve when he was abducted into the army. His relatives did not hear of him for more than five years. He came back after the cease-fire in 1992 at the age of seventeen.

57. Domingo, a twenty-year-old former UNITA soldier, interviewed by author in Malange in February 1998.

58. Milito, from Uige in Angola, fought alongside the FAA, the government army. He was sixteen when interviewed by the CCF team in Uige in October 1997. He had spent about four years in the military. Demobilized in 1996, Milito now lives in Uige with his older brother.

59. Manecas, a twenty-year-old former soldier from Huambo, Angola, interviewed by the CCF team in October 1997. He was abducted at the age of sixteen in his neighborhood while playing outside with friends and was forced to enlist. Another friend was abducted with him.

60. Jamba, a nineteen-year-old former UNITA soldier from Kuito, province of Biè in Angola.

61. Zita, a former boy soldier from RENAMO, Mozambique.

62. Nineteen-year-old Tuta from Kunje district in Biè, Angola, served in UNITA's army for five years and was interviewed by the CCF team in Kuito in 1998.

63. Júlio, a twenty-year-old who had fought alongside UNITA, is from the province of Huambo. When he left the military he became very depressed. Interviewed conducted by the CCF team in Huambo in January 1998.

64. Eduardo, from Biè, served in the government army.

65. Nineteen-year-old Noel from Nhamatanda in Mozambique was forced to fight alongside RENAMO soldiers.

66. Gito, a former young soldier from Moxico, Angola, served in UNITA's army. Gito was nineteen years old when he was interviewed by the CCF team in March 1998.

67. Sula, a young man from Moxico in Angola, was a soldier with UNITA for many years. In April 1998, when the CCF team interviewed him, Sula was nineteen years old. During the war, Sula's leg was seriously injured, and he was out of action for more than a month.

68. Dacosta, a former child soldier who served in RENAMO's army, is from Josina Machel Island in Manhiça, Mozambique. I conducted this interview in May 1999. Dacosta was kidnapped at the age of nine. I met with his whole family. His father is a priest in the local Zionist church, and his brother was a militiaman with the government. The father's dilemma, which the two boys shared, was whether one day his sons would have to confront each other on the battlefield. Fortunately, that never happened. Dacosta was demobilized when the war ended in 1992.

69. Gito, interviewed in March 1998 in Moxico by the CCF team.

70. Lucas was nineteen when the war ended in 1992. I interviewed him in Chibuto, Mozambique, in September 1995. He was kidnapped in 1982 at the age of nine and forced to join the RENAMO insurgent army. His mother, grandmother, and baby sister were also kidnapped on the same day, but he never saw them in the camp. He learned later of their death in the hands of RENAMO.

71. Zita, from Macia in Mozambique, interviewed by author in September 1995.

72. Sam, a friend of Lopes; Carlinda Monteiro and I interviewed both boys in Viana, at the IOM Transit Center in July 1997.

73. Nelito, a former soldier from Manjacaze, Gaza province in Mozambique, interviewed by author, 1995.

74. Pedro, a nineteen-year-old from Malange in Angola, interviewed by author in Malange in February 1998.

75. Ben, interviewed by author in Malange, Angola, in February 1998.

76. Ibid.

77. Anthony Giddens, *The Constitution of Society: Outline of the Theory of Structuration* (Berkeley: University of California Press, 1984).

78. Ibid., 9.

79. Ibid., 16.

80. Partha Chatterjee, *The Nation and its Fragments: Colonial and Postcolonial Histories* (Princeton, N.J.: Princeton University Press, 1993); Gayatri Chakravorty Spivak, *Outside in the Teaching Machine* (New York: Routledge, 1993).

81. De Certeau, *The Practice of Everyday Life*, xix.

82. Ibid., 37.
83. Ibid., 38.
84. On Timangane's story, see Júnior, "The Psychic Reconstruction," 62.
85. Jacinto, a seventeen-year-old former soldier from Malange, Angola, interviewed by the CCF team in January 1998.
86. Julio, a twenty-year-old former UNITA soldier from Huambo, Angola, interviewed by the CCF team in Huambo, January 1998.
87. Mario, a nineteen-year-old former UNITA soldier from Huambo, Angola, interviewed by the CCF team in Huambo, January 1998.
88. Nordstrom, *A Different Kind of War Story*.
89. Fernand Deligny, in De Certeau, *The Practice of Everyday Life*.
90. Achille Mbembe, "Provisional Notes on the Postcolony," *Africa* 62, no. 1 (1992): 3.
91. Kourouma, *Allah n'est pas obligé*.

Chapter 4

1. Anita, interviewed by author in May 1999 in Josina Machel Island.
2. Carol MacCormack and Marilyn Strathern, *Nature, Culture and Gender* (Cambridge: Cambridge University Press, 1980); Belinda Bozzoli, "Marxism, Feminism and South African Studies," *Journal of Southern African Studies* 9, no. 2 (1983): 139–71; Jill Dubisch, ed., *Gender and Power in Rural Greece* (Princeton, N.J.: Princeton University Press, 1986); Henrietta Moore, *A Passion for Difference: Essays in Anthropology and Gender* (Bloomington: Indiana University Press, 1994); Judith Butler, *Gender Trouble: Feminism and the Subversion of Identity* (New York: Routledge, 1990); Begoña Aretxaga, *Shattering Silence: Women, Nationalism and Political Subjectivity in Northern Ireland* (Princeton, N.J.: Princeton University Press, 1997); Judith DiIorio, "Feminism and War: Theoretical Issues and Debates," *Reference Issues Review* 20, no. 2 (1992): 51–68; Funmi Olonisakin, "Women and the Liberian Civil War," *African Women* (March/September 1995): 34–37.
3. Henrietta Moore, "The Problem of Explaining Violence in the Social Sciences," in *Sex and Violence: Issues in Representation and Experience*, ed. Penelope Harvey and Peter Gow (London: Routledge, 1994), 138–55.
4. Jean Bethke Elshtain, *Women and War* (Brighton: Harvester, 1987).
5. Meredeth Turshen, "Women's War Stories," in *What Women Do in Wartime*, ed. Meredeth Turshen and Clotilde Twagiramariya (London: Zed Books, 1998).
6. Jacklyn Cock, "Women, the Military and Militarization: Some Questions Raised by the South African Case" (paper presented to the Center for the Study of Violence and Reconciliation, seminar 7, 1992), 2.
7. Jacklyn Cock, *Colonels and Cadres: Women and Gender in South Africa* (Cape Town: Oxford University Press, 1991).
8. Sheila Rowbotham, *Women, Resistance and Revolution* (London: Penguin Books, 1972).
9. Susan McKay and Dyan Mazurana, "Girls in Militaries, Paramilitaries, Militias and Armed Opposition Groups" (background paper presented at the International Conference on War-Affected Children, Winnipeg, Manitoba, Canada, 2003). See also McKay and Mazurana, *Where Are the Girls?*
10. Yvonne Keairns, "The Voices of Girl Child Soldiers, Sri Lanka" (New York and Geneva: United Nations Quake Office, January 2003), available at http://www.quno.org/newyork/Resources/girlSoldiersSrilanka.pdf.

11. Human Rights Watch, Forgotten *Fighters: Child Soldiers in Angola* (New York: Human Rights Watch, April 2003).

12. In "Angola's Children Bearing the Greatest Cost of War," *Africa Security Review* 11, no. 3 (2003).

13. Vivi Stavrou, CCF in Angola, in an interview with The United Nations Integrated Regional Networks (IRIN) 4, March 2004.

14. Veena Das, "The Anthropology of Violence and The Speech of Victims," *Anthropology Today* 3, no. 4 (1987): 11–13. See also F. Ross, "Speech and Secrecy: Women's Testimony in the First Five Weeks of Public Hearings of the South African Truth and Reconciliation Commission," in *Remaking a World: Violence, Social Suffering and Recovery*, ed. Veena Das, Arthur Kleinman, Margaret Lock, Mamphela Ramphele, and Pamela Reynolds (Berkeley: University of California Press, 2001), 250–79.

15. Susan Brownmiller, "Making Female Bodies the Battlefield," in *Mass Rape: The War Against Women in Bosnia-Heregovina*, ed. Alexandra Stiglmay (Lincoln: University of Nebraska Press, 1994).

16. Honwana, "Untold War Stories: Young Women and War in Mozambique" (paper presented at the conference on "Children and Youth as Emerging Social Categories in Africa," Leuven, November 1999).

17. In Africa, Zionist churches fuse a Christian message with cultural practices and spiritual beliefs from local religious traditions.

18. *Muti* means a house or residential unit in Shangane, a southern Mozambican language.

19. See also Elisa Muianga, "Mulheres e Guerra: Social de Mulheres Regressadas das 'Zonas da Renamo' no Distrito de Mandhakazi" (Ph.D. diss., Universidade Eduardo Mondlane, Mozambique, 1996).

20. Nora, a seventeen-year-old woman interviewed by the author in Josina Machel Island in May 1999. She walked for more than three days before reaching the camp. On her way to the camp, she saw soldiers kill captives who were tired and could not walk anymore. Nora managed to escape during one of the girl's expeditions to fetch water for the camp.

21. Catarina, interviewed by author in May 1999 in Josina Machel Island.

22. Leia, interviewed by author in May 1999 in Josina Machel Island.

23. Ntombi, a talkative young women from Josina Machel Island, interviewed by author in May 1999.

24. Maria, a seventeen-year-old woman interviewed by the author in May 1999, in Josina Machel Island in Mozambique.

25. Anita, interviewed by author in May 1999 in Josina Machel Island.

26. Twenty-one-year-old Dinha, interviewed by the author in the island in May 1999.

27. Mats Utas, "Sweet Battlefields: Youth and The Liberian Civil War" (Ph.D. diss., Uppsala University, 2003).

28. Human Rights Watch, *"You'll Learn Not to Cry": Child Combatants in Colombia* (New York: Human Rights Watch, September 2003), 53.

29. Angolan girl child soldier quoted in Keiarns, "The Voices of Girl Child Soldiers," 15.

30. Elderly women from Josina Machel Island.

31. I interviewed Felista in the most remote area of Josina Machel Island where access is very difficult, especially during the rainy season, in May 1999. Almost everybody told me of her story. Felista was happy to share her war experiences with me. Unfortunately, I was unable to interview her husband, as he was away during my stay on the island.

32. Judite's story in Muainga, "Mulheres e Guerra," 30–31.

33. Ibid.

34. These women and a few others composed the women's wing commonly called DF; see ibid., 33.

35. Susan Brownmiller, *Against Our Will: Men, Women, and Rape* (New York: Simon & Schuster, 1975).

36. A film by Helke Sander and Barbara Johr, *Befreier und Befreite: Krieg, Vergewaltig-ung, Kinder* (Munich, 1991).

37. Ibid., 46; see also Ruth Seifert, "War and Rape: A Preliminary Analysis," in *Mass Rape*, 54.

38. Ustinia Dolgopol, "Women's Voices, Women's Pain," *Human Rights Quarterly* 17 (February 1995): 127–54.

39. Bownmiller, "Making Female Bodies the Battlefield," 180–82.

40. Seifert, "War and Rape," 55.

41. Brownmiller, *Against Our Will*, 14–15.

42. Seifert, "War and Rape."

43. M. R. Burt and B. L. Katz, "Dimensions of Recovery from Rape: Focus on Growth Outcomes," *Journal of Interpersonal Violence* 2 (1987): 57–81; Laura S. Brown, "Not Outside the Range: One Feminist Perspective on Psychic Trauma," *American Imago* 48, no.1 (1991): 119–33; L. Lebowitz and S. Roth, " 'I Felt Like a Slut': The Cultural Context and Women's Responses to Being Raped," *Journal of Traumatic Stress* 7, no. 3 (1994): 363–90.

44. Carolyn Nordstrom, "Girls Behind the (Front) Lines," *Peace Review* 8, no. 3 (1996).

45. Lina Magaia, *Dumba Nengue: Run for Your Life—Peasant Tales of Tragedy in Mozambique* (Newark, N.J.: Africa World Press, 1989); Carolyn Nordstrom, "War in the Frontlines," in *Contemporary Studies of Violence and Survival*, ed. Carolyn Nordstrom and Antonius C. G. M. Robben (Berkeley: University of California Press, 1995); McKay and Mazurana, *Where Are the Girls?*

46. William Minter, "The Mozambican National Resistance (RENAMO) as Described by Ex-participants" (Washington, D.C.: Ford Foundation and Swedish International Development Agency, 1999).

47. Mr. Diniz, interviewed at the primary school in Josina Machel Island by author in May 1999. Mr. Diniz had been stationed in the island since 1989 and lived through the worst of the war. He witnessed abductions of students who were forced to join the RENAMO rebels.

48. Zara, a sixteen-year-old girl interviewed by the author in May 1999 in the island.

49. Magaia, *Dumba Nengue*, 20.

50. For additional evidence of the systematic character of sexual abuse, see Magaia, *Dumba Nengue*; Stephanie Urdang, *And Still They Dance: Women, War, and the Struggle for Change in Mozambique* (New York: Monthly Review Press, 1989); Nordstrom, "Girls Behind the (Front) Lines"; and Muianga, "Mulheres e Guerra."

51. Helsinki Watch, *War Crimes in Bosnia-Herzegovina*, vol. 2 (New York: Human Rights Watch, 1993).

52. Letter from Natalie Nenadic, an American researcher of Croatian and Bosnian descent working with refugees, to Catharine MacKinnon in October 1992 and cited in Catharine MacKinnon, "Rape, Genocide, and Women's Human Rights," in *Mass Rape*, 185.

53. Nenadic's letter to MacKinnon in October 1992, in MacKinnon, "Rape, Genocide, and Women's Human Rights," 185.

54. Women's Rights Project/America's Watch, *Untold Terror: Violence against Women in Peru's Armed Conflict* (New York: Human Rights Watch, 1992).

55. Asia Watch/Women's Rights Project, *Double Jeopardy* (New York: Human Rights Watch, 1992).

56. Human Rights Watch, *"We'll Kill You If You Cry": Sexual Violence in the Sierra Leone Conflict* (New York: Human Rights Watch, January 2003); Human Rights Watch, *Stolen Children: Abduction and Recruitment in Northern Uganda* (New York: Human Rights Watch, March 2003).

57. Nordstrom, "Girls Behind the (Front) Lines," 151.

58. For works that examine the trauma that rape inflicts in social-psychological terms, see Burt and Katz, "Dimensions of Recovery from Rape"; Brown, "Not Outside the Range"; Lebowitz, and Roth, " 'I Felt Like a Slut.' "

59. Judith Herman, *Trauma and Recovery* (New York: Basic Books, 1992).

60. David Ntimana, interviewed by author in Josina Machel Island in May 1999. Bishop Ntimana is highly respected and involved in several community projects.

61. Mrs. Cuamba, interviewed by author in Josina Machel Island in May 1999.

62. Elsa, interviewed by author in Josina Machel Island in May 1999.

63. Cock, *Colonels and Cadres*; "Women, the Military and Militarization"; Cynthia Enloe, *Does Khaki Become You? The Militarization of Women's Lives* (Boston: South End Press, 1983); Jean Elshtain, *Women and War*; Barbara Roberts, "The Death of Macho-Think: Feminist Research at The Transformation of Peace Studies," *Women's Studies International Forum* 7(1984): 195–200.

64. Even in this revolutionary context, although the position of women in the public sphere gradually changed, relations between men and women in the domestic sphere did not change much. Women were often overburdened with domestic responsibilities. See, Signe Arnfred, "Women in Mozambique: Gender Struggle and Gender Politics." *Review of African Political Economy* 41 (1988): 5-16; Urdang, *And Still They Dance*; Rowbotham, *Women, Resistance and Revolution*; Allen Isaacman, and Barbara Isaacman, "The Role of Women in the Liberation of Mozambique," *Ufahamu* 13 (1984): 2–3.

65. B. Efraime and A. Errante, "Rebuilding Hope on Josina Machel Island" (unpublished manuscript, n.d.); Carrie Manning, "Constructing Opposition in Mozambique: RENAMO as a Political Party," *Journal of Southern African Studies* 24, no. 1 (1998): 161–89. McKay and Mazurana, *Where Are the Girls?*

66. McKay and Mazurana, *Where Are the Girls?*

67. Human Rights Watch, *"You'll Learn Not to Cry,"* 56.

68. See "Voices of Girl Child Soldiers."

69. Sri Lankan girl soldier quoted in Keairns, 15.

70. Michael Wessells, "Child Soldiers," *Bulletin of the Atomic Scientists* 53, no. 6 (November/December 1977): 32–39.

71. Roberts, "The Death of Macho-Think."

72. Cock, "Women, the Military and Militarization," 14.

73. Ibid.; Enloe, *Does Khaki Become You?*

74. These laws do not take into account current military doctrine, which includes a more fluid front line; first strikes can be ordered deep into the previously safe rear to knock out the enemy's supply line. "Precision" bombing, such as that used during the first Gulf War, and the exchange of Scud and Patriot missiles also show this fluidity of the front line. See Cock, "Women, the Military and Militarization."

75. Enloe, *Does Khaki Become You?*

76. Leia, interviewed by author in May 1999 in Josina Machel Island.

77. Berta, an eighteen-year-old woman from Josina Machel Island, interviewed by author in May 1999.

78. Rosa was fourteen when she was forced to join the RENAMO camp, where she lived for about a year. She was interviewed by author in Josina Machel Island in May 1999.

79. Ntombi, a young woman interviewed by the author in Josina Machel Island in May 1999.

80. See the discussion in chapter two on "new" and "old" wars and the blurring of distinctions between civilians and belligerents. Also see Wessells, "Child Soldiers."

81. DiIorio, "Feminism and War."

82. See discussion on agency in Chapter 3; Michel De Certeau, *The Practice of Everyday Life* (Berkeley: California University Press, 1988).

83. Muianga, "Mulheres e Guerra," 29.

84. Mrs. Cuamba, interviewed by author in Josina Machel Island in May 1999.

85. A girl quoted in Keiarns, "The Voices of Girl Child Soldiers: Angola," 15.

86. Marcela, a sixteen-year-old from Zanga, Angola, interviewed by the CCF team in Malange. Marcela's father was also killed in one of UNITA's military ambushes prior to this one.

87. Catarina, interviewed by the author in Josina Machel Island, May 1999.

88. Rosa, a sixteen-year-old, interviewed by author in Josina Machel Island in May 1999.

89. Tina, a seventeen-year-old, interviewed by author in Josina Machel Island in May 1999.

90. Mrs. Cuamba, interviewed by author in May 1999.

91. Marcela, interviewed by members of the CCF team in Malange, Angola in 1998.

92. Flor, a sixteen-year-old from Kilengues, in Hoila, Angola, interviewed by the CCF team in 1998.

93. Many Angolan children were victims of landmines. Through the thirty years of colonial and postcolonial war, more than five million antipersonnel landmines were planted in the territory; about 60 percent of them were concentrated in the provinces of Moxico, Kuando-Kubango, and Cunene. According to the 1997 UNDP report, the majority of landmine victims are not soldiers but civilian peasants, especially women and children. Many children encounter landmines in their daily activities: farming, searching for firewood and water, herding animals, or even playing in the fields.

94. Lena was nine years old when she lost her leg after stepping on a landmine in Kuíto-Biè, Angola. Her story was collected by the CFF team in Biè in 1997.

95. Rosa was interviewed by the CCF team in Huambo-Biè in December 1997.

96. UNDP, *Human Development Report 1997* (New York and Oxford: Oxford University Press, 1997).

Chapter 5

1. Marcos, interviewed by author, Manjacaze, Gaza province, Mozambique, September 1995. Marcos was about seventeen when this interview was conducted.

2. On social pollution, see Harriet Ngubane, *Body and Mind in Zulu Medicine* (London: Academic Press, 1977).

3. Soba Saldanha, interviewed by the CCF team in 1997, Uige Province Report, 1997, 1.

4. Soba Santos, in a group interview with the CCF team in Malange in 1997, Malange Province Report, 1997, 5.

5. Mr. Adam, Malange, Angola, interviewed by author, February 1998.

6. Alcinda Honwana, "Spiritual Agency and Self-Renewal in Southern Mozambique" (Ph.D. diss., University of London, School of Oriental and African Studies [SOAS], 1996). A version of the dissertation was later published as a book: Alcinda Honwana, *Living Spirits, Modern Traditions: Spirit Possession and the Politics of Culture in Southern Mozambique* (Maputo: Promedia, 2001; Lisbon: Ela Por Ela, 2003). See also Alcinda Honwana, "*Okusiakala O'ndalo Yokalye*, Let's Light a New Fire: Local Knowledge in the Post-War Reintegration of War-Affected Children in Angola," Consultancy Report for CCF Angola, 1998.

7. In southern Mozambique, this remote creator is called *Xikwembu or Nkulukumba.*

8. CCF field notes about death and mourning rituals collected in The Provinces of Biè and Malange atlest to this in Angola.

9. Michael Jackson, "An Approach to Kuranko Divination," *Human Relations* 31, no. 2 (1978): 117–38.

10. Pitango is the same youth, discussed in Chapter 3, who voluntarily enlisted in the government forces because he wanted to help protect his family from rebel attacks and get food and other necessities for them. He was fifteen when he left, so he was in the army for at least three years.

11. Pitango, of Cambandua, Biè, Angola, interviewed by the CCF team, March 1998.

12. Mr. Boaventura, interviewed by the author, Maputo Urban District Number Five, Mozambique, April 1993.

13. A. Kimbanda, interviewed by the CCF team, in Uige, Angola, in 1998.

14. Edward C. Green and Alcinda Honwana, "Indigenous Healing of War-Affected Children in Africa," *IK Notes* 10 (Washington, D.C.: World Bank, July 1999).

15. Vieira from Huambo, interviewed by members of the CCF team in 1997.

16. CCF Report on Formas Tradicionais de Cura (Traditional Forms of Healing), Huambo, September 1997, 1.

17. Soba Calei of Huambo, Huambo/Biè Report, 1997, 24.

18. Soba M. S. of Moxico, CCF Report, Formas Tradicionais de Cura (Traditional Forms of Healing), Moxico, Angola, 1997, 6.

19. Mr. A. R., a retired teacher from Biè, interviewed by author, July 1977.

20. Seculo Kazunzu, from Uige, interviewed by members of the CCF team in 1997.

21. Seculo Loloca. Uige Report, 1997, 2.

22. On rites of passage and rituals of transition, see Arnold van Gennep, *Les rites de passage* (Paris: É. Nourry, 1909), and *The Rites of Passage* (London: Routledge and Kegan Paul, 1977); Audrey Richards, *Chisungu: A Girl's Initiation Ceremony Among the Bemba of Zambia* (1956; London, Routledge, 1982); 248 Victor Witter Turner, *The Forest of Symbols: Aspects of Ndembu Ritual* (Ithaca, N.Y.: Cornell University Press, 1967); Victor W. Turner, *The Ritual Process: Structure and Anti-Structure* (Chicago: Aldine Publishing Co., 1969); Victor W. Turner, *Revelation and Divination in Ndembu Ritual* (Ithaca, N.Y.: Cornell University Press, 1975).

23. More specifically on liminality, see Turner, *The Ritual Process*.

24. Nzinga, a female healer from Malange, interviwed by author and Carlinda Monteiro, Malange, Angola, February 1998. We had several interviews with Nzinga and her nephew Pedro.

25. Mr. Chico from Malange, interviewed by author, February 1998.

26. Titos was conscripted into the Portuguese colonial army and fought against the national liberation movement until 1975. Conscription was mandatory for all young Mozambicans. Some young people had to flee the country to avoid fighting that war on the colonialists' side.

27. Using medicine to protect a soldier from injury could be dangerous. Sacamboa from Moxico, in an interview with the CCF team in 1997, pointed out that, if these forms of *feitico* (magic) were not undone after the war ended, the soldier might suffer from afflictions, including insanity.

28. Amèlia, a woman healer from Dhlavela in the Maputo area in Mozambique, interviewed by author, May 1993. Amèlia was a very helpful informant, dedicating many hours of her time to talk with me about all these issues.

29. Sacamboa of Moxico, interviewed by Fernando Miji, August 1996.

30. Gil, nineteen-year-old former government soldier from Huambo, Angola, interviewed by author and Carlinda Monteiro, Huambo, February 1998.

31. Ibid.

32. This type of Zionism has nothing to do with Jewish nationalism. These are syncretic religious groups that started in the city of Zion in the U.S.A, thus the name Zionist. From there it spread to southern Africa in the nineteenth century.

33. Various authors have given attention to this issue. Bengt Sundkler, *Bantu Prophets in South Africa* (Oxford: Oxford University Press, 1961) and Martin West, *Bishops and Prophets* (Cape Town: Davis Philip, 1975), who studied the Zionist phenomenon in South Africa, both detected strong similarities between the Zionist prophets and the ancestral mediums and diviners. These authors refer to parallels in the experience and training of the Zionist prophets and of the mediums and diviners and to a measure of overlap in their respective functions. James P. Kiernan, "Variation on a Christian Theme: The Healing Synthesis of Zulu Zionism," in *Syncretism/Anti-Syncretism: The Politics of Religious Synthesis*, ed. Charles Stewart and Rosalind Shaw (London: Routledge, 1994), 59–84, argues that the Zulu Zionists have fused the Bible and healing into a single, coherent system of meaning. See also Jean Comaroff, *Body of Power: Spirit of Resistance* (Chicago: Chicago University Press, 1985) on Zionist churches in Botswana. On religious syncretism in general, see Charles Stewart and Rosalind Shaw, eds., *Syncretism/Anti-Syncretism: The Politics of Religious Synthesis* (London: Routledge, 1994).

34. Bishop David from the Zionist church in Josina Machel Island, interviewed by author, May 1999. The bishop was involved in many activities aimed at helping the community recover after the long and devastating war.

35. J. Marrato, *Superando os Efeitos Sociais da Guerra em Mocambique: mecanismos e Estrategias Locais* (paper presented at the fourth Congress of Lusophone Social Sciences, Rio de Janeiro, September 1996).

36. Harriet Ngubane, *Body and Mind in Zulu Medicine* (London: Academic Press, 1977).

37. Nordstrom, *A Different Kind of War Story*.

38. Seculo Kapata from Moxico, Moxico Report, 1997, 2.

39. Seculo Samba, Huambo/Biè Report, 1997, 4.

40. Kimbanda Wambembe, Huambo/Biè Report, 1997, 5.

41. Soba Lohali from Kuito, Biè Report, 1997, 2.

42. Seculo Kapata from Luena, Moxico Report, 1997, 2.

43. Mr. Marimba from Huambo, Huambo/Biè Report, 1997, 6.

44. Henri Alexandre Junod, *The Life of a South African Tribe*, 2nd ed. (London: Macmillan, 1927), 382.

45. See Honwana, "Spiritual Agency."

46. Soba Chissico and Soba Chilombo of Biè, Huambo/Biè Report, December 1997, 2. These chiefs participated in a focus group discussion with the CCF team in November 1997.

47. Seculo Kalema from Moxico, Moxico Report, 1997, 3.

48. Interviews with C. Tchivunda and D. Tchissole, Moxico Report, December 1997, 2, 3.

49. Seculo Selundo, Huambo/Biè Report, 1997, 2.

50. Soba Camarada of Huambo, Huambo/Biè Report, 1997, 3.

51. Seculo Congo, Uige Report, 1997, 3.

52. Xitoquisana of Mukodwene, interviewed by author, Zona Verde, Maputo-Province, Mozambique, April 1993.

53. Damião, from Zibondzane in Manjacaze, interviewed by author, village of Massaka, district of Boane, Maputo-Province, Mozambique, May 1993.

54. Carlos, intervi wed by author, district of Boane, Maputo-Province, June 1993.

55. In the nineteenth century, the Nguni broke from the Zulu state of Shaka and migrated north towards Mozambique, conquering and dominating the peoples they encountered along the way. During this process, they subjugated the Ndau, a group from central Mozambique, and forced them south as slaves in the Nguni state of Gaza which they established in the southern region after dominating the Tsonga. For more information see J. K. Rennie, "Christianity, Colonialism and the Origins of Nationalism among The Ndau of Southern Rhodesia 1890–1935" (Ph.D. diss., Northwestern University, 1973); Antonio Rita-Ferreira, *Fixação portuguesa e história pré-colonial de Moçambique* (Lisboa: Instituto de Investigação Científica Tropical/Junta de Investigações Científicas do Ultramar, 1982).

56. Fabião, interviewed by the author, Munguine, district of Manhica, Maputo, Mozambique, May 1993. Fabião, a healer, was kidnapped by RENAMO soldiers and forced to work in the military camp to help treat soldiers and perform divinatory rituals to identify the location of the enemy and protect commanders. See Honwana, "Spiritual Agency," for Fabião's story.

57. A daily newspaper published in Maputo and distributed by fax.

58. Maconde is an ethnolinguistic group from northern Mozambique. The Maconde are located in the Mueda (Cabo Delgado) province.

59. For more on the practice of having a young girl become the wife of the spirit of the dead and tend his hut, see Honwana, "Spiritual Agency."

60. See R. Carvalho's article "Filho por filho," published in May 1996 by *Media tax*, a Mozambican independent newspaper distributed by fax.

61. Soba Kavingangi of Biè, Huambo/Biè Report, 1997, 12.

62. Such potentially fatal but necessary forays were so common that there is a specific term for them: *batidas*.

63. Kutximuila and Aurora, two female *kimbandas* (healers) from Kuito, interviewed by author and Carlinda Monteiro, Kuito, July 1997.

64. Soba Capumba, Huambo/Biè Report, 1997, 14.

65. Soba Kavingangi of Biè, Huambo/Biè Report, 1997, 15.

66. This sort of ceremony, which involves the entire community, is commonly organized by *sobas* (chiefs) in Angola. Similar ceremonies are held in cases of natural disaster, such as droughts and floods.

67. Règulo Chirindja, interviewed by author, Munguine, April 1993; also Fabião and others.

68. See Honwana, "*Okusiakala 'ndalo Yokalye*, Let's Light a New Fire."

69. L. Swartz, *Culture and Mental Health: A Southern African View* (Cape Town: Oxford University Press, 1998), 260.

Chapter 6

1. United Nations Operation in Mozambique (UNOMOZ), Technical Unit Database, Maputo, 1995. See also Miguel A. Máusse, Daniel Nina, and Elizabeth Bennett, *Child Soldiers in Southern Africa* (Pretoria: Institute for Security Studies, 1999).

2. Neil Boothby, Peter Upton, and Abucabar Sultan, "Boy Soldiers of Mozambique," *Refugee Children*, Refugee Studies Program, Oxford, March 1992.

3. Zita, a young former RENAMO combatant from Macia, Maputo, Mozambique, interviewed by author in Macia in September 1995.

4. Sula was nineteen years old when he was interviewed by members of the CCF team in Moxico in 1998. He was eighteen years old at the time of his demobilization.

5. Astro from Karilongue, Huambo. He was seventeen years old when the CCF team interviewed him in Huambo in 1998.

6. Pitango was from Cambandua in Biè; see his homecoming story in Chapter 5.

7. Ibid.

8. Soma, a nineteen-year-old from Huambo, Angola, interviewed by the CCF team in 1998.

9. Joao, a twenty-year-old from Huambo, Angola, interviewed by the CCF team in 1998.

10. Mario, a nineteen-year-old from Huambo, Angola, interviewed by the CCF team in 1998.

11. Miguel, from Uige, in an interview with the CCF team in 1998.

12. Mario, from Huambo.

13. Fonseca, a eighteen-year-old, from Kuíto, interviewed by the CCF team in 1998.

14. Joao, from Huambo.

15. A case study of Manuel was conducted in March 1998 by the CCF team in Malange.

16. A case study of Pedrito was conducted in April 1998 by the CCF team in Moxico.

17. Gabriel, a fourteen-year-old from Huambo, interviewed by the CCF team in 1998.

18. Mrs. Cuamba, mother of a former captive girl from Josina Machel Island, interviewed by author in the island in May 1999.

19. Elsa, a twenty-year-old former captive from Josina Machel Island, interviewed by author in the island in May 1999.

20. Jo Boyden (paper presented at the SSRC Cape Town workshop on Youth in Africa, 1999).

21. Neil Boothby, "Working in the War Zone: A Look at Psychological Theory and Practice from the Field," *Mind and Human Interaction* 2, no. 2 (October 1990); A. Dawes, "Helping, Coping and 'Cultural Healing,'" *Recovery: Research and Co-operation on Violence, Education and Rehabilitation of Young People* 1, no. 5 (1996); Bóia Efraime Júnior, "The Psychic Reconstruction of Former Child Soldiers," *Children, War, and Persecution—Rebuilding Hope: Proceedings of the Congress in Maputo, Mozambique, 1–4 December 1996* (Mozambique, s.n., 1996); Michael G. Wessells, "Child Soldiers," *Bulletin of the Atomic Scientists* 53, no. 6 (November/December 1997): 32–39.

22. G. White and A. Marsella, introduction to *Cultural Conceptions of Mental Health and Therapy*, ed. White and Marsella (Dordrecht: Reidal Publishing Company, 1982), 85.

23. For a definition of culture as a "pattern of meaning" that shapes human experiences and provides a framework for the understandings and beliefs which underpin people's actions, see Clifford Geertz, *The Interpretation of Cultures: Selected Essays* (New York: Basic Books, 1973).

24. Jo Boyden and Sara Gibbs, *Children of War: Responses to Psycho-Social Distress in Cambodia* (Geneva: United Nations Research Institute for Social Development, 1997).

25. White and Marsella, introduction to *Cultural Conceptions of Mental Health and Therapy*, 28.

26. Dawes, "Helping, Coping and 'Cultural Healing.'"

27. Patrick Bracken, Joan Giller, and Derek Summerfield, "Psychological Responses to War and Atrocity: The Limitations of Current Concepts," *Social Science and Medicine* 40 (1995): 1073–82.

28. A few veterans manifested these symptoms in the context of medically diagnosed major mental illnesses, such as paranoid schizophrenia, or physical illnesses that were eventually attributed to their battlefield exposure to dioxin-containing defoliants such as Agent Orange. But the diagnosis of PTSD was independent of other underlying mental and physical disorders; it was precisely its appearance in the ordinary lives of normal persons that was remarkable.

29. See, among others, Allan Young, *The Harmony of Illusions: Inventing Post-Traumatic Stress Disorder* (Princeton, NJ: Princeton University Press, 1995); Bracken, Giller, and Summerfield, "Psychological Responses to War and Atrocity."

30. Derek Summerfield, "A Critique of Seven Assumptions behind Psychological Trauma Programs in War-affected Areas," *Social Science and Medicine* 48 (1999): 1449–62.

31. Boyden and Gibbs, *Children of War*.

32. For a study of Mozambique, see J. Marrato, "Superando os Efeitos Sociais da Guerra," paper presented at the 4th Congress of Lusophone Social Sciences. (Rio de Janeiro 1996)

33. See also Carolyn Nordstrom, *A Different Kind of War Story* (Philadelphia: University of Pennsylvania Press, 1997); idem, "Girls Behind the (Front) Lines," *Peace Review* 8, no. 3 (1966).

34. J. K. Rennie, "Christianity, Colonialism and the Origins of Nationalism among the Ndau of Southern Rhodesia 1890–1935" (Ph.D. diss., Northwestern University, 1973).

35. S. Fainzang, *L'Interieur des Choses: Maladie, Divination et Reproduction Sociale chez les Bisa du Burkina Fasso* (Paris: Harmattan, 1986).

36. Michael Jackson, "An Approach to Kuranko Divination," *Human Relations* 31, no.2 (1978): 117–38.

37. Arnold Van Gennep, *Les Rites de Passage* (Paris: ÉNourry, 1909) and *The Rites of Passage* (London: Routledge and Kegan Paul, 1977).

38. Victor W. Turner, *The Ritual Process: Structure and Anti-structure* (Chicago: Aldine Publishing Co., 1969).

39. Alcinda Honwana, *Espíritos Vivos, Tradições Modernas: Possessão de Espíritos e Reintegração Social Pós-Guerra no Sul de Moçambique* (Maputo: Promèdia, 2002; Lisbon: Ela Por Ela, 2003).

40. Report of the Special Representative of the UN Secretary General for Children and Armed Conflict to the UN General Assembly, 12 October 1998.

41. Olara Otunnu, "Innocent Victims: Protecting Children in Times of Armed Conflict," in *United Nations 2000* (London: Agenda Publishing, 2000), 84.

42. Peter W. Singer, *Children at War* (New York: Pantheon Books, 2005); P. Collier, *Economic Causes of Civil Conflict and Their Implications for Policy* (Washington, D.C.: The World Bank, 2000); Julia E. Maxted, "Children and Armed Conflict in Africa," *Social Identities* 9, no. 1: (March 2003): 51–73; A. El Kenz, "Youth and Violence," in *Africa's New People, Policies and Institutions*, ed. Stephen Ellis (The Hague: *Ministry of Foreign Affairs*, DGIS 1996), 42–57.

43. Alcinda Honwana and Filip De Boeck, eds., *Makers and Breakers: Children and Youth in Africa* (Oxford: James Currey, 2005); Singer, *Children at War*; Maxted, "Children and Armed Conflict in Africa."

Index

abduction, 14, 38, 49–50, 54–57, 59–61, 138, 177n.70. *See also under* girls/young women

Adam, Mr., 105–6

adolescent/adult initiations. *See* initiation, social

Afghanistan, 30

Africa, 29–30, 41, 46–47, 52. *See also* Angolan civil wars; Mozambican civil wars

African Charter on the Rights and Welfare of the Child (1990), 36

African Independent Churches, 19

African National Congress (ANC), 8–9

African vs. European-American culture, 153–54

agency: of children, generally, 4, 18; of child soldiers, 50, 69–74, 96–97, 162; of girls/young women in war, 95–96, 102; and power, 69–70; silence as, 80, 97; women's silence as, 80

Agent Orange, 187n.28

ainê-cadet (older–younger generations) relationship, 126

AK-47 assault rifles, 31, 58

Allah n'est pasobligé (Kourouma), 74

Alto Naya (Colombia), 30

Amèlia (a *nyanga*), 116–17, 184n.28

American-European vs. African culture, 153–54

amnesty law (Mozambique, 1987), 20, 138

Ana (pseud.), 120–21

ANC (African National Congress), 8–9

ancestral spirits: harm from, 126; honoring of, 106, 114, 123–28; *ndomba* (house of), 111, 117; offerings to, 126; power

of, 155–56; protection by, 106–7, 127; returning soldiers' reintroduction to, 111–12; and the war-peace transition, 19

Angola: burial rituals in, 107–8, 123–25; childhood vs. adulthood in, 3, 40, 157; children's roles in, 41–42, 52; democratic government in, 12; Government of National Reconciliation and Unity established, 12; independence/postcolonial government of, 7, 11; map of, 13; war ethics in, 53–54. *See also* Angolan civil wars

Angolan civil wars: ceasefire of 1991–92, 12, 167n.13; ceasefire of 1997–98, 12; ceasefire of 2003, 12, 123; civilians attacked during, 5–6; civilians vs. combatants in, 76; Cuito Cuanavale siege, 12; death toll and social costs of, 12, 14; displacement resulting from, 14, 99, duration of, 11; Lusaka Protocol, 12; political background of, 7; sexual assault on village women during, 76; social norms violated in, 105, 106; traumatic circumstances following, 122–23; women's roles in, 79, 93 (*see also under* girls/young women). *See also* MPLA; UNITA; UPA-FNLA

Angola Popular Union–National Front for the Liberation of Angola, 11

Anita (pseud.), 75, 84–85

apartheid, 8, 9, 11, 47

Appadurai, Arjun, 45

Ariès, Philippe, 40

Asian civil wars, 30

Association of Former Combatants, 131

Association of Traditional Healers, 131

Acknowledgments

I owe this book to the contributions of many people. First and foremost, I offer my deepest appreciation to all the children who agreed to share their experiences of war with me. Without them, this study would have never been possible, and their stories, similar to those of so many children across Africa whose lives have been touched by such extraordinary levels of physical and psychological violence, would remain untold.

My gratitude goes to the Swiss Cooperation for Development in Mozambique for sponsoring my research on the impact of war on vulnerable groups in 1992–93, immediately after the ceasefire; Save the Children USA, which sponsored my evaluation of the Children and War Project (CWP) in Mozambique in 1995; Enny Pannizo, Agostinho Mamade, and the whole CWP team for their important contributions; and Frieda Draisma and Eunice Mucache, who also offered valuable insights.

I thank the Christian Children's Fund (CCF) for supporting my research in Angola. I am indebted to the CCF team that worked with me in the field during 1997–98: Carla, Jùlia, Filipe, Lourdes, Ezequiel, Engràcia, and Carlinda. I am especially grateful to Carlinda for sharing with me her intimate knowledge of the situation in Angola and for her generous contributions.

My colleagues at the Department of Social Anthropology at the University of Cape Town (UCT) enriched this work through frequent discussions while I was a faculty member there. I thank the UCT for the research grant it provided for my fieldwork in Mozambique in 1999.

The Mozambican NGO Reconstruindo a Esperança (Rebuilding Hope) provided generous assistance throughout my work in Josina Machel Island in 1999. I am especially grateful to Bóia Júnior and his colleagues for their support and assistance.

In 2000–2001, while working at the Office of the Special Representative of the United Nations Secretary-General for Children and Armed Conflict (OSRSG/CAC) on the design of a research agenda on this topic, I gained a more global perspective on the issue of children's participation in armed conflict. I thank Olara Ontunnu, the Special Representative, for his constant encouragement and all my colleagues at the OSRSG/CAC for their valuable support.

In preparing this book, I benefited from the contributions and sound advice of my colleagues at the Social Science Research Council, especially Ron Kassimir, Beverlee Bruce, Seteney Shami, and Paul Price. I also thank Sara Acosta, Ezra Simon, and Clarice Taylor for their assistance.

I am also indebted to Pamela Reynolds, Larry Aber, Francisco Gutierres, Andy Dawes, Jon Pedersen, Carolyn Nordstrom, and Nanette Barkey for their generous intellectual inputs. Grey Osterud worked with me throughout the process of writing this book, editing my chapters and helping pull the threads together. I am also thankful to Julie Fratrik and Danielle Zack for assisting me with the bibliographical research.

I have been greatly inspired by the pioneering work of Graça Machel on children and armed conflict. I thank her for her friendship and encouragement.

By offering me their unwavering support and unconditional love throughout our journey together, my husband, João, and my daughters, Nyeleti and Nandhi, made me believe in myself and gave me the inner strength to carry out this project. To my daughters I say, May the world be a better place for you, your children, and the children of your children.